NAVIGATING THE MARITAL JOURNEY

MAP:
A Corporate
Support Program
For Couples

Gary L. Bowen

Foreword by Jay A. Mancini

PRAEGER

New York
Westport, Connecticut
London

HQ
734
B7585
1991

Library of Congress Cataloging-in-Publication Data

Bowen Gary L.
    Navigating the marital journey : MAP, a corporate support program
for couples / Gary L. Bowen ; foreword by Jay A. Mancini.
        p.   cm.
    Includes bibliographical references and index.
    ISBN 0-275-93423-3 (alk. paper)
    1. Marriage—United States.   2. Interpersonal relations.   3. Group
relations training.   4. Work and family—United States.   I. Title.
HQ734.B7585   1991
306.81—dc20   91-3553

British Library Cataloguing in Publication Data is available.

Library of Congress Catalog Card Number: 91-3553
ISBN: 0-275-93423-3

First published in 1991

Praeger Publishers, One Madison Avenue, New York, NY 10010
An imprint of Greenwood Publishing Group, Inc.

Printed in the United States of America

∞™

The paper used in this book complies with the
Permanent Paper Standard issued by the National
Information Standards Organization (Z39.48-1984).

10 9 8 7 6 5 4 3 2 1

NAVIGATING THE MARITAL JOURNEY

To my parents, Lynwood and Augusta Bowen,
for their encouragement and loving support.

Contents

Foreword

Matters of the family and of work are pivotal aspects of adult life. A person's feeling of being successful is tied to thoughts and feelings about being a family member and to experiences in the work world. Today we read a great deal about struggling to balance the family and work realms—social and behavioral scientists contend that such a balance is necessary, and average people talk about how they are trying to find that balance. Yet with all the talk and concern about work and family issues, there appear to be few intervention activities and programs that focus on their nexus.

Navigating the Marital Journey tells about an enrichment program that is grounded in theory and research and that is designed expressly to address the worlds of work life and family life. This book's title is an apt one because marriage is processual, ever-changing, and in need of thoughtful attention. A marriage is surrounded by various social rules, personal expectations, internal strains, and outside pressures. These forces require couples to chart a course wherein needs and expectations of wives and of husbands are met, and wherein there is mutual support.

The primary vehicle for enriching marriages is the Marital Assessment Profile (MAP). Gary Bowen uses these words in describing the MAP program: understand, conceptualize, examine, appreciate, identify, increase awareness, and act. MAP leads its participants toward applying these mental and behavioral processes to marriage trends, the work and family dynamic, marital values, marriage behavior, relationship barriers and resources, congruency between behavior and values, marital teamwork, and relational satisfaction. The exploration of values and their juxtaposition with behaviors constitute the heart of the underlying theory and the accompanying enrichment program. How well matched these values and behaviors are is said to be a clear index of the quality of married life. Students of the family will appreciate the diversity of the books and articles that have been interwoven to develop the Value-Behavior Congruency Model of Marital Satisfaction (VBC). The model is quite complex but accurately reflects the complexity in today's marriages. Family professionals who develop and implement programs will appreciate this highly usable approach to enhancing marriage, and they will note how the program complements other enrichment endeavors.

I like the title that Gary Bowen has chosen for his book. The word *navigating* describes both the nature of marriage and the process of enriching a marriage. The word *journey* suggests a course of events and experiences, some predictable and some unanticipated. In these pages you will be challenged and benefitted by the theory and research context, and you will be enlightened by the rich detail on how to improve marital relationships.

Jay A. Mancini
Virginia Polytechnic Institute
and State University

Preface

This book presents a field-tested corporate support program for employees and their spouses: the Marital Assessment Profile (MAP). Its primary aim is to assist couples in realizing their full relational potential by helping spouses to better understand and achieve their individual and collective goals for marriage through values clarification, self-development, and marital teamwork and growth.

Anchored by a theoretically derived conceptual model, the program is based on an explicit consideration of marital-related values. Marriage is likened to a journey over the life course with both trials and tribulations as spouses work to navigate toward desired individual and collective goals within the context of personal, relational, and environmental resources and constraints. MAP is a metaphor representing a planned and systematic change effort, a guide for helping couples chart and navigate toward marital destinations.

Like other marital enrichment programs, MAP focuses on helping couples to better understand the dynamics of contemporary relationships and to negotiate a relationship that fosters both individual and relational growth and satisfaction. Enablement and empowerment are key process dimensions.

Unlike other marital enrichment programs, MAP is tailored to the corporate sector. Assuming an ecosystem perspective, a key component of the program is helping couples to examine the nature of the work and family interface in their lives—and the implications of this interface for achieving their individual and collective goals in marriage. An underlying aim of the program is to forge a more productive and supportive work and family partnership, a win-win equation for both the company sponsor and the program participants.

The support program provides the organizing theme for the book. However, its core is directed toward setting the context for the development of the

program and outlining its key objectives, theoretically and empirically grounding the core assumptions from the conceptual framework that anchors the program, empirically exploring selected assumptions from this framework, and
linking the development and implementation of the program with trends in
corporate America today.

Following an introductory chapter (Chapter 1) that sets the context and in-
troduces MAP and its development, an overview of MAP is presented in
Chapter 2. Chapter 3 provides the underlying theoretical and conceptual foundation for MAP: the Value-Behavior Congruency Model.

In Chapters 4 and 5, selected assumptions from the Value-Behavior Congruency Model are explored empirically through the use of samples of married couples from both the U.S. Army and the corporation in which MAP was
first field-tested. These two chapters will be most salient to scholars interested
in strategies for testing key assumptions from the Value-Behavior Congruency
Model and the challenges posed by such inquiry, especially the use of discrepancy scores. Applied practitioners who wish to evaluate the underlying
assumptions of MAP on their face validity may forego a review of Chapters
4 and 5 without sacrificing an understanding of the program itself and its
theoretical and conceptual foundation.

Chapter 6 provides the rationale for the expansion of marital support programs like MAP in the workplace. It links the development and implementation of such programs with trends and developments in both corporate America
and work and family life today. The book concludes with a postscript that (1)
stresses the need for studies that evaluate the effectiveness of the program, and
(2) reviews strategies for implementing MAP in the workplace.

Taken together, the contents of this book represent an attempt to integrate
theory, research, and practice in the development and grounding of the intervention program. Although such attempts are recognized as important tasks
in disciplines such as family science and social work, segregation rather than
integration of these three domains has been the rule rather than the exception
in the behavioral and social science literature.

Its contents also represent an attempt to cross closely related disciplines,
especially in providing theoretical and empirical support for the conceptual
framework that undergirds MAP. The development of the Value-Behavior Congruency Model has been greatly enriched by developments across a number
of fields of inquiry, especially family science and the science of close relationships, social and organizational psychology, sociology, and social work. Based
on the present experience, it is concluded that academicians and professionals
within the various behavioral and social sciences have much to gain by creating
alliances and increasing their flow of communication with others in closely
aligned fields.

This book should be especially relevant to the growing number of marital
enrichment specialists who are looking for more theoretically and empirically
grounded support programs, especially those that have been field-tested in

the expanding marketplace of workplace programs for employees and their families. It should also be a valuable resource to senior managers and human resource professionals in both the private and the public sector who are looking for both a rationale and ways to strengthen the nature of organizational supports for employees and their families. As a text, this book should be highly applicable in graduate curriculums in schools of social work; departments of educational, clinical, and counseling psychology; departments of educational psychology; departments of applied sociology; schools of marriage and family therapy; and schools of pastoral counseling.

Acknowledgments

Grateful appreciation is expressed to the many colleagues and friends who have participated with the author on projects and experiences that were the basis for this book. In particular, I would like to thank Gerald Croan, Barbara Janofsky, Richard Carr, and Dennis Orthner, who helped design and perform the study on variations in family values that was sponsored by the Office of Chief of Chaplains, Department of the Army. This study led to the development of the Value-Behavior Congruency Model that anchors the Marital Assessment Profile (MAP) and to the early specification of the enrichment program that is the focus of this book. This study would not have been possible without the leadership of Chaplain (COL) Gary Bowker, Chaplain (LTC) Bill Hufham, and Ms. Ida Butcher from the Office of Chief of Chaplains.

Special thanks also go to Herman B. Maynard, who supported an early field test of MAP in a corporate setting and who encouraged the author to further develop the program. In addition, Scott and Vicki Golden are acknowledged for their work with the author in designing and implementing the spouse initiative in which MAP was an integral component and was first field-tested.

I would like to recognize the critical feedback on sections of the book provided by Peter Neenan, Jay Mancini, Phyllis Raabe, Walter Schumm, and Jack Richman; the thorough library research provided by Joanne Carrubba and Angelina Palmiero, my graduate student assistants; and the editorial assistance provided by Nancy Fischer and Kathrine Short. Joanne Carrubba was particularly helpful in framing Chapter 2, which provides an overview of MAP.

I am also most appreciative of the feedback on the Value-Behavior Congruency Model that I receive from my graduate social work students who take my class Family Stress, Social Support, and Coping. These students continually push me to translate abstract theoretical assumptions and concepts into practice-based wisdom.

Last but not least, I am appreciative of the support from my editors at Praeger, Anne Davidson and Alison Bricken, who believed in this book and who provided encouragement and evidenced patience in seeing this project to completion. In closing, I would like to express my indebtedness to Dennis Orthner, John Scanzoni, Rebecca Smith, and E. M. "Bud" Rallings, who challenged me in my graduate school education to become more ambitious in my thinking about relational dynamics and the contextual influences on these dynamics. Their work continues to inspire my theoretical and conceptual development.

1

Introduction

The rise of the modern corporation is a twentieth-century phenomenon. A corporation's success depends in large part upon its personnel. The recruitment of the best qualified, the productivity and task performance of those hired, and the retention of the best performers are essential to corporate success in an increasingly competitive world economy.

To achieve their objectives, corporations in the United States have relied from the outset upon theories and research from the behavioral and social sciences in designing their personnel practices and approaches to management. From the tenets of scientific management to the human relations approach, the human resources/capital movement, and the sociotechnical perspective, these practices and approaches have largely centered either on employee proficiency and task requirements; employee motivation and morale, including the interpersonal relationships among employees in the workplace; or the interaction between task attributes and organizational structure (Kanter, 1977a; Litwak, Messeri, Wolfe, Gorman, Silverstein, & Guilarte, 1989; Moos, 1986a; Taylor, 1947).

This introductory chapter sets the context and provides an overview of a marital enrichment program that was first developed and pilot tested in a small work group in a large, multinational, Fortune 500 company in response to high reported levels of marital stress and conflict among married employees and their spouses that paralleled a corporate change initiative. Recognizing the important link between marital success and corporate success, senior managers in the work group requested the development of a support program for married employees and their spouses that would enhance the level of "teamwork" in marriage and would expand corporate-sponsored enrichment activities to the family members of employees. The program has since been further expanded and revised through subsequent presentations and experiences.

The program, the Marital Assessment Profile (MAP), is based on a theoretically derived model of relationship satisfaction: the Value-Behavior Congruency Model (VBC). The model was originally developed and empirically evaluated through a study on variations in families values in the U.S. Army; the study was funded by the Office of Chief of Chaplains (Bowen & Janofsky, 1988). Although undergirded by many of the same principles and procedures that are the basis for promoting team building and enhancing job satisfaction in work organizations, the program deviates considerably from precedent in the corporate world by expanding the work boundary to directly involve both employees and their spouses in the program.

BOUNDARIES BETWEEN WORK AND FAMILY LIFE

Despite the traditional importance assigned to "informal organization" (Kanter, 1977a, p. 23) and team building in organizations that stress the importance of the emotional and relational aspects of employee behavior to organizational performance and retention (Bedeian, 1987), relatively little attention has been given to expanding the concepts of informal organization and team building to the employees' external system of family relationships. Until recently, the family situations of employees have been virtually ignored both in the study of organizational behavior and in the design of organizational interventions to promote the well-being and performance of employees (Kelly & Voydanoff, 1985; Kopelman, Greenhaus, & Connolly, 1983; Rapoport & Rapoport, 1965; Renshaw, 1976).

Nearly 20 years ago, Culbert and Renshaw (1972) described the asymmetrical nature of the boundary between work and family that continues to persist today:

A double standard of participation has left the families open to exploitation. On the one hand, their strengths are drawn upon to make or implement critical organizational decisions which the employee cannot manage by himself. On the other hand, they are denied formal channels of participation, and, therefore, can neither initiate nor react to proposals that affect them. (pp. 321–322)

Kanter (1977b) referred to the boundary tensions between work and family life as "the dilemma of fusion versus separateness in the work-family relationship" (p. 126): "Is the family, the intimate tie, to be included in the organization to make more committed members, or is it to be discouraged, kept away, so that participants will feel no competing pulls?" (p. 125)

This segregation of the family from the internal world of work paralleled the emergence of the large corporation as the "dominant organizational form" in the early twentieth century (Kanter, 1977a). The development of the modern corporation was imbued with both a strong "masculine ethic" (Kanter, 1977a) and a "separate worlds" orientation between work and family life (Kanter, 1977b). Combined, these perspectives stressed: the primacy of work for men;

the availability of wives to attend to home and family responsibilities so that men could devote their time and energy to the organization without family repercussions; the subordination of family needs to organizational requirements; the importance of rational and unemotional analysis, efficiency, and task-oriented relationships in the workplace; and an "antithetical" relationship between bureaucratic organizations, like the modern corporation, and primary groups, like the family (Aldous, 1969; Burke & Greenglass, 1987; Kanter, 1977a; Litwak & Meyer, 1966; Sussman, 1977).

According to Aldous (1969, p. 707) and supported by others (Litwak & Meyer, 1966; Sussman, 1977), although contrasts between the occupational setting and family life were probably exaggerated, the culture and requirements of the occupational setting were seen by both management leaders and social scientists as simply "at variance" with the "highly charged affective relations" in the family, where decision making was more typically based on emotional rather than rational analysis. Consequently, although relying on the family for instrumental support of the employee and for emotional management of the tensions and stresses incurred by family members in their work roles (Sussman, 1977), work organizations denied the potential conflict between the goals of the organization and those of the individual (Whyte, 1956) and were designed to minimize the intrusion of family life into the workplace (Burke & Greenglass, 1987; Kanter, 1977b).

However, such continued boundary rigidity between work and family life is particularly surprising given contemporary demographic and social trends in work and family life and the increasing recognition in the scientific literature of system interdependency among different aspects of the employee's life (Bowen, 1988c; Burden & Googins, 1987; Cooper & Marshall, 1978; French & Bell, 1984; Moos, 1986a; Renshaw, 1976). For example, over the last several decades, there has been a substantial growth in the labor force participation of married women, including those with young children in the household (Glick, 1989; Hayghe, 1986; Teachman, Polonko & Scanzoni, 1987); a significant increase in the proportion of employed women in professional and higher paying occupations (Glick, 1989; Powell, 1988; Reubens and Reubens, 1979); the emergence of dual career couples in which both spouses are career-oriented (Sekaran, 1986); a convergence of new, more egalitarian gender-role preferences among men and women toward work and family roles (Bowen, 1987; Bowen & Neenan, 1988; McBroom, 1984; Scanzoni & Fox, 1980; Thornton, 1989); greater emphasis on individualism and personal fulfillment by men and women (Bellah, Madsen, Sullivan, Swidler, & Tipton, 1985; Glenn, 1987b; Shouksmith, 1987; Yankelovich, 1981); the desire by an increasing number of men and women to better balance work and family demands (Nieva, 1985; Shinn, Wong, Simko, & Ortiz-Torres, 1989; Yankelovich, 1979); rising demands by employees for a more responsive family-oriented workplace (Blankenhorn, 1986); and a move toward more democratic and participatory styles of management and decision making in work organizations that follow more of a human relations model of management (Crouter, 1984; McGregor, 1960; Ouchi, 1981).

In addition to these contemporary demographic and social trends, there have been numerous studies and reviews over the last decade that suggest a congruency between events and satisfaction in the work and family sphere for employees (Bowen, 1988c; Burden & Goggins, 1987; Burke & Greenglass, 1987; Crouter, 1984; Kopelman, Greenhaus, & Connolly, 1983; Lambert, 1990; Louis Harris and Associates, Inc., 1981; Piotrkowski, Rapoport, & Rapoport, 1987). Although there has been relatively greater focus on the impact of work demands and dynamics on family life than vice versa, research is accumulating that demonstrates the importance of adding family-oriented variables to corporate success equations. For example, based on their review and research, Burke and Weir (1977b; 1982) concluded that the nature of the husband and wife helping-process in marriage contributes not only to their personal and marital well-being, but also to their job well-being.

Other research has identified spouse support of the partner's occupational pursuits as a highly significant mediator of conflicts between work and family roles (Holahan & Gilbert, 1979a; 1979b), a reducer of stress (Berkowitz & Perkins, 1984), and an enhancer of job commitment and stability (Arnott, 1972; Bowen, 1986; Orthner & Pittman, 1986). In addition, the affective quality of marital interaction (e.g., happiness and satisfaction) has been shown to be strongly and positively related to the physical and psychological well-being of adults, especially for females (Gove, Hughes, & Style, 1983; Gove, Style, & Hughes, 1990; Kessler & Essex, 1982), outcomes that are instrumental to effective role performance in the workplace.

Such findings make it difficult for work organizations to ignore the influence of families on workplace dynamics. Nevertheless, relatively few corporations have sponsored marital enrichment and support experiences in the workplace that are designed to strengthen the marital bond and the ability of spouses to work more effectively as a team in achieving their collective and individual work and marital goals. As concluded by Burke and Weir (1977a), "the husband-wife help-relationship . . . is an aspect of marriage that often remains undeveloped or at best is left to evolve haphazardly" (p. 924). In strengthening the productive interface between bureaucratic organizations, like work, and primary groups, like the family, such that each may better perform their separate yet complementary tasks, Sussman (1977) cites research by Eugene Litwak and associates that stresses the importance of organizational intervention within the ecosystem of the primary group through face-to-face interaction.

In general, the increased responsiveness of corporate America over the last decade to the family responsibilities of employees has been largely directed to expanded corporate benefits (e.g., extended maternity leave) and support policies (e.g., work hours) that enable employees to better integrate work and family demands (cf. Bowen, 1988c; Galinsky, 1986; Kamerman & Kahn, 1987; Kingston, 1990). While they are important baseline initiatives, these supports need to be further buttressed by corporate support programs that allow family members to permeate organizational boundaries and that are designed to foster more cooperative relationships between spouses and between the organization and the marital system. Corporate-sponsored marital enrichment activities for married employees and their spouses represent one such opportunity.

By recognizing the interface between the work and family systems and by reinforcing their complementarity in supporting one another in achieving their respective values and goals, such support programs have the capacity to reduce the "social distance" between the values and goals of the work organization and those of spouses in marriage (Litwak & Meyer, 1966). However, despite the interest of both employers and employees in such programs (Galinsky & Hughes, 1987; Orthner & Bowen, 1982b; Vocational Education Work and Family Institute, 1983), opportunities for marital enrichment have only recently begun to be introduced in the corporate sector.

In the context of increasing recognition by employers of the extent of marital problems experienced by employees and their effect on organizational effectiveness (Brown, 1985; Finkelstein & Ziegenfuss, 1978; Vocational Education Work and Family Institute, 1983), more corporations should be interested in such programs in the future. Given the differential ability of work organizations as formal groups to mount organized and efficient social interventions (House, 1981), and given the established role that many companies already have in health and mental health promotion (Byers, 1987; Moos, 1986a), such programs offer rich potential in the years ahead.

MAP: BACKGROUND AND RATIONALE

The Corporate Scenario: A Change Initiative

In 1985, a new work group of approximately 50 employees was created from the integration of several product-based divisions to field-test a new market-based approach to business. Historically, the larger organization had been product-oriented: Products were first developed and then a market for these products was found. However, as a consequence of increasing competition in the international business world and a declining share of the market as compared to competing companies, the group was created to field-test a new market-based approach to business. From this approach, products would be developed based on customer needs.

The establishment of the new group coupled with the change in business focus resulted in major disruptions in the security and performance of employees as they faced a number of personal- and system-level stressors in making the organizational shift: the merging of diverse work groups and individuals to create a new business, the unfamiliarity of some of the new transfers from other divisions with the nature of the products in the new business, the general lack of expertise of many of the employees with marketing concepts and strategies, the early retirement of some senior figures in the work group, the challenge of having to develop an internal organizational structure capable of accommodating diverse organizational divisions and the new market orientation, the fact that change was experimental, boundary ambiguity with other business groups in the organization, and employee insecurities about the consequences of the change for their future with the organization (summary based on verbal and written communication with a senior manager in the pilot corporation). The process of establishing a new organizational order and transforming the work group from a loosely organized and inexperienced collection of talented individuals into a coordinated and effective work team required a combination of both business and personal growth on the part of all members of the team, including senior managers, over a two-year period. During these two years, growth experiences created heavy demands upon the time, energy, and emotion of employees.

A Work and Family Life Survey

To understand better the potential marital and family repercussions of such work demands, a senior manager in the work group contracted with the author to conduct an exploratory survey of 34 employees and their spouses who had expressed interest in participating in some marital enrichment and growth experiences. Although there were no baseline data for purposes of longitudinal comparison, it was hypothesized (based on both the perceptions of the senior manager and the results from the survey) that the demanding business activities and travel had taken a heavy toll on the family lives of the employees, especially their spouses. Nearly one-quarter of employees and their spouses reported that they were either somewhat dissatisfied or dissatisfied with the relationship with their spouse, and more than one-quarter reported frequent family conflict. In addition, spouses reported high levels of stress, especially tiredness and fatigue, perhaps as a consequence of role overload from having a frequently absent spouse. Overall, more than one-half of the employees and their spouses reported that they were less than satisfied with the organization's attitude toward families and family problems. In fact, nearly one-third felt that their family lives would improve to a great extent, or at least to some extent, if they or their spouse would leave the organization.

On the positive side, the survey results indicated a high level of commitment of employees to the organization, and nearly two-thirds of the spouses were very supportive of their employee spouse continuing his or her employment with the organization. Given that employees who completed the survey had worked for the company for an average of 18 years and were mostly in management positions (81 percent), these findings were not particularly surprising. However, the survey results also showed strong correlations between the employees' level of organizational commitment and their level of family life satisfaction and the level of spouse support that they received for continuing their careers with the organization. A finding of particular interest to management was the link between the satisfaction of spouses with the organization's attitude toward families and family problems and the level of spouse support of the employee for continuing his or her career: The higher the satisfaction of the spouses with the organization's attitude, the higher their level of support.

The Challenge

Given their general understanding of the transactional nature of work and family linkages and their own family experiences over the last two years, it is not surprising that the conclusions of several senior managers were supported by the findings: Something should be done for spouses. Unfortunately, the "science," as one senior manager with a background in engineering put it, of how to provide direct support to families was unclear; others were concerned about possibly being perceived by employees as interfering with their private lives. Although the organization offered an impressive pay and benefit package to employees and had traditionally sponsored corporate events for families around holidays and other special occasions, the spouses of employees were neither active participants in organizational decision-making nor were they invited to attend personal developmental activities that the organization frequently sponsored for its employees. Based on the concern of one senior manager about the family lives of employees in the work group, the author was hired even before the survey was conducted to help develop a marital support program for employees and their spouses based on the "science" of family support. He was asked to coordinate his activities with a private consulting group that had previously conducted personal development seminars for employees in the organization. If employees and their spouses found the program helpful, it was anticipated that the program would be marketable to other work units and divisions within the company.

THE MARITAL ASSESSMENT PROFILE: MAP

The development of a spouse program based on the science of family support presented a significant challenge. Although the field of marital enrichment has expanded greatly over the past decade (Denton, 1986; Hof & Miller, 1981; Hoopes, Fisher, & Barlow, 1984), many marital and family enrichment programs lack an explicit theoretical or empirical framework for anchoring the program (L'Abate, 1990).

Many of these programs are primarily skill-based, placing heavy emphasis on the development of effective communication and problem-solving skills through experiential activities. Fewer of these programs are designed to help couples examine the nature of work and family linkages in their lives and to better understand relational dynamics and the nature of their affective responses to their marriage, to their relationship with their spouse, and to their spouse.

Although skill-based programs are essential to helping couples effect change in their relationship, these programs should be logically integrated into conceptual frameworks that spouses can use in understanding relational dynamics and the impact of broader ecosystem influences on these dynamics. In addition, enrichment programs need to respect possible variation and diversity in marital values and preferences among couples. Many enrichment programs to date have had a tendency to homogenize the rich variation and diversity among married couples, equating optimal marital functioning with the presence (or absence) of certain characteristics and attributes.

Since many of the managers had been through corporate team-building seminars and exercises, it was decided that this familiar technology could be broadened to include the marital arena. With marriage being conceptualized as a special type of two-person group (Levinger, 1965), the general goal of the spouse program that evolved through discussions with the senior manager responsible for initiating the effort was to help spouses forge a more supportive marital team for achieving individual and relational goals and interests.

Paralleling Gordon Lippitt's (1982) concept of "organizational renewal" as "the process of initiating, creating, and confronting needed changes so as to make it possible for organizations to become or remain viable, to adapt to new conditions, to solve problems, to learn from "experiences" (cited in French & Bell, 1984, p. 18), the concept of "marital renewal" (cf. Carnes, 1981) was used to describe this change process. The primary aim was to help couples develop a cognitive "map" for better conceptualizing, planning, and navigating their marriages toward what Constantine (1986) and Kantor and Lehr (1975) describe as an "enabled marriage": a marriage where husbands and wives support one another through joint disclosure and cooperation in accomplishing both their collective goals as a couple as well as their individual goals as spouses in such a way that neither the needs of the collective nor the needs of the individual are systematically neglected. An underlying aim was to help employees and their spouses better understand the nature of the work and family interface, to include spouses as members of the corporate team by expanding learning opportunities to them, and to help create a more productive partnership among employees, their spouses, and the corporation in meeting their respective needs and obligations.

To achieve these goals, a marital enrichment program was developed that was undergirded by many of the same principles and procedures that are the basis for team building in organizations: (1) specification of group mission and functions, (2) clarification of both collective and individual values for the group, (3) behavioral assessment in terms of identified mission and values, (4) identification of personal, relational, and environmental conditions that mediate achieving collective and individual values, and (5) development of an action plan to increase the level of value and behavior congruency.

The key objective of this program is to enhance the level of satisfaction that spouses experience from their marriage. Paralleling definitions of job satisfaction in the field of organizational psychology (Locke, 1969, 1976) and the analysis of close relationships in the field of social psychology (Berscheid, 1983, 1985; Berscheid, Gangestad, & Kulakowski, 1984, Kelley et al., 1983), marital satisfaction is defined as a "pleasurable or positive emotional state" (Locke, 1976, p. 1300) that is a function of the extent to which spouses perceive that they are able to realize their individual and collective values for marriage in behavior. As a function of the perceived congruency between what is valued and what is experienced in marriage, marital satisfaction is conceptualized on a continuum from low to high. It is important to underscore that this value-based definition of marital satisfaction contrasts greatly with more static definitions of this concept in the literature that imply a fixed set of interactions and feelings as the point of reference (Bowen, 1988b).

An important feature of the program is its relatively value-free position. A key objective is to assist spouses in better understanding their own value positions toward marriage and how their values in marriage may have evolved over the marital career. Intervention with couples is geared to helping spouses identify strategies and requisite resources and skills to better realize their defined individual and collective values and goals for marriage in behavior.

CONCLUSION

The MAP program is undergirded by a model of corporate-family partnership. Based on team-building principles and procedures, the program extends the corporate boundary to include the spouses of employees as members of the corporate team. Although MAP was developed in response to the situation in one corporation, its development is consistent with changing trends in work and family life in contemporary society.

Its development is also consistent with the recognition of the role of primary groups, like the family, in providing instrumental and emotional support to its members. Although the corporate world has historically relied on such support from the family, especially the wife, changing trends and dynamics in families have made the provision of such support more conditional on the willingness of employers to cooperate rather than compete with families for the time, energy, and resources of the employee.

No longer is "spouse support" synonymous with "wife support" (House, 1981). The labor force participation rate of married women is beginning to parallel the rate for married men (Kingston, 1990). In addition, an increasing number of women are central players in the occupational world and are "full partners" with their husbands in marriage (Scanzoni, Polonko, Teachman, & Thompson, 1989). As compared to the wife of the "organization man" who was described by William Whyte (1956) more than three decades ago, wives today are not as easily subjugated by the husband's employer and are less willing to exchange their instrumental and expressive support to share vicariously in the occupational successes of the husband.

Marriage today is increasingly a two-way street between spouses, where "the support of women by men is as necessary as the support of men by women" (House, 1981, p. 106). Husbands and wives may need assistance in understanding changing trends and patterns in intimate relationships and help in accommodating to a more equitable balance of power in their relationship and to changing roles and expectations in marriage.

Through MAP, corporations can play a proactive and catalytic role in assisting couples in better understanding the dynamics of contemporary relationships and in developing more supportive and enabling relationships. Not only is it assumed that such assistance strengthens and enriches relationships, but also it is highly plausible that such assistance will provide dividends to the employer through increased marital teamwork and spouse support for the work demands and commitment of the employee.

It is important to underscore that MAP is not in any way an attempt to subordinate the interests of the spouse of the employee to the needs of the corporation, to displace responsibility for employee problems on the marriage, or to blame marital problems on the corporation. It does represent an attempt to recognize the valuable role that spouses play as a support system for the employee, the relationship between corporate and marital success, and the reality that family members may need support in order to provide support. By paying dividends to the couple in the form of marital education and enrichment, it is assumed that the corporation helps to produce a "win-win" situation for both the couple and itself—an equitable partnership in the work-family equation.

MAP: The Marital Assessment Profile

The field of marital enrichment has expanded considerably since the first weekend retreats were conducted for married couples nearly three decades ago. Numerous enrichment programs exist today, some of which have served thousands of couples (Denton, 1986; Hof & Miller 1981; Hoopes, Fisher, & Barlow, 1984; L'Abate, 1990; Mace & Mace, 1986). This expansion represents an increased interest by marital and family practitioners in assuming a "salutogenic" or preventive perspective in working with couples as compared to the more traditional remedial or treatment perspective (Antonovsky & Sourani, 1988; Denton, 1986; Guerney, 1985).

Although programs vary in terms of sponsorship, structure, and content, all are broadly based on the assumption that marriage is a dynamic and growth-oriented process. Their underlying goal is to help couples achieve a more satisfying and meaningful relationship, a mutually supportive relationship that fosters the ability of spouses to better realize their individual and collective potential and ambitions. Content and activities in these programs are geared generally toward helping spouses to better understand the dynamics of marital interaction, to gain greater self-awareness, and to develop concrete skills for problem solving and relational enhancement (Giblin, 1986).

MAP springs from the rich foundation of many existing enrichment programs (e.g., Dinkmeyer & Carlson, 1986; Guerney, 1977; Hof & Miller, 1981; Hoopes, Fisher, & Barlow, 1984; LeCroy, Carrol, Nelson-Becker, & Sturlaugson, 1989; Stuart, 1980). However, unlike existing programs, this program is specifically tailored to the corporate setting. It is also designed as an intensive, short-term enrichment experience.

Assuming an ecosystem perspective, a key focus of the program is the work and family interface and its influence on marital dynamics and interaction.

Fitting the description by Mace (1983, p. 20) of marital enrichment as a process of "experiential education," integrating the acquisition of new information with modeling and the practice of alternate behaviors and patterns of interaction, the program applies technology on team building in organizations to promoting teamwork and cooperation in marriage. An underlying aim is to foster a more productive partnership between the work organization and spouses in marriage.

Participation in the program is promoted as an important step for couples who wish to foster their marital well-being and growth. By participating in the program, spouses should develop a better appreciation of relational dynamics and the personal, relational, and environmental conditions that either facilitate or restrict their opportunities to achieve a satisfying marital relationship. Although spouses learn techniques for promoting more positive marital interaction, the program is more conceptually based than skill-oriented. There are many excellent skill-based programs on the market that spouses may decide to pursue after attending, MAP, such as the Couples Communication Program (Miller, Nunnally, & Wackman, 1979) and the Relationship Enhancement Program (Guerney, 1977). As such, MAP is intended to complement rather than duplicate the skill-based strengths of many existing programs. At the close of MAP, spouses are provided with a list of community resources, including enrichment opportunities and marital counseling resources, that they may decide to pursue as a consequence of their participation in MAP.

This chapter provides an overview of MAP. After reviewing the philosophy underlying the program and outlining its objectives, the structure and format of the program are presented, followed by an overview of a sample program that is responsive to MAP's objectives.

PHILOSOPHY AND OBJECTIVES

MAP is designed to help married couples maximize their relational potential by becoming a cohesive and cooperative marital team. It likens marriage to a journey with both opportunities and challenges, helping couples to develop a cognitive "map" for better conceptualizing, planning, and navigating their marriages toward what is termed an "enabled" marriage: a marriage where spouses support one another in realizing their individual and collective marital goals through joint disclosure and cooperation (Constantine, 1986; Kantor & Lehr, 1975).

The program is built upon an explicit consideration of marital-related values (i.e., organized preferences for how individuals wish to conduct their marital lives) and goals (i.e., lower-tier values that are more manifest and explicit). It is given coherence by a theoretically derived conceptual framework: the Value-Behavior Congruency Model (see Chapter 3). This model is grounded both in a larger person-environment fit perspective to capture the ecological context of marital interaction and in social exchange theory to capture the micro-level interactions between husbands and wives in marriage. From the perspective of this model, marital life is conceptualized as a dynamic, fluid, interactional process between spouses who are attempting to achieve desired individual and collective ends in an ever-changing personal, relational, and ecological context (Mace & Mace, 1978). As such, intervention is directed toward helping couples move toward relational growth and fulfillment.

The program provides an opportunity for spouses and couples to:

1. Better understand contemporary patterns and trends in marital and family relationships and the changing dynamic between work and family life in contemporary society.
2. Understand the dynamics of group cohesiveness and stability.
3. Conceptualize the "enabled" marital system and use the Value-Behavior Congruency Model as a framework for understanding marital dynamics and relationship satisfaction.
4. Examine their values and goals for marriage and how these values and goals may have changed over the marital career.
5. Better appreciate individual differences in marital values and goals within and between couples.
6. Examine their present behavior in marriage in the context of their individual and collective values and goals.
7. Identify personal, relational, and environmental resources and barriers to realizing defined individual and collective values and goals for the marital relationship in behavior.
8. Increase awareness of new options and strategies for promoting value-behavior congruency in marriage.
9. Develop an action plan for navigating the marital relationship toward a higher level of marital teamwork and relational satisfaction.

PROGRAM ORGANIZATION

Sponsorship

An underlying objective of the program is to open the boundary between work and family life by forging a more productive partnership among the employee, the spouse, and the employer. Consequently, corporations are asked to sponsor the enrichment program for their married employees and their spouses as an employee benefit. Although individuals at various levels of the organization may be the catalyst to sponsoring the program, it is important to receive corporate support for the program at the highest level possible. Such sponsorship is important in promoting changes in the work organization that both recognize spouses of employees as members of the corporate team and promote a better fit between family capabilities and needs and corporate demands and supports.

Group Composition

To ensure responsiveness to individual questions and concerns, no more than four to six couples should participate in the program in any one session. Because large corporations often have multiple subcultures that vary by location, division, and rank (Schein, 1985), it is recommended that employees be self-selected from the same division or unit and from a similar level in the corporate hierarchy. A point of contact (POC) is established in the corporation to publicize the program, to recruit employees and their spouses to attend, and to handle the necessary logistics. A letter should be forwarded by the POC to all employees and their spouses who are eligible to participate, explaining the purposes of the program and criteria for participation. Employees and their spouses should also be advised that participation in the program is voluntary and that no adverse consequences will occur to anyone not electing to participate. In addition, the letter should explain that an independent consulting group is conducting the program and that any assessment instruments completed by employees and their spouses will be seen only by the consulting group.

Assessment Instruments

Approximately two weeks before the scheduled session, it is recommended that each participant spouse be mailed several assessment instruments to complete and return to the program leader(s). Spouses are asked to complete these assessment instruments without consulting one another. A self-addressed, stamped envelope is provided to both the husband and wife to return their completed instruments. For purposes of evaluation, it is recommended that the assessment instruments be re-administered approximately six weeks after the workshop.

Assessment Instruments Used in the Sample Program

Moos and Moos' (1986) *Family Environment Scale (FES)* (Ideal Form and Real Form). This instrument assesses the preferences of spouses toward the ideal family environment (Ideal Form) and their actual perceptions toward the social-environmental features of their own families (Real Form). The Ideal and the Real Forms are parallel to one another and are comprised of ten subscales, each with nine true/false items, across three underlying sets of dimensions: the relationship dimensions (cohesion, expressiveness, and conflict), the personal growth dimensions (independence, achievement orientation, intellectual-cultural orientation, active-recreational orientation, and moral-religious emphasis), and the system maintenance dimensions (organization and control). The Ideal and Real Forms may be used together to identify discrepancies between the type of family environment that spouses would prefer ideally and their perceptions toward their actual family life. Spouses are provided special instructions to respond to the Ideal and Real Forms from a "couple" rather than a "family" perspective. An FES manual, including copies of the Ideal and Real Forms, answer sheets, scoring stencil, and profile sheets, is available from Consulting Psychologists Press, 577 College Avenue, Palo Alto, California 94306.

Schumm and Associates' (1986) *Kansas Marital Satisfaction Scale* (KMS). Three items ask spouses to evaluate their level of satisfaction with their partner as a spouse, with their marriage, and with their relationship with their spouse. A seven-point evaluation scale is used for evaluating each item, ranging from "Extremely Dissatisfied" to "Extremely Satisfied."

Highly Suggested Assessment Instruments

Bowen's Marital Assessment Profile (MAP) (see Chapter 5). A 26-item self report instrument that is designed to assess each spouse's perception of the importance of specified marital interaction patterns and behaviors (Marital Values Profile) as well as the degree to which these patterns and behaviors are actually evidenced in the marriage (Marital Behavior Profile). Four underlying subdimensions of marital functioning and interaction are identified on the MAP: (1) Marital Integration, (2) Achievement Orientation, (3) Active-Religious Orientation, and (4) Extended Family. A complete description of the profile is provided in Chapter 5, including its development, administration and scoring.

Bowen and Janofsky's (1988) *Problem-Solving Skills in Marriage Scale*. Spouses are asked to evaluate the extent to which they see themselves in marriage as: (1) A Good Listener, (2) An Effective Problem-Solver, (3) A Compromiser in Resolving Family Problems, and (4) Open to the Views of Others. Each item is evaluated on a five-point response scale, ranging from "Very Little Extent" to "Very Great Extent." These items may either be used as separate indicators or sum averaged as a scale (see Chapter 4).

Moos' (1986b) *Work Environment Scale (WES)* (Employees Only). Parallel to the FES, three sets of dimensions are assessed by the WES: the relationship dimensions (involvement, peer cohesion, and supervisor support), the personal growth dimensions (autonomy, task orientation, and work pressure), and system maintenance and change dimensions (clarity, control, innovation, and physical comfort). Each dimension is assessed by nine true/false items, and the scale is normed on more than 3,000 employees. A WES manual, including forms, answer sheets, scoring stencil, and profile sheets, is available from Consulting Psychologists Press, 577 College Avenue, Palo Alto, California 94306.

Olson and Associates' (1985, 1986) *FACES III: Family Adaptability and Family Cohesion Evaluation Scores* (Ideal and Perceived Forms, Couple Version). Assessing the dimensions of cohesion and adaptability in families, FACES III is comprised of 20 items. It is administered twice to spouses. First, working separately, spouses respond to the items based on their ideal expectations for family life. Next, they respond to the same items based on their perceptions toward their family. A measure of family satisfaction may be derived for each spouse by calculating the discrepancy between ideal expectations and actual perceptions toward the family. FACES III is copyrighted. Permission to use or duplicate the scale may be obtained by writing to: Dr. David Olson, Family Social Science, University of Minnesota, 290 McNeal Hall, St. Paul, Minnesota 55108. A manual is available that explains the development, validity, reliability, administration, scoring, and interpretation of FACES III.

Format and Structure

The workshop can be designed as either a weekend experience that requires an evening and one full day or as four two- to three-hour evening sessions. Each format also involves a follow-up dinner for participants that is scheduled either at the conclusion of the workshop (weekend format) or for a separate evening (evening format). In the evening format, time should be allowed at the close of each session to outline the agenda for the next meeting and to allow for informal discussion and dialogue. Given the number of dual earner couples with young children in today's workforce, it is often more convenient for participant couples to attend the more intensive weekend format that is scheduled typically for a Friday evening and a Saturday.

The sponsoring corporation is requested to locate a site for the workshop. It is recommended that the workshop be held in a pleasant and private conference room in the corporation or at an off-site location, such as a meeting room in a hotel. The room should have comfortable chairs for participants organized around a U-shaped table. Such a design facilitates face-to-face contact among participants. The workshop leaders operate from the top of the U, and they should have an overhead projector available as well as an easel pad for recording group process. The availability of fresh fruits and hot and cold drinks promotes a relaxed and friendly atmosphere.

Given the short duration of the program, the workshop is highly structured and goal-directed. In addition, the focus is more on the individual couples than on group interaction. However, it is important that couples have opportunities to share information, provide positive feedback to one another, and build peer support and group cohesion (Yalom, 1970). Consequently, time should be provided in the workshop for the exchange of information among couples, and breaks between program units provide for the informal processing of information with one another and with the group leaders. It is important for group leaders to create a safe and supportive environment in which participants feel comfortable with disclosure among group members.

The closing dinner, which is preceded by a social hour, is an important aspect of the program. In the weekend format, dinner is scheduled at the conclusion of the workshop. In the evening session format, a closing dinner is scheduled for a separate evening following the fourth and final session. This dinner should be scheduled in a private room in a hotel or restaurant and should be sponsored by the corporation. It provides couples with an opportunity to informally process the workshop and to share insights and learning experiences. It is also a celebration of the commitment that couples have shown by their attendance in the workshop to strengthen their marriage and to forge a more supportive partnership between themselves and the work organization.

Leadership

Forms of leadership in marital enrichment programs vary from formally trained professionals to untrained nonprofessional volunteers, from husband/wife pairs to individual male/female facilitators (Dyer & Dyer, 1986). Although no formal training program is currently available for MAP leaders, it is imperative that leaders understand the theoretical and conceptual foundation for MAP (see Chapter 3), understand the nature of work and family dynamics (see Chapters 1 and 6), and have experience in group leadership and process. It is expected that group leaders will have a background in one of the helping professions, such as social work, psychology, counseling, or nursing. A manual for workshop leaders is currently under development.

Ideally, leadership is provided by a husband and wife pair who share responsibility for workshop content and who model cooperative marital behavior. However, it is also possible for the workshop to be directed by an unmarried male and female pair. Although it is possible for the workshop to be conducted by a single individual, this is not the preferred leadership structure. It is critical that leaders have ample time to informally converse with participants during breaks and to monitor group process for one another.

A sense of humor and a willingness to share one's own relational issues and dilemmas is an important aspect of group leadership. Marriage is full of trials and tribulations, and workshop leaders need to acknowledge the challenges of having an enabled marriage.

Community Resource Assessment

Before the workshop is held, it is important that workshop leaders assess available community resources for couples and families. An important responsibility of the workshop leaders is to serve as information broker for couples who wish to pursue further marital development or assistance following the workshop. A sheet is prepared for distribution to couples at the conclusion of the workshop that lists public agencies and nonprofit associations in the local community that sponsor various marital enrichment and support opportunities. A useful starting point in generating this resource list is the local telephone directory, which typically publishes a list of social, health, and mental health services and information sources in the community.

PROGRAM OUTLINE

The program is divided into four parts. Part 1 includes units 1 and 2; each requires a 50-minute time segment. Part 2 includes units 3 and 4, which require approximately three hours to complete. Part 3 includes units 5 and 6. At least two-and-one-half hours should be allowed to complete these units. Part 4 includes units 7, 8, and 9. Approximately two hours should also be allocated to complete this aspect of the program. A break is suggested between each unit of activity.

For purposes of presentation, the weekend program format is presented below. Table 2.1 provides a sample program schedule for this format.

PART 1

Unit 1: Getting Acquainted

Objectives:

- To introduce the workshop leaders and participants.
- To provide an overview of the MAP and the program agenda.
- To set ground rules for the workshop.
- To challenge participants toward relational growth and enhancement and to generate excitement in participants about promoting a more positive marital experience.

Time: 50 minutes

Activities: The leaders first introduce themselves and the MAP program. MAP is described as an enrichment program for helping couples better conceptualize, plan, and navigate their marital path. It is intended to promote higher levels of marital teamwork and relational satisfaction among participant couples, and a better understanding of work and family dynamics. A MAP analogy is drawn that conceptualizes marriage as a journey, one that can be navigated in a planned and purposeful manner by identifying one's present location, collective and individual goals and destinations for marriage, a route of travel, anticipated or experienced obstacles and barriers in the journey, and resources and processes for overcoming these obstacles and barriers. An overview of workshop objectives should be provided, followed by a brief overview of the program agenda. Overheads should be prepared that outline the workshop objectives and the program agenda.

Participants are asked to introduce themselves and their expectations for the program. These expectations should be recorded by the workshop leaders for revisiting at the conclusion of the workshop. Ground rules are established for the workshop, including confidentiality, respect for differences of opinion, sharing of discussion time, voluntary participation in activities, and adherence to the program schedule. An underlying assumption of systems theory is suggested by the workshop leaders that is congruent with the Value-Behavior Congruency Model: Equifinality—there is more than one way to get to a final goal or destination. Participants are asked to be accepting of individual differences and to avoid giving advice to other couples.

Unit 2: The Value-Behavior Congruency Model

Objectives:

- To understand the dynamics of group cohesiveness and stability.

Table 2.1
Sample Program Agenda

Friday Evening

Part 1

7:00-7:50   Unit 1: Getting Acquainted

8:00-8:50   Unit 2: The Value-Behavior Congruency Model

Saturday

Part 2

8:30-9:50   Unit 3: Values: A Driving Force in our Lives

10:00-11:30   Unit 4: Value-Behavior Congruency in Marriage

Lunch

Part 3

12:30-1:20   Unit 5: Personal and Relational Resources and
                            Barriers

1:30-3:00   Unit 6: Corporate Culture

Break

Part 4

3:15-3:50   Unit 7: Coping with Value-Behavior Incongruity

4:00-5:00   Unit 8: A Plan of Action

5:10-5:30   Unit 9: Close

Social Hour and Dinner

- To conceptualize the enabled marital system.

- To use the Value-Behavior Congruency Model as a framework for conceptualizing marital teamwork and relational satisfaction.

Time: 50 minutes.

Activities: The VBC model provides the conceptual underpinning for the workshop. Consequently, its presentation should provide a framework for the enrichment experience. An overhead is used for presenting the model (see Figure 2.1). Following the discussion in Chapter 3, each feature of the model is discussed, including definitions and assumptions, an ecological and social exchange perspective, influences on value-behavior congruency in marriage, coping with value-behavior incongruity, and a life course perspective. Couples are involved in the discussion where appropriate, as in defining "values" and "goals" and in giving examples of "dispositional" and "motivational" transformation in marriage (see Chapter 3). Special attention is directed toward understanding the dynamics of marital cohesion and dissolution (Levinger, 1965, 1979a, 1979b), the changing interface between work and family life in society today (see Chapters 1 and 6), the spillover nature of work and family linkages (see Chapters 1 and 6), and the influence of organizational culture on marriage (see Chapter 3). Spouses should be provided with an opportunity to ask questions about the model and to offer comments about its implications. This should be a "user friendly" presentation; for many spouses, it may be their first exposure to paradigms for understanding marital interaction and dynamics.

PART 2

Unit 3: Values: A Driving Force in our Lives

Objectives:

- To help spouses become more aware of their marital values (the relational "menu"), the origin of these values, and how these values may have changed over the marital career.

- To increase the openness of spouses to understanding value similarities and differences in their marriage, and the influence of these similarities and differences on marital teamwork and relational satisfaction.

- To better appreciate individual differences in marital values and goals across couples.

Time: 80 minutes

Activities: Based on the earlier presentation of the VBC model, a working definition of values is provided, including a discussion of their origin and level of abstraction. Johari's Window (Luft, 1969) is presented to conceptualize an important goal of MAP: to increase the insight of spouses into their own values and to share this awareness with their spouse (to increase open areas). Spouses are presented with their preferred ("ideal") family environment profile from the Family Environment Scale (FES) (Moos & Moos, 1986). Standard scores are derived for each of the ten subscales from norms provided by Moos and Moos (1986). For purposes of interpretation, a summary profile for the group is presented using an overhead transparency, and each of the ten FES subscales

Figure 2.1
Value-Behavior Congruency Model

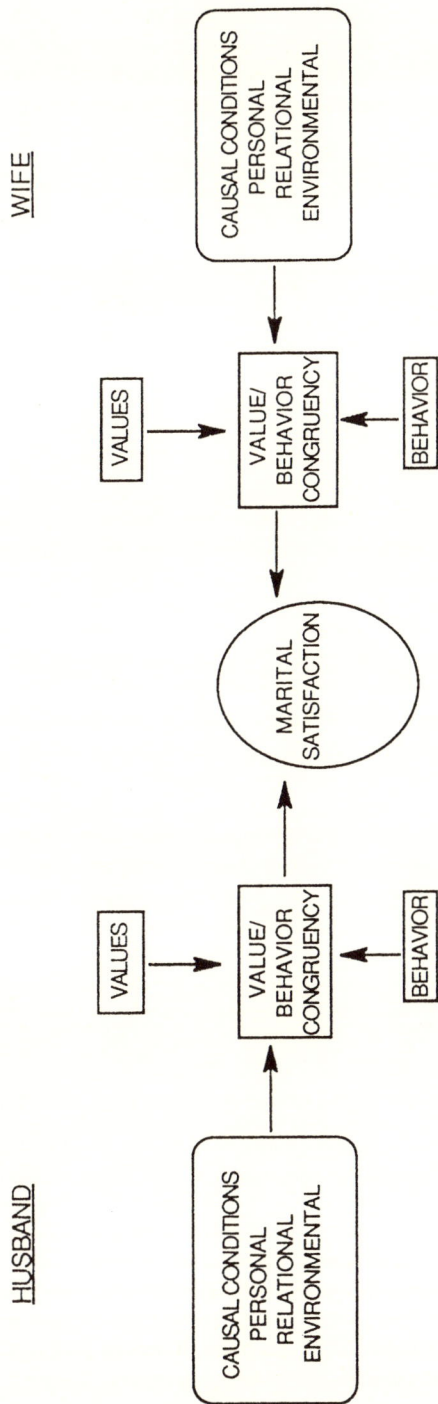

HUSBAND

WIFE

across the three underlying sets of dimensions are defined. Before discussing their profile with their spouse, spouses are asked first to mark on their profile where they perceive their spouse scored on each subscale (higher or lower or about the same as themselves). Spouses in each couple are then asked to get together to share their profiles, their projection of the other's score by subscale, changes in both their values as an individual and the pattern of their values as a couple over the duration of the marriage, and the implications of value similarities and differences for marital teamwork and relational satisfaction. For those who are comfortable with group disclosure, couples are asked to share insights with the group.

Unit 4: Value-Behavior Congruency in Marriage

Objectives:

- To identify levels of value and behavior congruency in marriage.
- To identify consequences of value-behavior congruency and incongruity in marriage.

Time: 90 minutes

Activities: Derived from Johari's Window, a two-by-two figure of value-behavior congruency is presented. The value dimension is located on the horizontal axis (yes, no), and the behavioral dimension is listed on the vertical dimension (yes, no). From the figure, value-behavior congruency is represented where either the marital-related value is preferred and realized in behavior or where the value is not preferred and not realized in behavior. Value-behavior incongruity results from a discrepancy between values and actions. From the VBC model, marital satisfaction is dependent on realizing values in behavior. Consequently, the focus of intervention is helping spouses to reduce situations where marital-related behaviors fall short of preferences. Spouses are presented with their actual ("real") and preferred ("ideal") family environment profiles from the Family Environment Scale, which are combined on the same graph (Moos & Moos, 1986). Standard scores are derived for both profiles across each of the ten subscales from norms provided by Moos and Moos (1986). For purposes of interpretation, a summary profile for the group is presented using an overhead transparency. These profiles enable participants to identify areas where behaviors and interactional patterns in marriage fall short of goals. Before sharing their profiles with one another, spouses in each couple are asked to think about areas in which their spouse may report the most difficulty in realizing his or her values in behavior. Spouses are then asked to share their profile with one another, to consider how their profile may have changed over the marital career, and to discuss the implications of value-behavior congruency and incongruity as indicated by their respective profile for their marriage. At this point, spouses may share learning experiences and insights from the exercise with the larger group. This concludes Part 2 of the workshop. Before separating for lunch (weekend format), an overview of Parts 3 and 4 is provided and spouses are encouraged to continue conversing about their learning experiences over lunch.

Lunch: Couples Enjoy Lunch Together

Objectives:

- To provide informal time to meet with workshop leader(s) and other participant couples for purposes of sharing and discussion of learning experiences.

• To promote social support and group cohesion.

Time: 60 minutes

PART 3

Unit 5: Personal and Relational Resources and Barriers

Objectives:

• To identify personal and relational resources that facilitate the ability of spouses to realize their individual and collective values and goals for marriage in behavior.

• To identify personal and relational obstacles and barriers that may be restricting their ability to realize their values and goals for marriage in behavior.

Time: 50 minutes

Activities: Based on the earlier presentation of the VBC model, spouses are asked to identify at least two personal and/or relational resources and two personal and/or relational barriers that influence their ability to realize their individual and collective values and goals for marriage in behavior. From this analysis, spouses come together with their partners to discuss their personal resources, to share perceptions about relational strengths, and to develop strategies for overcoming identified personal and relational barriers. Feedback from the partner in marriage is a critical aspect of this exercise. Couples are asked to share with the group at least one identified relational resource that they perceive themselves as having.

Unit 6: Corporate Culture

Objectives:

• To identify the values, norms, and informal rules that govern interaction in the host corporation and their influence on realizing individual and collective values and goals for the marital relationship in behavior.

• To have spouses compare their perceptions toward corporate culture with one another and to understand the influence of environmental conditions on the marital relationship.

• To determine the level of agreement among participants about the culture of the sponsoring corporation.

• To have couples make recommendations for improving the level of fit between corporation demands and resources and their values and goals for marriage.

Time: 90 minutes

Activities: Following the discussion of environmental constraints in Chapter 3, an overview of corporate culture is provided by the workshop leaders. Following this introduction, spouses are administered the Organizational Culture Profile (OCP) (see Chatman, 1989; O'Reilly, Chatman, & Caldwell, 1990). The instructions for administering and using the OCP have been altered from those suggested by its developers for purposes of its use in the workshop. Using a Q-sort method, the profile involves 54 descriptive value statements (e.g., "fairness," "tolerance," "being demanding," "working long hours") that are listed on cards and are sorted by participants into nine categories, ranging from "most characteristic" to "most uncharacteristic" of the corporation supporting the workshop. The continuum follows the normal distribution such that fewer cards are sorted into the extremes of the distribution than into the central part of the distribution (2–4–6–9–12–9–6–4–2). Spouses are asked to share their profiles with their partners by exchanging seats, focusing particularly on those value statements that have been sorted in the more extreme categories, to discuss their profile similarities and differences, and to discuss the implications of their descriptive assessment of corporate culture on their ability to realize their values and goals for marriage in behavior. After sharing their findings with the larger group, spouses are asked to sort another set of the same 54 items on a second, nine-point, Q-sort continuum that follows the same distribution pattern (2–4–6–9–12–9–6–4–2). This time, however, spouses are instructed to sort the cards from "most desirable" to "most undesirable" corporate culture for enhancing their ability as spouses to realize marital-related values and goals in behavior. Once again, spouses are requested to share the results of their Q-sort with their partners, to discuss discrepancies between their preferred and their perceived assessment of corporate culture, and to consider the implications of these discrepancies, if any, for marital life. After sharing insights with this group, spouses are asked to work together as a couple to draft a letter to the corporation outlining three recommendations for how the corporation can better support their marriage, how these changes would benefit both the corporation and themselves, and strategies for implementation. After having couples share their recommendations with the group, the workshop leaders collect the letters (no names are recorded) to prepare a summary briefing of recommendations to corporate sponsors. Further information about the Organizational Culture Profile (OCP) may be obtained from the reference articles just cited or by writing to: Professor Jennifer Chatman, J. L. Kellogg Graduate School of Management, Northwestern University, Leverone Hall, 2001 Sheridan Road, Evanston, Illinois 60208-2011, Phone 708-491-3470, Fax 708-491-8896.

Break: Fresh Fruits and Drinks

Time: 15 Minutes

PART 4

Unit 7: Coping with Value-Behavior Incongruity

Objectives:

- To review mechanisms by which spouses cope with their lack of success in realizing their values and goals for marriage in behavior.
- To have spouses discuss their attempts to cope with incongruities in marriage, and the implications of these strategies for desired personal and relational outcomes.

Time: 35 minutes

Activities: Using the presentation in Chapter 3 of "Coping with Value-Behavior Incongruity" as a guide, a discussion of coping styles and strategies is led by the workshop leaders. Following this discussion, spouses discuss with their partners how they have attempted to deal with value-behavior incongruities in marriage. Spouses are asked to identify their general coping styles and the effects of these styles on achieving their marital ambitions. Spouses are requested to propose to one another and receive feedback on alternative coping strategies that may facilitate their ability to better realize their marital-related values in behavior. Spouses are asked to share the results of their discussion with the group.

Unit 8: A Plan of Action

Objectives:

- To practice developing action plans for navigating the marital relationship toward increased levels of marital teamwork and relational satisfaction.
- To revisit the Value-Behavior Congruency Model as a framework for marital negotiation and problem solving.

Time: 60 minutes

Activities: Working separately, spouses in each couple are asked to select an area in marriage where they are experiencing difficulty achieving their goals for the relationship in behavior. Spouses are asked to identify a specific goal, to specify it in behavioral terms, and to determine the higher-order value from which the goal is derived. They are asked to think about this goal from a life cycle perspective and how its salience may have changed over time. They are asked to identify two barriers (personal, relational, or environmental) that hinder them from realizing this goal in behavior, and strategies for removing these barriers. They are also asked to identify two resources (personal, relational, or environmental) that they may draw upon in promoting behavior in support of their goal. In addition, they are asked to specify one thing that they want their spouse to do that will help them better realize this important marital-related goal. They are asked to be clear, concise, and direct in framing this request. From this analysis, they are asked to develop a plan of action for better achieving this goal in behavior. They are then asked to present this plan to their spouse. If cooperation is needed from the spouse, they are asked to negotiate this request and to identify any contingencies for the supportive actions of their spouse. Finally, they are asked to work together with their partner to develop a time frame for implementing the plan of action, a strategy for evaluating the success of their actions, and a plan for reinforcing themselves for goal achievement and their spouse for providing the necessary support and cooperation. Spouses are asked to share their final plan of action and their insights with the group.

Unit 9: Close

Objectives:

- To review the basic principles of MAP.
- To reinforce the learning experience.
- To inform participants about additional enrichment experiences and resources in their local community.

Time: 20 minutes

Activities: The workshop leaders review the basic principles of MAP and re-emphasize the challenges of the marital journey. The major theme in closing is reinforcing the hard work of participants in the workshop as an important step in their commitment toward enhancing their marital relationship. In addition, couples are encouraged to continue their journey toward reaching their full relational potential through clarifying and working to achieve their individual and collective values and goals for marriage. It is suggested by the workshop leaders that some couples may wish to continue to meet together informally to share their journey toward a more enabled marriage and to provide support and encouragement to one another. A listing of additional enrichment opportunities and therapeutic resources in the local community is distributed and reviewed with participants. Couples are informed that a second set of questionnaires will be mailed to them in approximately six weeks to help determine the impact of the workshop on their marital relationship. Evaluation forms of the workshop experience, including suggestions for strengthening the workshop, are distributed to participants. These are to be returned to the corporate point of contact. Participants are provided an opportunity to comment on the workshop and to ask questions. The workshop is adjourned for a social hour and dinner.

Social Hour and Dinner

Objectives:

- To provide couples with an opportunity to interact with one another and to discuss learning experiences and insights from the workshop.
- To provide workshop leaders with an opportunity to interact with the participants in an informal and relaxed manner.
- To reinforce the hard work of participants and their commitment to a better marriage.

Time: 150 minutes

FOLLOW-UP AND EVALUATION

Approximately six weeks after the workshop, each spouse is mailed a copy of the pre-workshop assessment instruments to complete and return to the workshop leaders. The purpose of this assessment is to help determine the potential influence of the workshop on the couple's relationship, in particular its effects in promoting greater value-behavior congruency in marriage and higher levels of marital teamwork and relational satisfaction. If possible, a control group of couples waiting to receive the workshop can be used as a comparison group and can receive both pre- and the post-instruments. Such a design increases the ability of workshop leaders to draw conclusions about the implications of the workshop for enhancing marital teamwork and relational satisfaction. These results are then presented to corporate sponsors.

CONCLUSION

MAP is considered responsive to the need for short-term marital enrichment programs that are specific to the corporate environment and that complement more extensive skill-based programs that are currently on the market. It is given coherence by a model that is grounded in the theoretical and empirical literature, the Value-Behavior Congruency Model. It also incorporates an evaluation component, and it emphasizes the responsibilities of workshop leaders to consult with the corporation based on the feedback of participants to build a set of policies and practices that promote the marital well-being of employees and their spouses.

Although specific program units and activities have been outlined, they should be seen as merely suggestive. At this point in its development, the program is designed to be flexible; as such, workshop leaders are encouraged to experiment with alternative program formats and activities. In addition, program leaders are encouraged to develop alternative measures and exercises to assess the level of value-behavior congruency in marriage. Although the Family Environment Scale (Moos, & Moos 1986) is recommended as one such measure (see Moos, 1990 and Roosa & Beals, 1990 for a critique of the FES), it is important to adapt the scale to represent a couple reality. This should involve not only changing the instructions (as described above), but also eventually rewording the items. In addition, with continued use it should be possible to develop norms for computing standard scores that are based on the responses of spouses who have participated in the program rather than the norms provided by Moos and Moos (1986).

The corporate sector represents a tremendous opportunity for marital and family enrichment specialists to work on behalf of families. Research suggests that both the corporation and the family can benefit from programs that are designed to enhance marital teamwork and relational satisfaction. By building on concepts that are familiar to corporate leaders, such as teamwork, by not requiring large investments in time or money by either the corporation or the participants, and by complementing rather than duplicating existing enrichment programs, MAP is considered to have tremendous market potential in the work world.

3

The Value-Behavior Congruency Model: A Theoretical and Conceptual Foundation for MAP

MAP draws upon a general theory of interrelationship between the person and the environment. Traced to the work of Henry Murray (1938) and Kurt Lewin (1951) in organizational psychology and to the work of Mary Richmond and Bertha Reynolds in social work (see Bartlett, 1970; Hartman & Laird, 1983), the key assumption of this theory is that the "goodness of fit" between the characteristics of a person and the characteristics of his or her environment affect a person's level of stress and satisfaction (Caplan, 1987; French, Caplan, & Harrison, 1982; Harrison, 1978). Within this perspective, MAP focuses on the level of fit or congruence between the marital values and goals of spouses and their opportunities in the marriage to behaviorally realize these values and goals.

This perspective has recently been incorporated into a model by Gary Bowen (1988a, 1988b, 1989a) that serves as the theoretical anchor for MAP: the Value-Behavior Congruency Model of Marital Satisfaction (VBC). The core assumption of this model is that the level of marital satisfaction is enhanced in situations where spouses are able to realize their collective and individual marital-related values and goals in behavior.

This chapter defines key concepts in the model and discusses its underlying assumptions. The model is grounded both theoretically and empirically, and factors are discussed that may influence the level of value-behavior congruency in marriage. This discussion is followed by a consideration of both potential coping responses to value-behavior incongruity in marriage and the importance of a life course perspective in the study of relational dynamics. Implications of the model are discussed for enriching marriages through educational and experiential activities.

DEFINITIONS AND ASSUMPTIONS

Values

A key concept in MAP is that of values. Although there is little consensus in the literature concerning the definition of values and related concepts, values are defined from the perspective of the value-behavior congruency model as organized sets of preferences for how individuals wish to conduct their lives (Christensen, 1964; Kluckhohn, 1951; Mindel & Habenstein, 1976). These preferences are conceptualized as cognitive and evaluative, serving as a basis for choice and as a guide for action (Kluckhohn & Strodtbeck, 1961; Kohn, 1969; Locke, 1976; Rokeach, 1968, 1973; Scheibe, 1970; Spiegel, 1971, 1982; Turner & Musick, 1985).

In addition, the values held by each individual are assumed to be logically ordered from the most abstract to the most concrete and to be connected across levels of abstraction (see Montgomery, 1982, pp. 75–81 for a more detailed discussion). Although "higher-order" values are considered to serve as a general "frame of reference" for the individual (e.g., the importance of family integration), they operate as general assumptions and are seldom made explicit (McDonald & Cornille, 1988; Montgomery, 1982, pp. 76–77). However, they do provide an overarching structure for ordering and evaluating lower-tier values—values that operate at a higher level of consciousness, that are more manifest and explicit, and that are more open to direct consideration and discussion than higher-order values (e.g., preferences for spending time together as a family).

Lower-tier values refer to specific objects, actions, or conditions that are connected to a broader and more abstract class of objects, actions, or conditions that are valued by the individual (cf. Nye, 1967). They are referred to in the literature by a variety of closely related concepts: goals, aims, preferences, priorities, attractions, interests, desires, ambitions, wants, and aspirations (Dunst, Trivette, & Deal, 1988; Nye, 1967). In the present discussion, the concept of "goals" will be used to refer to these lower-tier values.

According to Pervin (1987), goals have three associated components: cognitive, affective, and behavioral.

The cognitive component consists of the mental representation of the desired endpoint and constructions of paths toward that point (plans). The affective component consists of the specific affects associated with goals and the plans involved in reaching these goals. The behavioral component consists of the behaviors associated with the plans or routes associated with achieving goals. (p. 228)

At each level of abstraction, values are conceptualized as hierarchically arranged from most important to least important: the assumption of transitivity (Montgomery, 1982; Ravlin & Meglino, 1989; Stein, 1985). All else being equal, it is assumed that individuals are likely to behave in ways that validate their values at the highest level (D. Friedman, 1987; Montgomery, 1982).

Although they are learned primarily from parents and significant others in childhood and adolescence through processes of identification, role modeling, and reinforcement, neither values nor their respective importance within levels of abstraction are considered fixed. They are defined as variables that may change in response to a variety of familial and extra-familial influences, including changes in the interactional dynamics in families, differential associations with both others and groups in the larger society over time, and shifts in cultural norms and societal expectations. In addition, the values of an individual are not assumed to be necessarily compatible. As a consequence, behavior in accordance with values at one level may preclude or limit behavior in accordance with values at some other level.

In agreement with Nye (1967), it is important not only to define a concept in terms of what it means, but also to distinguish it from concepts that are used in its place or synonymously with it. In the case of values, both the concepts of "expectation" and "need" meet this criterion. In discussing job satisfaction as the product of the interaction between the person and the environment, Locke (1969), an organizational psychologist, perhaps most clearly distinguishes the concepts of "expectations" and "needs" from the concept of "value."

The view that evaluations results [sic] from a discrepancy between what is perceived and what is expected . . . is based on a failure to distinguish between cognitive and evaluative concepts. Expectation is a term denoting one's beliefs about what will occur in the future. What is expected, however, may or may not correspond to what is wanted. Conversely, what is valued may or may not correspond to what is expected. . . . Empirically, values and expectations often coincide, because most people value only that which they have some reasonable chance of attaining. . . .

Some investigators have argued that satisfaction is a function of the discrepancy between needs and outcomes. . . . Biologically the concept of need derives from the fact that living organisms require certain objects and conditions to maintain their physical health and survival. The analogous meaning of need at the psychological level would pertain to conditions required for a healthy consciousness. In both cases the concept refers to the objective requirements of an organism's well-being.

A conscious living organism may or may not be aware of all its needs. Need frustration produces discomfort, but it does not automatically produce a conscious desire for the needed object. . . .

The concept of need should be . . . distinguished from the concept of wish or value. A value is that which a man actually seeks to gain and/or keep or considers beneficial. A value presupposes an awareness, at some level, of the object or condition sought. A need does not. . . . Whether or not a man's values correspond to needs, it is his values which regulate his actions and determine his emotional responses. (pp. 319-321)

It is assumed that spouses have an "emotional response" to their ability to realize marital-related values in behavior. Based upon discussions by both

Berscheid and associates (1983, 1984, 1985) and Bradbury and Fincham (1987), emotion is defined as an affective response to the level of facilitation or interruption that a presenting stimulus or event poses to an individual's plans or goal-directed activities. This response is predicated on the cognitive interpretation of the presenting stimulus or event by the individual on a continuum of supportiveness to one's plans and goal-directed activities and may be associated with physiological arousal and behavioral action (see Hochschild, 1983 for a review of models of emotion).

Emotions in marriage may have either a positive, neutral, or negative valence, and positive and negative emotions may vary in the level of their intensity. When one spouse supports the other in achieving a collective and/or individual goal for marriage, it is hypothesized that a positive emotion, such as joy or satisfaction, may be generated toward the supportive spouse. On the other hand, when one spouse hinders or disrupts the other from achieving a collective and/or individual goal for marriage, it is hypothesized that a negative emotion, such as anger or frustration, may be directed toward the nonsupportive spouse.

Although it seems logical to hypothesize that spouses may have a neutral or benign emotional response in the absence of either facilitation or interruption by the other of their collective and/or individual goals, such events may assume either a positive or negative valence depending upon one's interpretation of the other's response. In MAP, it is assumed that the level of marital satisfaction experienced by husbands and wives is a function of this emotional response.

Marital Satisfaction

The penultimate objective of MAP is to help spouses increase the level of satisfaction that they experience from their marriage. Paralleling the work of Locke (1969, p. 320; 1976, p. 1300) in defining job satisfaction, marital satisfaction is conceptualized as a "pleasurable or positive emotional state" that is a function of the perceived ability of spouses to realize their individual and collective values for marriage in behavior. Consistent with a person-environment fit perspective (Harrison, 1978), this definition draws a theoretical distinction between the level of value-behavior congruency in marriage and the emotional state that results from this level of congruency. For purposes of definition, marital satisfaction ranges from high to low, and the overall level of marital satisfaction is a result of satisfactions experienced by spouses from more specific domains in marriage over time.

Based on the conceptual discussion by Spanier and Cole (1976) and the empirical work by Schumm and associates (1986) that forms the basis of the Kansas Marital Satisfaction Scale, the overall level of marital satisfaction for spouses is conceptualized as a composite of three distinct components: satisfaction with their spouse, satisfaction with their relationship with their spouse, and satisfaction with their marriage. Although it is assumed that the level of satisfaction for each component may vary for a given spouse, the level of satisfaction in each is assumed to be the product of the same process: the level of value-behavior congruency. Research by Schumm and associates (1986) suggests that these three components are highly interrelated, and for purposes of the present discussion they are used interchangeably.

Thus, marital satisfaction is defined as an emotional outcome of a dynamic, fluid, interactional process between spouses who are constantly working to achieve desired marital-related ends in the context of ever-changing and emerging marital-related values (Mace & Mace, 1978). Although marital satisfaction is defined from an individual perspective, it is likely that the overall level of satisfaction for each spouse is enhanced in situations where both spouses are able to move toward realizing their collective and individual values for marriage in behavior. This assumption is consistent with Constantine's (1986) definition of an ''enabled'' family system:

An enabled family system is one which: (1) on the average, is able to meet most of its collective or jointly defined needs and goals; (2) on the average, enables most of its members to meet most of their individual needs and individually defined goals; and (3) does not consistently and systematically disable any particular member(s) from meeting individual needs and goals. (p. 26)

This approach to defining marital satisfaction proposes that neither couples nor spouses in the same marriage necessarily share similar values for marriage. In addition, values are viewed in neither ''good'' nor ''bad'' terms. The marital-related values of spouses both within marriages and between marriages are seen as ''different than'' rather than ''better than'' or ''worse than'' one another. However, they are considered to influence behavior and to serve as criteria for evaluating one's own experiences in the relationship. This motivational aspect of values is reflected in the work of Hess and Handel (1959, p. 3):

in his relationship in the family an individual member strives toward predictability of preferred experience, attempting to discover or create circumstances which fit his image of what the world around him should be—how it should respond to him and provide opportunity for expression of his own preferences. (cited in Galvin & Brommel, 1986, p. 38)

This value-based definition of marital satisfaction contrasts greatly with other conceptualizations of marital satisfaction in the literature. By focusing on a fixed set of interactions and feelings as a point of reference, there has been a tendency in both models of marital functioning and self-report measures of marital outcomes, like marital satisfaction, to homogenize the rich variation and diversity among couples (Adams, 1988; Larzelere & Klein, 1987).

Despite the growing respect for diversity in family values, perceptions, needs, and process in the United States (e.g., Bowen & Janofsky, 1988; Constantine, 1986; Langman, 1987; McGoldrick, Pearce, & Giordano, 1982; Wilkenson, 1987), definitions and measures of marital satisfaction in the literature have tended to neglect variations in the normative values of families. Marital satisfaction has tended to be defined and operationalized on the basis of either the presence of positive attributes, the absence of negative attributes, or a score that represents a statistical average (cf. Epstein, Bishop, & Baldwin, 1982; Walsh, 1982; see Sabatelli, 1988b for a review of issues in the measurement of marital outcomes). As recently pointed out by Karpel (1986), models and measures of family functioning often assume that there is some ideal way that families should function; all other ways are seen as somewhat less than desirable. Such assumptions can promote the design and implementation of enrichment programs for couples that are static and nomothetic in orientation rather than dynamic and sensitive to the unique situation and values of spouses in marriages.

Although the level of value-behavior congruency of spouses serves as the benchmark for evaluating their marital satisfaction, the proposed conceptualization of marital satisfaction recognizes the potential influence of "causal conditions" in the interface between values and behavior (Kelley et al., 1983). Kelley et al. (1983, p. 49) define a "condition" as "something that must exist if something else is to be or to take place, an affecting influence, something that limits or modifies the existence or character of something else." It is assumed that the spouses pursue their values in their marriage within a larger "causal context" that may serve to either facilitate or constrain their ability to behave in ways that are consistent with their values (McClintock, 1983, p. 95). Kelley et al. (1983) and McClintock (1983) discuss three broad categories of causal conditions that will be examined in a subsequent section: personal, relational, and environmental.

A SOCIAL EXCHANGE PERSPECTIVE

The importance of using values as a contingent variable in conceptualizing marital satisfaction is consistent with tenets of social exchange theory (e.g., Berscheid, 1983; Blau, 1964; Chadwick-Jones, 1976; Edwards, 1969; Heath, 1976; Homans, 1958, 1961; Kelley, 1979; Kelley et al., 1983; Kelley & Thibaut, 1978; La Gaipa, 1977; Lawler, 1973; McDonald, 1981; Nye, 1978, 1979; Scanzoni, 1972, 1978, 1979a, 1979b; Thibaut & Kelley, 1959; Walster, Walster, & Berscheid, 1978). From this perspective, it is assumed that:

1. Spouses in marriage are "strategic" (cf. Kanter, 1977a, p. 252) and often have complex and competing value systems that influence decisions about behavior.
2. Goals are specific outcomes within a broader category of outcomes that are valued by spouses in marriage (Nye, 1967).

3. Behavior by spouses in marriage is "not random," but "purposive" and "goal directed" (Edwards, 1969, p. 518).

4. Spouses are brought into interdependence by the pursuit of individual and collective goals in marriage (Berscheid, 1983; Edwards, 1969; Scanzoni, 1979a).

5. Spouses vary in the level of instrumental and expressive support that they provide to one another in working to achieve their individual and collective goals in marriage. This support may either facilitate, hinder, or have no influence on the ability of spouses to achieve their individual and collective goals for marriage (Kelley et al., 1983).

6. Spouses have emotional responses to their ability to achieve their goals for marriage as a result of their behavior (cf. Berscheid, 1983).

7. When spouses define their interaction with the other as facilitative to their individual and collective goals for marriage, personal and/or joint profit from the relationship tends to increase, and spouses are likely to experience more positive emotional responses toward their marriage. On the other hand, where spouses define their interaction with one another as creating more interference than facilitation of their individual and collective goals for marriage, personal and/or joint profit from the relationship tends to decrease, and spouses are likely to experience more negative emotional responses toward the marriage. Levinger (1986, p. 175) refers to the relative level of facilitation and interference that spouses pose to one another in realizing their marital-related values and goals as the "facilitation-interference ratio."

8. The more positive the emotional response to the marriage, the more spouses will define the marriage as being satisfying.

An implicit proposition in the work of Homans (1961) is the influence of "value" on the amount of profit that partners receive from interaction. As elaborated by Burr (1973), the value of interaction between partners influences the amount of profit from the interaction and the level of positive sentiment. In other words, the impact of actions in relationships is influenced by the relative value that partners attach to these actions (Burr, 1973). Burr suggests this to be a positive and monotonic relationship.

The influence of values from the exchange perspective on the salience and consequences of actions or lack of actions in relationships is related to the underlying conceptual link between values and goals. Nye (1967, p. 242) distinguishes values from goals as a matter of degree: Goals are specific outcomes that are connected to a "broader category" of outcomes that are valued by the individual. For example, one who values family integration may set a goal of devoting every Friday night to interact with the children.

At the most general level, it would be proposed from an exchange theory perspective that the level of marital satisfaction will be dependent upon the relative perceptions that spouses have of their ability to realize important marital-related values in behavior. In situations where spouses are able to consistently realize marital-related values and goals that are defined as important in behavior, it is predicted that there is a building up of positive sentiments toward the marriage. On the other hand, the consistent failure of spouses to realize important marital-related values in behavior is likely to result in frustration and disappointment, leading to less rewarding interaction and the development of negative sentiments toward the marriage. Thus, consistent with the premises of exchange theory, satisfying marital relationships may be conceptualized as profitable and reciprocal exchanges based on the ability of spouses to realize their marital-related values in behavior (Bagorozzi & Wodarski, 1977; Walster, Walster & Berscheid, 1978).

It is assumed that spouses in a relationship may have differential success in realizing their goals for marriage in behavior. Although "equity" theory would assume that both "overbenefitted" as well as "underbenefitted" spouses would be less satisfied with their marriage than spouses who are "equitably treated" (Hatfield & Traupmann, 1981; Walster, Walster, & Berscheid, 1978), a cumulative series of studies by Cate and associates of relationship satisfaction among participants in premarital relationships yields some interesting qualifications to this assumption (Cate, Lloyd, & Henton, 1985; Cate, Lloyd, & Long, 1988; Lloyd, Cate, & Henton, 1982).

Their research suggests that the level of rewards that participants receive from the relationship ("reward level") is a better predictor of relationship satisfaction than their perceptions about "equity" in the relationship (Cate, Lloyd, & Long, 1988). In addition, they also provide support for an exchange principle found in the work of Leik and Leik (1977), Levinger and Snoek (1972), Rubin (1973), and Scanzoni (1979a): The contribution of "fairness" considerations to relationship satisfaction may become more attenuated over time.

As they hypothesized, Cate and associates (1988) found that equity in exchange decreased in its contribution to relationship satisfaction over a three-month period of time. However, in support of their hypothesis, they found that an individual's reward level remained a strong and significant predictor of relationship satisfaction over the same time frame. Although Hatfield and Traupmann (1981) also suggest that "equity" considerations may become less important to relationship satisfaction over time, they propose that issues of "fairness" remain important until "very late" in the life of the couple (p. 173). Future research should re-examine the findings by Cate and associates among married respondents and among participants in longer-term relationships.

Based on the research by Cate and associates, it is assumed for purposes of the VBC model that although the marital satisfaction of each spouse *may* be maximized when *both* spouses in the relationship are able to realize their individual and collective goals for marriage (a situation that approximates a condition of equity), it is not assumed that equity is a necessary condition for spouses to experience high marital satisfaction. From the perspective of the VBC model, the ability of spouses to achieve their values for marriage and family life in behavior is considered to correspond to Cate and associates' (1988) concept of reward level.

However, in agreement with Hatfield and Traupmann (1981), in the long run, inequitable arrangements may lead to distress and low satisfaction, especially for the underbenefitted spouse, and it is likely that efforts will be directed by one or both spouses to establish a more equitable arrangement (Hatfield & Traupmann, 1981). In addition, it is likely that as the marriage matures in years, partners become more interdependent and the relationship becomes more "we" than "I" oriented (Levinger & Snoek, 1972; Scanzoni, 1979a). Consequently, across time, there will be a proportional increase in the ratio of collective to individual marital goals in longer-term relationships, increasing the likelihood that each spouse will benefit by the success of the other in realizing their marital-related goals.

From this perspective, it is important to underscore that the exchange patterns in marriage are not static; they may change through either implicit or explicit bargaining to permit one or both parties to experience greater rewards and fewer costs (Chadwick-Jones, 1976; Scanzoni, 1978). For example, Levinger (1986) discusses not only the changing nature of values for partners over time, but also how the values of partners can converge over the course of the relationship through a process of accommodation. According to Levinger, such accommodation of partners may result from a long-term convergence over the marital career in the values or goals of one or both partners ("dispositional transformation") or by deliberate actions of one or both partners to adapt to the needs and wishes of the other for a period of time ("motivational transformation").

Moreover, exchange relationships may not have an immediate payoff. Specifically, one spouse may provide the other with a reward, trusting that the other will reciprocate in some future transaction, a phenomenon that helps explain actions by family members that are not congruent with their professed values. This indebtedness is interpreted as binding actors together and giving solidarity to their relationship (Scanzoni, 1979a).

Last, social exchanges do not occur in a vacuum, but within a larger "structural," "normative," and "temporal" context (McDonald, 1981, p. 826). Cultural norms, societal expectations, and alternative suppliers of rewards play an important part in the process of social exchange by influencing definitions of what is preferable, what is profitable, and what is equitable (Edwards, 1969; Scanzoni, 1979b).

CONCEPTUAL AND EMPIRICAL SUPPORT

The concept of "value" is regarded by Hinde (1979) as central to the understanding of interpersonal relationships. The nature and impact of values in marriage and family life have been an important focus of study in family science. They have been studied in relation to mate selection as well as to various dimensions of marital well-being and stability (e.g., Adams, 1979; Bowen & Orthner, 1983; Levinger, 1986; Lewis & Spanier, 1979). For example, the level

of husband and wife value consensus has been correlated with various dimensions of marital quality and stability (e.g., Lewis & Spanier, 1979).

The pioneering work of Don Byrne (1971), George Levinger (1965, 1966),
and others (e.g., Grush & Yehl, 1979) has led to the conclusion that value congruency operates as a reward in relationships; it leads to interpersonal attraction and stability because it provides "consensual validation" for one's point
of view. Levinger (1986) recently hypothesized that the greater the fit between
the values of partners, the greater their relational involvement as well as their
level of compatibility.

Empirical support for the VBC model of marital satisfaction goes at least
as far back as the studies by Terman and associates (1938) of correlates of marital
happiness. These investigators found a strong correlation between the discrepancy between the desired and the actual frequency of sexual intercourse and the
level of marital happiness. In addition, in a comprehensive review of theory
and research on mate selection and marital satisfaction in 1963, Tharp concluded "that marital satisfaction is a function of the satisfaction of needs and/or
expectations specific to husband and wife roles" (p. 115). More recently,
Spanier (1976), in his development of the dyadic adjustment scale, found that
scale scores on the dyadic consensus subscale were influenced by weighting
the component items by their respective importance to respondents, suggesting
the mediating role of values to relational assessment.

In studying how the individual perceptions of family members toward the
family unit mediate the impact of family experiences on family-related outcomes, research conducted by Van Der Veen, Hubner, Jorgens, and Neja
(1964) in the early 1960s also provides important historical support for the proposed conceptualization of marital satisfaction. Using small clinical and
nonclinical sample groups, the investigators found that the greater the discrepancy between the ideal expectations of parents toward the functioning of the family
unit and their actual experiences, the greater the level of family dissatisfaction
and family maladjustment. Van Der Veen and colleagues recommended that
an important focus of clinical intervention with families is in helping members
to recognize their different expectations toward the family unit, and to focus
on those areas where family functioning falls short of ideal expectations.

Conceptual and empirical support for the proposed framework of marital
satisfaction is also found in more recent literature, including the theoretical
and empirical work by Berscheid (1983, 1985), Berscheid, Gangestad, and
Kulakowski (1984), McCubbin and Thompson (1987), Moos and Moos (1984,
1986), Olson (1986), Olson and associates (Olson & Portner, 1984; Olson,
Russell, & Sprenkle, 1983), and Sabatelli (1984, 1988a). Overall, the work
of these behavioral and social scientists clearly suggests that family members,
even those within the same family, may in fact differ in their preferences toward
marital and family life; they may also have differential success in realizing their
preferences for marital and family life in behavior. Although much of the work
reviewed below relates specifically to family dynamics rather than marital

dynamics per se, the processes described should have similar relevancy for couples. Satir (1972) maintains that one of the best ways to enhance family life is to strengthen the relationship of the husband and wife, who are the "architects" of the family.

Berscheid and Associates

Ellen Berscheid (1983) and Berscheid, Steven W. Gangestad, and Donna Kulakowski (1984) present an analysis of emotion in close relationships that underscores an underlying assumption of the VBC model of marital satisfaction: the importance of understanding the values and goals of participants in the relationship. Berscheid describes participants in a relationship as having "higher-order plans" or "goals" that reflect their values and to which they are committed to some degree. Although varying in their level of abstraction, organization, and specificity, these plans or goals are connected across levels of abstraction and influence the behavior or "intrachain sequences" of the individual.

The "intrachain behavioral sequences" of participants in the dyad that are connected to some degree to these higher-order plans or goals are presented by Berscheid as operating parallel to one another (e.g., the husband is preparing dinner and the wife is watching the evening news). Since "interdependency" or mutual impact between participants is a key feature of close relationships, the goal-directed behaviors of these participants will become interconnected to some degree over time. Depending upon the nature of the relationships between the participants and their level of interdependency, these "interchain causal connections" between participants may either facilitate, interrupt, or have no influence on the higher-order plans or intrachain sequence of events of one another.

The concept of "emotion" is central to Berscheid's analysis. Drawing upon George Mandler's (1975) cognitive approach to emotion, the "interruption hypothesis" is a critical feature in Berscheid's analysis of emotion. As presented by Berscheid, Mandler proposes that the interruption of "higher-order plans" or "organized behavior sequences" is sufficient to result in peripheral physiological arousal, which is associated with the autonomic nervous system (ANS). This arousal is a necessary, but not sufficient, condition for an emotional experience.

The degree to which individuals experience an emotional response to events that trigger autonomic arousals depends upon their cognitive appraisal of both the presenting stimulus or event as a threat as well as their ability to control or modify the interrupting stimulus through action. Lazarus and Folkman (1984) refer to the former appraisal as primary, the latter appraisal as secondary. Mandler suggests that a complex interaction exists between the physiological responses of individuals to events and the meaning analysis that they apply to these events.

From Berscheid's model, both negative and positive emotions are produced from the same process: interruptions of higher-order plans or organized behavior sequences. However, drawing upon Mandler's control hypothesis, Berscheid notes that for positive emotion to occur the interrupting stimulus must be defined by the individual as benign or controllable, not as a threat to the individual's higher-order plans or organized behavioral plans, which are assumed to develop in service of the individual's well-being and survival. In addition, based on Berscheid's completion hypothesis, positive emotion will occur if the interruption either removes an interrupting stimulus that interferes with accomplishing higher-order plans or organized behavior sequences or facilitates completion of these plans or sequences earlier than anticipated. In both cases, the interrupting stimulus should be viewed as benign.

Since most interrupting stimuli are not under the individual's immediate control, Berscheid hypothesizes that most interruptions lead to negative rather than positive emotions. In addition, as a consequence of increased autonomic arousal during the time individuals are seeking solutions to stimuli that pose a threat but that are not under their immediate control, negative emotions are likely to be experienced more intensely than positive emotions.

As already stated, interruption is a necessary condition for the experience of emotion, either positive or negative. Although interchain causal connections between participants in relationships may be interruptive and thus result in autonomic activity, they may also be either facilitative to the other's higher-order plans or organized behavioral sequence or have a benign influence on these plans and sequences. In situations where the behavior of one participant actually facilitates the goal-directed activity of the other, but is expected or anticipated, Berscheid suggests that the recipient of the supportive action may experience a "cool" as compared to a "hot" emotion, such as appreciation or satisfaction. Hot emotions, such as anger or joy, will occur only under situations of interruption that trigger physiological arousal.

Berscheid distinguishes the concept of "emotional investment" from the concept of "emotion." Emotional investment is defined as "potential" for participants to experience emotion in the relationship or the extent to which the intrachain sequences of each participant in the relationship are tied to the other through interchain connections and thereby are vulnerable to interruption (the wife depends upon the husband to pick up the children from nursery school on Tuesday and Thursday because she attends night classes at the university).

Since the nature and extent of these interchain to intrachain connections may vary for each participant, it is possible for participants in the dyad to have different levels of emotional investment in the relationship. In addition, because interruption is a necessary precursor for the experience of emotion by participants in a relationship, participants may have a high level of emotional investment but a low frequency and intensity of emotion.

The conceptual distinction between emotion and emotional investment presents an interesting challenge for participants in relationships. From

Berscheid's analysis, a partner is only able to produce emotion in the other through an interrupting stimulus. As noted previously, the interruptive stimulus may either facilitate or limit the other in achieving their intended plans and goals. However, to produce positive emotion, this interruptive stimulus must not only be facilitative, but also unexpected. Since the behavior of participants becomes relatively predictable over time and since past behaviors influence future expectations for behavior, an interesting paradox is presented in relationships: Behavior in the past that produced positive emotion in the other may become relatively benign over time. On the other hand, if the behavior is withdrawn, it may actually produce negative emotion. Berscheid et al. (1984) state: "we can predict that while the capability of the partner to produce positive emotion should decrease over time, the capability of the partner to produce negative emotion should increase as the relationship grows closer and older" (p. 454).

Over time, relational partners may become quite "meshed" in the nature of their interchain causal connections, leading to high emotional investment but higher potential for negative rather than positive emotion. Based on this analysis, Berscheid et al. (1984) conclude:

Only those people who continue to dream and plan throughout their lives, and who continue to strive for long-term goals, are capable of staying emotionally alive. And within close relationships, perhaps only those people who continue to dream dreams whose fulfillment depends upon their partner can stay emotionally alive within their relationship. Even these people, unfortunately, cannot be guaranteed the experience of intense positive emotion. (pp. 452–453)

The work of Berscheid and Berscheid and associates provides conceptual support for the proposed definition of marital satisfaction as a "pleasurable emotional state" (Locke, 1969, p. 320) that is a function of the extent to which spouses perceive that they are able to realize their individual and collective values for marriage in behavior. It underscores that the behavior of participants in close relationships is directed by higher-order plans and goals that may vary over the life cycle.

The pursuit of these plans and goals brings participants into interdependency. In situations where participants are able to support one another in realizing their plans and goals, it is likely that they will experience less negative emotion. However, herein lies the paradox from Berscheid's analysis: They still may not experience positive emotion unless some element of the unexpected is built into their responses to one another.

Over time, participants may develop a high potential for emotion through increasing levels of emotional investment but may actually experience little emotional intensity because their behaviors may become so well synchronized. According to Berscheid et al. (1984, p. 453), this "emotional tranquility" may lead participants to feel that something is wrong with the relationship and move it toward termination. In addition, Berscheid suggests that some relationships experience not only little emotion but also little potential for emotion. In these relationships, participants have few interchain causal connections, a necessary but not sufficient condition for the experience of emotion within the relationship.

Berscheid and associates' analysis of emotion has rich implications for relationship enhancement. As with the VBC model, it is important to help couples to understand and possibly negotiate their individual and collective plans and goals for their relationship. In addition, it is important to help them examine their behavior outcomes and to identify obstacles and constraints to identified discrepancies between higher-order plans and goals and their outcomes, especially those liaisons and commitments outside the relationship that may provide competition for the partner.

Perhaps, most important, couples may benefit from learning more about the "paradoxical" nature of relationships over time and may plan strategies for keeping their relationship emotionally viable and satisfying. Since participants are likely to be less consciously aware of "facilitative interconnections" than "interfering interconnections" within the relationship because of differential ANS arousal, couples may need help in appraising the nature of their relationship. The greater intensity usually associated with negative emotions as compared to positive emotions may cause these emotions to be weighted too heavily in the overall evaluation of the relationship.

McCubbin and Thompson

In their innovative construction of family typologies, Hamilton I. McCubbin and Anne Thompson (1987) explicitly recognized the importance of shared values by family members for the successful management of family tension and strain. In addition, the authors' fourfold typology of rhythmic families (one of the four family typologies discussed by the authors) is operationalized on the basis of the level of balance between valuing family time and routines and the actual efforts of the family to routinize family life into predictable activities. In McCubbin and Thompson's typology, families that both value family time and routines and that embrace these values in behavior were labeled "rhythmic" families.

In their analysis, McCubbin and Thompson compared families that placed little value on family time and routines and little behavioral emphasis on such practices (i.e., "unpatterned" families) as well as families that evidenced value and behavioral incongruity with respect to family time and routines (i.e., "structured" families and "intentional" families, respectively) to rhythmic families. The authors found that rhythmic families as compared to the other family types evidenced greater family-related outcomes in the following domains: traditions and celebrations, bonding, flexibility, hardiness, coherence, family satisfaction, marital satisfaction, child development satisfaction, community satisfaction, and overall family well-being.

When the category of rhythmic families was compared across the family life cycle (i.e., single, couple, preschool and school-age children, adolescence and launching, and empty nest and retirement), the highest proportion of rhythmic families was found among couples with preschool and school-age children, as well as among couples in the empty nest through retirement period of life. The lowest proportion of rhythmic families was found in the adolescent through launching phase of the family life cycle; in this stage, families with low levels of family time and routines and low valuing of these routines and investments in family life (referred to as "unpatterned" families) were the most prevalent.

McCubbin and Thompson's emphasis on the link between family-related values and behavior in their development of family typologies provides an important conceptual and empirical foundation to the proposed conceptualization of marital satisfaction. As in the work by McCubbin and Thompson, it will be important to evaluate the ability of the proposed framework to make predictions about marital-related outcomes.

An important finding by McCubbin and Thompson is the significance of examining the congruency of family-related values and behaviors in the context of the family life cycle. Their findings suggest that family members may have particular difficulty realizing their values in behavior at certain stages of the family life cycle. For example, families that greatly emphasize the value of family time and routines, but that actually practice these patterns with little frequency (intentional families), were most prevalent among childless couples. In the proposed framework, these families may be particularly likely to face a high number of system-level constraints both from their families of origin as well as from their beginning careers that limit their ability to realize important family-related values.

Olson and Associates

An important empirical foundation of the present conceptualization of marital satisfaction is reflected in the work of David H. Olson and associates. Their integration of normative expectations of family members as an additional design feature of both FACES II and III—modifications of the original Family Adaptability and Family Cohesion Evaluation Scores—explicitly responds to the importance of considering family-related values as a contingent variable in understanding marital and family dynamics (Olson, 1986; Olson & Portner, 1984; Olson, Russell, & Sprenkle, 1983). Recognizing the tremendous variation in family values across different cultural groups, the researchers have designed the 30-item FACES II and the 20-item FACES III not only to assess how individual family members perceive their family, but also to assess the level of discrepancy between how family members actually see their family (perceived) and how they would like it to be (ideal).

According to Olson and associates, the level of satisfaction with the family system is determined by comparing the perceived with the ideal across all family members—the less the cumulative discrepancies for family members, the higher the family's level of satisfaction with their current family system (Olson & Portner, 1984). Because the perceptions of family members often vary toward how they perceive the family system as well as how they would like it to be, Olson and associates stress the importance of obtaining the perceptions of all family members in determining the level of family life satisfaction (Olson, Russell, & Sprenkle, 1983).

Olson (1986) reports the results of a study by Caron and himself (1984) that provide empirical support for his ideal-perceived discrepancy hypothesis about family life satisfaction. Using a 14-item measure of family life satisfaction that assessed both dimensions of "cohesion" and "change," Olson (1986) reported that they found, as hypothesized, a "high negative correlation between family satisfaction scale and the ideal-perceived discrepancy on cohesion ($r = -.58$) and on adaptability ($r = -.64$)" (pp. 341–342).

The explicit recognition by Olson and his associates of how both family members as well as families may differ in their values for family life underscores the importance of assessing relational satisfaction from the vantage point of values. In agreement with Olson and associates, it is likely that families will function quite adequately as long as there is a high level of congruence between the family-related wishes and outcomes for all family members (Olson, Russell, & Sprenkle, 1983).

Moos and Moos

The self-administered 90-item family environment scale (FES) by Rudolf Moos and Bernice Moos (1986) is composed of ten subscales that assess the perceptions of family members toward the social-environment features of their family. These ten subscales assess three underlying sets of dimensions: the relationship dimensions (cohesion, expressiveness, and conflict), the personal growth dimensions (independence, achievement orientation, intellectual cultural orientation, active-recreational orientation, and moral-religious emphasis), and the system maintenance dimensions (organization and control).

The Real Form (Form R), which measures the perceptions of family members toward their families of origin or orientation, is most commonly used. However, two special reworded forms of Form R are available to determine both the type of family environment that family members would ideally like (Form I)—to assess the "goals" and "value orientations" of family members—as well as the type of family environment that they expect (Form E).

Although Moos and Moos (1984, 1986) do not explicitly discuss how these forms may be combined to assess the level of relational satisfaction, they do suggest that Form I can be used with Form R to identify discrepancies between what family members prefer and what they actually experience. They contend that such an understanding of discrepancies between the actual and preferred provides important information for guiding clinical intervention. In addition, they suggest that Form E could be used productively in premarital counseling sessions to facilitate discussion between prospective spouses about their expectations for family life.

For each form, it is possible both to calculate scores for each family member and to calculate family averages. These profiles can then be used to compare the perceptions of individual family members as well as to draw comparisons across families.

Sabatelli

Recent conceptual development and empirical research by Ronald Sabatelli (1984, 1988a) support the viability of applying a social exchange perspective to understanding and evaluating relationship satisfaction. Based on the "comparison level" concept of Thibaut and Kelley (1959), Sabatelli (1984, 1988a) proposes that individuals evaluate their relationship experiences on the basis of the expectations they have for those relationships. Sabatelli defines expectations as "a person's subjective impressions of what they feel is realistically obtainable from a relationship" (1988a, p. 219). In cases where relationship experiences consistently exceed expectations, relationship satisfaction is hypothesized to be enhanced; where relationship experiences consistently fall below expectations, relationship satisfaction is hypothesized to decline.

To assess the degree to which individuals perceive their relationships as meeting their expectations, Sabatelli (1984) developed the Marital Comparison Level Index (MCLI). Using this instrument, Sabatelli (1984, 1988a) has demonstrated not only significant differences in the relationship expectations of dating and married couples, but also high correlations between the ability of spouses to realize their expectations in marriage and measures of relational equity and marital commitment.

However, it is important to note that Sabatelli's definition of expectations is clearly different from the definition of values presented previously in this chapter (i.e., organized sets of preferences for marriage and family life irrespective of whether they are viewed as realistically obtainable in the marriage). Sabatelli's definition of expectations also differs from the conceptualization of expectations by Van Der Veen et al. (1964), Olson (1986), and Olson and associates (Olson & Portner, 1984; Olson, Russell, & Sprenkle, 1983). By incorporating the notion of "ideal" as compared to Sabatelli's "realistically obtainable" as the basis of their definitions of expectations, the use of the term by Van Der Veen et al., Olson, and Olson and associates is more conceptually similar to the previous definition of values than to Sabatelli's definition of expectations.

As discussed by Locke (1969) in defining job satisfaction, it is argued that the "value-based" definition is more heuristic as an approach to conceptualizing relationship satisfaction than Sabatelli's expectation-based definition. For one thing, as defined previously, values are conceptualized as being hierarchically arranged from most important to least important across levels of abstraction. This definitional property of values reflects the potential differential salience of relational attributes and patterns to spouses and allows for a richer assessment and understanding of relationship satisfaction than the expectation-based approach outlined by Sabatelli.

Unlike Van Der Veen et al., Olson, and Olson and associates, Sabatelli's definition of expectations fails to incorporate the notion of differential salience of expectations across relationship domains. As a consequence, all relational attributes and patterns are treated as equally salient in their potential impact on relationship satisfaction—an assumption that the value-based approach is designed to circumvent.

In developing the MCLI, however, Sabatelli (1984) did measure the relative importance of each item on the index to sample respondents—a value perspective. In fact, he found variation in the importance that respondents assigned to the specified relationship attributes and patterns represented as items on the MCLI (albeit skewed toward high importance). Yet, he downplayed this variance, choosing neither to differentially weight the items by their respective importance ratings, nor to examine the correlations between weighted and unweighted items, nor to consider the calculation of discrepancy scores between the ''importance'' and the ''expectations'' ratings for their potential implications in explaining relational outcomes. In other words, he chose to treat all items on the MCLI as equally salient and additive in determining relational outcomes.

Besides the definitional distinctions between values and realistic expectations in marriage, values as defined previously and expectations as defined by Sabatelli may also differ in their relative stability over time. Although both are subject to change, expectations are considered to be more situationally influenced than values. For example, the failure to realize marital-related values in behavior over time is more likely to lead a person to ''expect'' less from the relationship in question than to modify values per se. However, all else being equal, this lessening of expectations should not promote more relationship satisfaction—it should only help spouses to anticipate the likelihood that they will not have their values for marital life met behaviorally. In addition, too-low expectations for marriage may serve as a personal-level constraint to realizing important family-related values in behavior—a self-fulfilling prophecy.

Despite the conceptual differences between the value-based approach and Sabatelli's expectation-based approach to understanding relational outcomes, the work of Sabatelli suggests the potential richness of conceptually distinguishing between values and realistic expectations in the same model. In the following section, expectations about what is realistically obtainable from the relationship in question are identified as a causal condition that may mediate the relationship between value and behavior congruency for spouses in marriage as well as the relationship between value/behavior congruency and relational outcomes.

INFLUENCES ON VALUE-BEHAVIOR CONGRUENCY IN MARRIAGE

In marriage, spouses may have different levels of success in realizing their individual and collective goals for marriage in behavior. For purposes of practice, it is important to consider some of the factors that may either facilitate or hinder goal-directed behavior activity in marriage. Only then can educational and enrichment activities be directed at helping couples to identify and influence those forces that are associated with goal attainment.

Based on the work of Harold Kelley et al. (1983) and Evie McClintock (1983) on the nature of interaction in close relationships, three broad categories of such factors are discussed: personal, relational, and environmental. Kelley et al. and McClintock refer to these factors as "causal conditions" to behavioral sequences and interaction patterns in close relationships: "relatively enduring causal factors that exercise constraints on P and O across time and limit randomness and variability of their behavior" (McClintock, 1983, pp. 95–96).

Several caveats are necessary in applying the work of Kelley et al. and McClintock to the present analysis. First, these authors would include the values of participants in a relationship as such causal conditions. Second, causal conditions are considered by these authors as independent variables for purposes of explaining variance in both the behavioral sequences of the participants in the relationship and in their interactions with one another. Although it is entirely appropriate from the perspective of the VBC model to conceptualize the values and goals of participants as causal conditions, from the perspective of the model they are treated as the primary independent variable in explaining both behavioral and interactional variance, not as one of many potential independent variables. While Kelley et al. and McClintock focus on a range of causal conditions that may account for behavioral and interactional variance as independent variables, both independently and in mutual interaction with one another, the present review focuses only on selected causal conditions that are hypothesized to mediate value-behavior congruency in marriage.

Although there are a number of potential causal conditions, the specification of causal conditions is further limited to those that are considered most applicable to influence from participating in MAP. As mediators, these causal conditions may influence either the nature or the strength of value-behavior congruency of participants in marriage. While they are reviewed in separate subsections that follow, it is assumed that these causal conditions operate simultaneously and in reciprocal interaction with one another at any given point in time and both influence and are influenced by an individual's values for marriage over time.

Personal Factors

There are a number of potential causal conditions that exist at the individual level of analysis that may influence the ability of spouses to realize their values for marriage in behavior. Many of these influences have been identified in past studies of stress and coping (e.g., Lazarus & Folkman, 1984; McCubbin and McCubbin, 1987; Pearlin & Schooler, 1978), and they include a broad array of personal traits, resources, and abilities. In MAP, two potential causal conditions serve as a focus of attention at the individual level: (1) beliefs about one's self, about marriage in general, about the relationship with one's spouse, and about personal control, and (2) expectations about one's ability to realize values and goals for marriage in behavior. These two sets of causal conditions are considered to be motivational in their influence and are hypothesized to operate in dynamic and reciprocal interaction with one another over time, mediating the level of congruency between values and behavior in marriage. Their discussion reinforces both the importance of distinguishing values from closely related concepts and the potential richness of including such concepts in the same model.

Beliefs

As defined by Lazarus and Folkman (1984), beliefs are "cognitive configurations . . . [that represent] preexisting notions about reality which serve as a perceptual lens . . . [about] 'how things are' in the environment, and they shape the understanding of its meaning" (p. 63). Although the beliefs of individuals operate as cognitive filters in their appraisal of events in their environments, they are unlikely to be aware of their influence on their subjective interpretation of environmental events and experiences unless their beliefs are challenged in some way by these events and experiences (Lazarus & Folkman, 1984).

Based on the work of Bem (1970), Lazarus and Folkman (1984) distinguish between "primitive" and "higher-order" beliefs. Primitive beliefs are generally not subject to question and generally operate as stable conceptions of one's world; they are more likely to be based on conformity to "external authority" than to be derived from personal experience. On the other hand, as compared to primitive beliefs, higher-order beliefs are generally derived more from experience than from conformity to external authority, are more likely to be seen as debatable and fallible, and are more subject to influence and challenge from new experiences and evidence. However, over time, higher-order beliefs that are not challenged may become primitive beliefs.

Two specific sets of beliefs are an important focus of attention in MAP: (1) those that spouses hold about themselves as spouses in marriage, about marriage in general, and about their relationship with their spouse, and (2) those that spouses hold about their capacity to change the nature of their relationship with their spouse or the nature of other causal conditions, such as influences from the environment, that influence their ability to realize their values for marriage in behavior.

It is assumed in the VBC model that beliefs in these areas that have little basis in reality and that rest on irrational premises may seriously constrain the ability of spouses to realize their values in behavior. This line of reasoning is consistent with what is referred to in the literature as cognitive therapies (see Mahoney & Arnoff, 1978; Baucom & Epstein, 1990), such as those by Ellis (1962, 1970, 1971, 1977, 1978), Ellis and Harper (1961, 1979), and Beck (1970, 1976). These therapies focus on surfacing and challenging such irrational beliefs, helping clients to gain insight into the negative consequences of such beliefs for personal and/or relational fulfillment and growth, and restructuring or modifying such beliefs to promote higher levels of psychological and emotional well-being.

For example, a wife may believe that her husband of 20 years only married her because she became pregnant by him during the time they were dating in graduate school. After they were married, the husband dropped out of graduate school to take on a job. The wife believes that the husband secretly blames her for his failure to complete his graduate studies. She has never confronted him about her beliefs.

In reality, the husband planned to ask his wife to marry him all along; the pregnancy just gave him a reason to advance the timetable. From his perspective, the marriage and his failure to complete his graduate studies were unrelated, associated only by a common time period; he had lost interest in his graduate studies and had planned to drop out. Although he is sensitive to the conflicts that he and his wife experience around issues of marital commitment and relational priority, he is unaware of his wife's beliefs about his motivation for marriage and the wife's assumption about the relationship between the marriage and his failure to complete his graduate studies.

Beliefs such as those by the wife that remain unchallenged may lead to negative attributions or attribution biases about specific events in marriage or about specific actions by the spouse. As such, they may create an undercurrent of tension and conflict between spouses in marriage, influencing the behavior of each spouse through their reciprocal interaction (see Bradbury & Fincham, 1990 for a comprehensive review of attributions in marriage). Such situations can greatly limit the willingness and ability of the husband and wife to work effectively as a team in supporting one another in achieving their individual and collective goals for marriage. For instance, suppose that the wife wishes to return to school to complete her studies that were interrupted 20 years ago when she became pregnant. Instead of interpreting her husband's encouragement for her to return to school as a supportive act, she may interpret it as a move on his part to help her become more financially independent. He can then leave her without a guilty conscience because she assumes he never wanted to marry her anyway.

In addition to the beliefs spouses have about themselves as spouses in marriage, about marriage in general, and about their relationship with their spouse, in their book about stress, appraisal, and coping, Lazarus and Folkman (1984) discuss how the individuals' beliefs about their level of "personal control" over events in their lives will greatly influence their appraisals of presenting situations.

Other researchers have labeled such beliefs as locus of control (Rotter, 1966), sense of mastery (McCubbin & McCubbin, 1987; Pearlin & Schooler, 1978), sense of coherence (Antonovsky, 1979, 1987; Antonovsky & Sourani, 1988), and hardiness (Kobasa, 1979; Kobasa, Maddi, & Currington, 1981). For example, Antonovsky and Sourani (1988) specify "sense of coherence" as consisting of three components (comprehensibility, manageability, and meaningfulness) and define it as:

a global orientation that expresses the extent to which one has a pervasive, enduring though dynamic feeling of confidence that (1) the stimuli deriving from one's internal and external environments in the course of living are structured, predictable and explicable [comprehensibility]; (2) the resources are available to one to meet the demands posed by these stimuli [manageability]; and (3) these demands are challenges, worthy of investments and engagement [meaningfulness]. (p. 80)

From the VBC model, all else being equal, it would be hypothesized that spouses who have general and event-specific beliefs about their ability to influence the events in their marriage or larger environment that are based in reality will be more likely to negotiate arrangements with their partners that lead to higher levels of value-behavior congruency in marriage.

From the perspective of person-environment fit, an important consideration in examining beliefs is not only the "accuracy of self-assessment" (the level of fit between objective and subjective person), but also the "contact with reality" (the level of fit between objective and subjective environment) (Harrison, 1978, p. 176). For example, spouses may overestimate as well as underestimate their ability to effect changes in self and/or their environment. It is important to provide spouses with opportunities to distinguish rational from irrational beliefs that influence their ability to realize marital-related values in behavior at both levels of fit.

Expectations

If values are defined as "what is desirable" and if beliefs are defined as "what is true," expectations are defined—based on the work of Sabatelli (1984, 1988a)—as "what is possible or realistically obtainable." Although these three variables are presented as conceptually distinct for purposes of discussion here, they are assumed to be reciprocally related and highly interdependent in mediating the congruency between values and behavioral outcomes over time.

Drawing upon the work of Tolman (1932) and Lewin (1935), which has culminated in a number of expectancy theories of motivation (see Lawler, 1973), expectations are considered at two levels from the perspective of the VBC model. First, spouses are assumed to hold expectations about the marital-related outcomes that they consider desirable (outcome expectancy). Second, spouses are assumed to hold expectations about the link between their actions in marriage and/or their capacity for action and the likelihood that these actions will produce desired outcomes (action expectancy). Expanding upon expectancy theory for purposes of the present model (Lawler, 1973), outcome and action expectancy are assumed to combine interactively with the value, or "valence" of desired outcomes to influence motivation and behavior. From the perspective of the VBC model, the greater the congruency between valued outcomes in marriage and outcome/action expectancy, the more motivated the individual will be to pursue marital-related goals. All else being equal, this should lead to higher levels of value-behavior congruency by spouses in marriage over time.

It is important, however, to add a caveat in this link between values and expectations. Although values are assumed to be more stable than expectations over time, especially highly internalized values, low outcome or action expectancy may lower the salience of certain values related to marriage over time, especially those that are less central in the spouse's value hierarchy. This is likely to produce a higher level of value-behavior congruency, but not necessarily a commensurate increase in the level of marital satisfaction. Vroom (1964), an expectancy theorist, refers to the relationship between first-order outcomes, such as value-behavior congruency, and second-order outcomes, such as marital satisfaction, as an "instrumentality." Over time, the level of instrumentality influences the salience of the first-order outcome (see Lawler, 1973, p. 47 for additional discussion of this point).

The preceding discussion suggests that there will be a high correlation between the belief by spouses about their level of personal control over their marital and environmental situation and their action expectancies in terms of specific marital-related goals. Low levels of personal confidence in ones' abilities are likely to lead spouses to expect their actions to show little correlation with preferred outcomes. Over time, all else being equal, this dynamic is likely to decrease motivation and to increase perceptions of helplessness and hopelessness in marriage.

In a similar vein, one's beliefs about self and marriage are likely to influence as well as be influenced by one's expectancy outcomes. For example, a spouse may believe that most marriages are unhappy. As a consequence, that spouse may expect low levels of fulfillment in his or her marriage. Over time, this can decrease motivation to initiate actions considered by the individual as important for happiness and/or lower action expectancy leading to a self-fulfilling prophecy and confirming the belief. However, the spouse may still value a happy marriage, resulting in a lower level of marital satisfaction as a result of value-behavior incongruity. It is critical to the VBC model that we better understand how such beliefs and expectations influence actions by spouses in marriage and mediate the relationship between value and behavior congruency in marriage.

From the perspective of the VBC model, it is important for spouses to examine both their outcome and action expectancies for marriage. As with beliefs, the subjective perceptions of spouses should be compared with objective realities, and spouses may benefit from exploring the basis of their outcome and action expectancies. In order to achieve higher levels of value-behavior congruency, spouses may benefit from restructuring their outcome expectancies to become more ambitious; they may also benefit from re-examining their action expectancies in the context of other action expectancies that may be more efficacious in producing desired outcomes.

Relational Attributes

The identification of relational attributes and patterns that are associated with positive marital and family outcomes has been an important focus of attention among family scholars (e.g., Angell, 1936; Beavers & Voeller, 1983; Curran, 1983; Epstein, Bishop, & Baldwin, 1982; Hill, 1949, 1971; Koos, 1946; Lewis, Beavers, Gossett, & Phillips, 1976; Mace & Mace, 1980; Olson, 1986; Olson & McCubbin, 1983; Otto, 1975; Stinnett, 1979; Stinnett & DeFrain, 1985; Stinnett & Sauer, 1977). As described by Kelley et al. (1983), these relational attributes and patterns emerge from the interaction between participants in relationships over time, producing outcomes that are beyond the influence of either participant in the relationship. This description by Kelley et al. captures the essence of the person-environment fit perspective.

From the VBC model, the key focus from a relational perspective is on the degree of accommodation and adaptation that spouses make to one another in marriage over time in providing a supportive context by which they are able to realize their collective and individual goals for marriage. Such accommodation and adaptation are necessary if spouses are to develop into an effective marital team for accomplishing their jointly and individually defined goals, providing one another with high levels of instrumental and socioemotional support.

In our application of social exchange theory as a theoretical foundation for the VBC model, two types of interpersonal transformations were introduced from the work of Levinger and associates (Borden & Levinger, 1990; Levinger, 1986) in the study of relationship development and compatibility in close relationships: "motivational transformation" and "dispositional transformation." Each is discussed as a causal condition that influences the ability of spouses to realize marital-related values and goals in behavior. Although both represent changes within the individual, they are processes that can only be understood within a relational context (Borden & Levinger, 1990). As discussed in the following sections, these two types of interpersonal transformations are not necessarily processes that are independent of one another.

Motivational Transformation

The nature of values and goals for marriage are not always in agreement or compatible between spouses in marriage. To the extent that the actions of spouses are interdependent such that the actions of one influence or are influenced by the actions of the other, the success of spouses in realizing their goals in marriage will depend in part on the cooperation of the other (Borden & Levinger, 1990).

Based on the work of Kelley and Thibaut (1978) and Kelley (1979), Borden and Levinger (1990) describe the process of motivational transformation wherein spouses adapt their actions for a period of time to support the other in accomplishing some aim or goal. For example, suppose the husband and wife have very different preferences for attending church on Sunday mornings. The wife was raised in a family where religion played an important role and where the family attended church together on a weekly basis. For the wife, it is important to have a spiritual and religious base in marriage, and she feels that couples should attend church together. She wants her husband to attend with her. On the other hand, the husband was raised in a family that had little spiritual or religious foundation. Church was attended only on special occasions, usually marking special events in the family such as marriages and funerals, and on holidays. For the husband, Sunday mornings are his only time for relaxation; the only religious experience he desires is reading the *New York Times*. Although both husband and wife share the same religious affiliation, they are at an impasse. It is interesting that neither spouse may have ever predicted before their marriage that religious issues would emerge as a major source of conflict.

Using the concept of motivational transformation, the couple can resolve their stalemate in one of several ways. Either the husband or wife could adapt his or her actions to be supportive of the interests of the other, or they could reach some compromise solution—the husband could attend church with the wife every other Sunday, for example. It is important to underscore that motivational transformation refers to the degree to which spouses in marriage accommodate themselves to each other's goals; it does not involve a convergence of their goals (Levinger, 1986).

In working with couples in enrichment, it is important not only to consider the level of motivational transformation in the marital relationship, but also to consider some of the causal conditions that are likely to promote the level of negotiation and problem solving between partners in marriage. In his work on family decision making (Scanzoni & Szinovacz, 1980) and behavioral interdependence between partners in relationships (Scanzoni, 1979a), John Scanzoni draws broadly on social exchange and conflict theory to discuss several dimensions that may influence the willingness of partners to transform their behavioral actions to support the other in better realizing their marital-related goals. Three of these dimensions are cooperation, trust, and empathy. According to Scanzoni and Maximiliane Szinovacz (1980), the evaluation by spouses of these dimensions is based in large measure upon their past negotiations and experiences with each other in marriage, and they are conceptualized by Scanzoni and Szinovacz as being interrelated.

The first of these is the level of "cooperation" between spouses in marriage (Scanzoni & Szinovacz, 1980, p. 35). In early phases of relationship development, individuals are usually more concerned with maximizing individual profit. However, as the relationship develops and the level of interdependence increases, the bargaining demeanor of spouses in relationships with higher levels of interdependence tends to shift from "maximum individual profit" to "maximum joint profit" (Scanzoni, 1979a, p. 77). From a perspective of maximum joint profit, spouses negotiate their divergent interests and goals based on the best interests of both parties and the relationship in general. It is likely that spouses will be more likely to transform their actions to support one another if, from their past experience, the other has shown an orientation more toward "we" than "I."

A second dimension discussed by Scanzoni & Szinovacz is "trust" (1980, p. 36). Although motivational transformation can be rewarding in itself, it also can lead to an expectation that the other will reciprocate one's supportive actions in some future transaction. In fact, one's willingness to redirect one's actions toward greater support of the other's goals may be contingent upon a negotiated arrangement. For example, I will attend church with you on Sunday if you do not ask me to do housework on Saturday. Through their interactions over time, spouses develop a level of trust in each other that reflects their confidence that the other will follow through with their bargains and commitments. To the extent that motivational transformation in marriage depends on some future reward or exchange, this level of trust will influence the willingness of spouses to negotiate and bargain in the interest of maximum joint profit.

In addition, according to McDonald (1981), the development of mutual trust between spouses in the relationship should enhance the level of "commitment" that each spouse has in maintaining the relationship, transforming the "exchange relationship from one of direct, short-term transactions to an indirect long-term exchange orientation" (p. 833). McDonald (p. 834) cites Leik and Leik (1972, p. 5), who define commitment as "the extent to which an actor has shifted from (1) interest in a relationship because of the goals it mediates to (2) maintenance of the relationship as the dominant goal." Such interpersonal commitment should facilitate the level of motivational transformation and cooperation between spouses in marriage.

A third dimension discussed by Scanzoni and Szinovacz is "empathy," which they define as being based on both "communication" and "understanding" (1979, p. 39). As with dimensions of cooperation and trust, the level of empathy that spouses exercise in their marriage evolves over the marital career and is determined in part by their prior exchanges with one another. In situations where spouses are able to communicate openly with one another and are open to each other's views, motivational transformation is likely to be facilitated. To the extent that the ability of spouses to realize their marital-related goals depends upon the motivational transformation of the other, they must not only clearly communicate their goals to the other and clarify their expectations for the other's response, but also the other must understand the nature of these goals and what is expected of him or her. Too often in marriage, communication is hampered by the inability or unwillingness of spouses to clearly articulate their marital-related goals and their behavioral expectations for the other.

In addition to these specific relational context dimensions, the ability of couples to experience higher levels of facilitating interaction will depend on their specific "problem-solving" skills in marriage (Lazarus & Folkman, 1984; Levinger, 1986). From the perspective of the VBC model, the concept of "problem" is defined based on the work of Klein and Hill (1979) as "any situation involving an unachieved but potentially attainable goal in which the means for overcoming barriers to achieving the goal, though not immediately apparent, are considered feasible" (p. 495). Based on this definition, the authors define problem solving as "goal-directed behavior" (p. 496). It is likely that spouses who attempt to clearly define problems by gathering the necessary information, who look constructively at both sides of an issue, who search together for solutions to presenting concerns and consider the potential outcomes and impacts of decisions, and who attempt to resolve differences in an equitable fashion, will reach the most satisfactory solutions in dealing with their potentially divergent agendas and in realizing their individual and collective goals in marriage (see Klein & Hill, 1979 for a comprehensive review of problem-solving effectiveness in families). It is likely that problem-solving in marriage will be facilitated where spouses have greater convergence in their values and goals for marriage (McDonald & Cornille, 1988).

Dispositional Transformation

As compared to motivational transformation, dispositional transformation is defined by Borden and Levinger (1990) and Levinger (1986) as the changes in values and goals of one or both individuals in the relationship over time toward greater similarity and compatibility. This convergence is likely to be facilitated by the mate selection process itself, where potential spouses are more likely to be attracted to those who share similar values and goals (see Adams, 1979 for a review of this literature; see Levinger, 1983 for some important qualifications to this literature). It is further promoted by the differential association of spouses in marriage, where each influences as well as is influenced by the other, and it is reinforced by their shared experiences in marriage over the years.

Unlike the behavioral shifts that accompany motivational transformation, dispositional transformation represents a shift in the "internalized" values and goals of the individual spouse (Borden and Levinger, 1990). According to Borden and Levinger (1990) and Levinger (1986), the greater the convergence of values and goals of spouses, the less likely it is that they will have to transform their motivations to adapt to the needs and wishes of the other.

Dispositional transformation may follow motivational transformation. In the discussion of motivational transformation, we mentioned the wife who wanted the husband to attend church with her on Sunday morning. Let's assume that the husband agreed to do this even though his preference to stay home, relax, and read the paper remained unchanged (a motivational transformation). However, over time, as the husband attended church with his wife, he became involved in activities at church that he began to enjoy. Pretty soon he began to value his experiences at church, and both his and his wife's preferences toward attending church became increasingly convergent: an occurrence of dispositional transformation.

From the perspective of the VBC model, it is important to help spouses identify their level of convergence in values and goals for marriage. Given the process of dispositional transformation over time, it is recommended that spouses be given opportunities to explore how their values and goals for marriage may have changed over the marital career. Although these value shifts are reported by Levinger (1986) as most often moving toward convergence, they may, in certain domains or interest areas, move toward divergence (Borden & Levinger, 1990). For example, a husband may have been initially attracted to his wife because of her nonassuming personality in interaction with others—she did not have to be the center of attention. However, he now criticizes her constantly when friends are visiting, because he feels that he always has to take the lead in conversation. In reality, little has changed in the wife's disposition; what has changed is the husband's values toward his wife's disposition. Such divergence may lead to serious conflict over the course of the relationship unless spouses are able to identify and understand these relational changes and to motivationally transform their actions in marriage to provide higher levels of instrumental and socioemotional support to the values and goals of the other.

Environmental Context

Past conceptualizations and studies of interpersonal relationships have largely neglected the broader social context of these relationships (La Gaipa, 1981). Instead, there has been a tendency to focus either on the personal attributes of participants in the relationship (such as their traits, attitudes, beliefs, values, and needs) or on characteristics of the relationship itself (such as communication patterns, companionship, and consensus); social contextual factors have been notably absent among determinants of interpersonal processes or have been simply assumed to operate as "common denominators" for the subjects under investigation (Andreyeva & Gozman, 1981, p. 47).

This is especially the case in the application of social exchange principles to the understanding of interpersonal relationships (Emerson, 1976; McDonald, 1981). According to McDonald (1981), "Social exchange theory has largely focused upon the interpersonal transaction, or exchange, as though it were occurring in a social vacuum" (p. 826).

However, relationships do not exist in isolation. Every relationship exists in the context of other relationships and may be affected by the relationships that its participants share with others (Hinde, 1981). In addition, every relationship exists in a larger social context that poses normative demands and constraints on the nature of interaction (Hinde, 1981). Drawing from an ecological perspective, Garbarino (1983) views such a contextual perspective as essential to understanding intimate relationships: "We cannot account for or understand intimate relationships without understanding how the conditions surrounding the social interaction affect interaction between individuals, and how these conditions shape and 'press' patterns of interaction" (p. 8). As a consequence, it is important to consider how the dynamic of value-behavior congruency in marriage may be influenced by conditions in the social environment that penetrate and frame the values, behavior, and interactions of spouses in marriage.

Although a number of such environmental conditions may impinge on spouses in marriage, given that MAP is a corporate program for couples, the focus is on the nature of "organizational culture" in the work setting or settings in which spouses are employed. Based on a spillover perspective of work and family linkages (Bowen, 1988c; Voydanoff, 1987), it is hypothesized that the nature of organizational culture in the work setting of one or both spouses shapes a set of conditions in the workplace that may not only influence the values and goals of spouses in marriage, but also may either facilitate or constrain their ability to realize marital-related values in behavior. At a minimum, this set of conditions includes: (1) the assumptions, values, norms, and expectations that guide both the nature of reinforcement and the nature of interpersonal relationships in both work and non-work domains (e.g., Aldous, 1969; Aldous, Osmond, & Hicks, 1979; Harrison, 1972; Kohn, 1963, 1969; Miller & Swanson, 1958; Peters & Waterman, 1982; Schein, 1984, 1985); (2) the nature and level of organizational responsibilities and demands that both employees and their spouses face (Bowen & Orthner, 1989; Orthner, Bowen, & Beare, 1990; Segal, 1989); and (3) the level of sensitivity and responsiveness of employers to helping employees better balance work and family demands and responsibilities (Bowen, 1988c; Kamerman & Kahn, 1987; Raabe & Gessner, 1988).

The concept of organizational culture has grown in popularity in recent years as a key to understanding organizational dynamics and excellence in the business world (Deal & Kennedy, 1982; O'Toole, 1979; Peters & Waterman, 1982; Schein, 1984, 1985). Although definitions of organizational culture vary in the literature (see Bowen and Orthner, 1991), Schein (1985) may provide the most comprehensive definition:

the pattern of basic assumptions that a given group has invented, discovered, or developed in learning to cope with its problems of external adaptation and internal integration and that have worked well enough to be considered valid, and, therefore, to be taught to new members as the correct way to perceive, think, and feel in relation to those problems. (p. 3)

Influenced by the deliberate actions of leadership and sustained by the ongoing interaction of group members, this culture expresses both the rules and expectations for behavior within the work group and the nature of the organization's interface with its environment, including the family environment (Harrison, 1972; Schein, 1984, 1985; Silverzweig & Allen, 1976). It may have considerable impact upon the values and behavior of employees in both work and nonwork domains (Bowen & Orthner, 1991; Chatman, 1989).

In a recent review of the effects of organizational culture on fathering behavior, Bowen and Orthner (1991) highlighted several important caveats to the study of organizational culture that are particularly appropriate to its examination as a causal condition to behavioral sequences and interaction patterns in marriage. Several of these caveats are addressed and expanded for purposes of the present discussion.

First, multiple subcultures may exist within any one organization that may be more or less compatible (Schein, 1984; Silverzweig & Allen, 1976). As spouses advance in their careers within an organization or transfer across organizational divisions, they may face different sets of conditions for both their behavior and the behavior of their spouse that may have a considerable influence on their behavior and interaction in marriage. For example, Kanter (1977a) describes the career progression of the wife of the corporate executive who may evolve from having little direct interface with the organization to becoming an active player in the organization itself.

In addition, in marriages where both the husband and wife are wage earners, spouses may be influenced by multiple organizational cultures, each with its own distinctive set of conditions. The impact of these organizational cultures on spouses in marriage may vary depending on the need for and the attractiveness of rewards for conformity, the perceived costs for nonconformity, and the attractiveness of alternatives, including the nature of the marital relationship (Harrison, 1972; Schein, 1984, 1985). It is likely in situations where both the husband and wife are employed that one employer will exercise relatively more influence on the life of the couple than the other (Orthner, Bowen, & Beare, 1990). Dominating organizations, especially those that engulf both the employee and the spouse within their cultures, may become a source of role strain and conflict for spouses in marriage. In addition, they may have a tremendous impact on the marital-related values of both husbands and wives over time and may pose serious constraints on their ability to realize marital-related values in behavior. Coser (1974) labeled such organizations as "greedy." These organizations "seek exclusive and undivided loyalty and they attempt to reduce the claims of competing roles and status positions on those they wish to encompass within their boundaries" (p. 4).

Third, although it is assumed that the nature of organizational culture may have a large impact on the values and behavior of spouses in marriage through shaping the set of associated conditions in the workplace, spouses may not be completely aware of its impact on their marriage. For example, in the workshops that have been conducted with MAP, corporate executives and their spouses have often been surprised to discover how conditions in the organization have influenced the nature of their values and behavior in marriage over time. In some cases, spouses are confronted with the realization that the nature of the organizational culture has framed and penetrated their marriage in ways that have seriously constrained their individual and collective goals for marriage.

On the other hand, spouses may seem to have a high level of awareness of the impact of organizational culture on their marriage but may misconstrue its objective impact. Harrison (1978) refers to the discrepancy between the "objective" environment that exists independently of the person's perception of it and the person's subjective perception of that environment as representing one's "contact with reality" (p. 176). Spouses may blame the organization for causing a high level of value-behavior incongruity in marriage when, in fact, the reasons for such incongruity are more complex. In his studies of military families, Ridenour (1984) refers to this process as "triangulation" (p. 5).

Last, it is important to emphasize the dynamic and fluid nature of organizational culture and its associated conditions. It represents, at best, a negotiated order among individuals in the organization; it does not exist independently of the individuals who create and sustain it through their behavioral actions (O'Toole, 1979; Schein, 1984). As such, it can be influenced and changed over time through an ongoing process of negotiation. As concluded by Mangam (1981, p. 200): "personal relationships acting in the social process create and uphold the rules, the rules do not create the process."

As a proposed causal condition to the level of value and behavior congruency of spouses in marriage, it is recommended from the perspective of the VBC model that spouses be encouraged to examine the underlying culture in their respective work organizations and the impacts of this culture on their values, behavior, and interactions in marriage. An important focus is on the level of person-environment fit between the nature of organizational values and demands that are reflective of its culture and the values and goals of each spouse for marriage (cf. Chatman, 1989). For example, there may be a lack of fit between (1) the organization's value that work demands should be superordinate to family demands and responsibilities of employees and (2) a given employee's value on time together and companionate activities in marriage. Such an organizational value may lead to policies that neglect to consider the implications of organizational demands (such as travel and overtime work) on the marital and family lives of employees and their spouses.

Exercises may be structured to assist spouses in examining both the nature of organizational culture and the level of person-organizational fit. For example, spouses can be asked to list five adjectives or short phrases that best describe their work organization (cf. O'Toole, 1979) and then evaluate these adjectives and phrases on a scale of personal desirability. In addition, structured instruments are available for examining the nature of organizational values and norms and their level of fit with the values of individuals. The Organizational Culture Profile (OCP) is one of these (see Chatman, 1989). Such exercises and structured instruments can serve as valuable tools to increase the awareness of spouses of the impacts of organizational culture on their marriage, which constitutes a critical first step in effecting organizational and behavioral change.

COPING WITH VALUE-BEHAVIOR INCONGRUITY

Given the number of potential constraints that spouses face in realizing values and goals for marriage in behavior, it is likely that they will often face a lack of fulfillment or negative emotion in working toward their individual and collective goals. A critical issue for purposes of education and enrichment is to better understand how spouses cope with the realities of their situation.

The definition of coping from the perspective of the VBC model is derived from definitions of the concept offered by Lazarus and Folkman (1984) and Harrison (1978). It involves those behavioral and cognitive activities that are constantly directed toward the environment and/or the person in an attempt to: (1) increase the level of positive emotion by facilitating value-behavior congruency in marriage and/or (2) reduce the level and/or the outcomes of negative emotion that spouses are assumed to experience from their inability to behaviorally realize their individual and collective goals in marriage. As implied by this definition of coping, emotions are assumed to have a motivational quality that prompts the individual to act.

In discussions of coping from a person-environment fit perspective, a distinction is made between objective and subjective reality. Drawing on the work of French, Rogers, and Cobb (1974), Harrison (1978, pp. 178–179) states that individuals may increase their level of objective person-environment fit by changing either the objective person (''adaptation'') or the objective environment (''environmental mastery''). Harrison restricts his use of the term *coping* to only those action-oriented activities that are directed toward either adaptation or environmental mastery.

On the other hand, individuals may increase their level of subjective person-environment fit either through their perceptions of better objective fit (which is a product of coping activities) or though intrapsychic mechanisms (which Harrison refers to as ''defences''), subjectively distorting their perceptions of either the objective person or the objective environment. Although improved levels of subjective person-environment fit that result from distorted perceptions of either person and/or environment may help the individual to feel better about his or her situation, they are not assumed by Harrison to affect the level of objective person-environment fit experienced by the person.

Unlike Harrison, but consistent with the proposed definition of coping, Houston (1987) refers to responses directed toward both the objective and subjective realities of the individual as coping. He identifies two broad categories of coping strategies that parallel, yet expand, those proposed by Harrison and that are consistent with theoretical work by Lazarus (1976): ''overt, action-oriented responses'' and ''covert, within organism responses'' (Houston, 1987, p. 386).

The work of Harrison (1978) and Houston (1987) provides a useful framework for considering some of the potential responses of spouses in marriage who are experiencing difficulties in behaviorally realizing their individual and collective goals for marriage. First, spouses may attempt to increase their level of value-behavior congruency through overt, action-oriented responses. These responses may entail adaptation, such as changing their own behavior or seeking consultation from others about self-limiting beliefs and expectations. They may also involve environmental mastery, such as influencing the behavior of their spouse or working to modify relational and/or environmental constraints.

These responses are not necessarily independent. For example, a wife who wishes to experience more companionship with her husband (a goal that is related to high-order value) may begin by limiting the number of hours she works at home during the evening. In order to make more free time available during the evening, she may begin to delegate a greater proportion of her work responsibilities to subordinates. Because she highly values her work as well as her companionship with her husband, it is important to her that the work gets done. In addition, she tells her husband about her desire to experience more companionship together and, because he also often works at home during the evening, she suggests that he likewise attempt to better confine his workload to the office. Because he also values spending time together and because he often works at home at night only because she is unavailable for joint activities, he has little difficulty responding to her request. Such a resolution should lead to a higher level of value-behavior congruency in the area of marital companionship for both the husband and the wife.

If, for some reason, the husband is unable or unwilling to support his wife in realizing greater companionship in the marriage, the wife might respond in one of several ways. The first three of these are overt behavior responses. First, depending on the importance of companionship to her, she may intensify her negotiation strategies, making the husband's unresponsiveness more costly (Scanzoni & Szinovacz, 1980). Depending on the wife's willingness to escalate her negotiation strategies and the husband's ability to resist redefining the relationship, it is likely that this strategy will result in some objective changes in the environment and/or person over time. Second, over time, she may turn to others to help meet her desire for greater companionship and affiliation. Although it is an adaptive response, such a coping strategy may actually limit opportunities for marital companionship over time and may lead the wife to form relationships with others that may threaten the stability of the marriage. Third, she may choose to cope directly with the negative emotions that accompany her inability to experience more companionship with her husband through exercise or through an emotional or behavioral outlet, such as eating. Although this response is an adaptation to the emotional outcomes that result from the inability to experience more companionship with the husband, the use of such "emotion-focused" strategies has little or no potential to change the presenting situation (Moos & Billings, 1982). Fourth, she may attempt to cope with the situation by distorting her perceptions of either the objective environment, the objective self, or the emotional consequences: a covert coping response.

Covert coping mechanisms constitute an interesting class of coping responses, and a number of these mechanisms have been identified in the literature, such as avoidance, denial, projection, rationalization, and detachment (Boss, 1988; Harrison, 1978; Houston, 1987; Lazarus, 1976). Although the use of these mechanisms results in neither individual adaptation nor environmental mastery as defined by Harrison (1978), by helping the individual to cognitively reframe the presenting situation, they may enhance the individual's subjective perception of person-environment fit and thereby decrease the negative emotions assumed to be associated with the inability of spouses to behaviorally realize marital-related values and goals.

For example, one means by which the wife could deal with her husband's reluctance to share more companionate activities would be by "devaluing" or "denying" the importance of companionship in marriage. Rodman (1963, 1971) has described such processes as part of a phenomenon that he refers to as "value stretch:" stretching one's values to accommodate the presenting situation. Although such strategies represent "compromise solutions" (Harrison, 1978, p. 179) and may be quite functional in dealing with some of the realities of one's situation in the short run, overuse of these covert mechanisms may lead to feelings of "inauthenticity" (Erickson & Wharton, 1989, p. 8) and "decreased contact with reality" over time (Harrison, 1978, p. 179).

From the perspective of the VBC model, an important intervention with spouses is to help them better understand their coping strategies in marriage and the implications of these strategies for both desired personal and relational outcomes. It is important not only to help them look at their own coping responses with respect to specific situations, but also to become more aware of their "coping styles" in marriage: "generalized coping strategies, defined as typical, habitual preferences for ways of approaching problems" (Menaghan, 1983, p. 114). Menaghan defines such coping styles as "general and relatively stable qualities of individuals which they bring to situations" (1983, p. 120). These coping styles lead individuals to respond to situations in very predictable ways, and the merging of coping styles in marriage may lead spouses to develop highly structured interactional patterns in their negotiations with one another and with their presenting situations.

A LIFE COURSE PERSPECTIVE

Change is a key concept in the VBC model of marital satisfaction. As suggested by proponents of social exchange principles (Leik & Leik, 1976; Scanzoni, 1979a), the personal and collective agendas of spouses in marriage are dynamic, and patterns of exchange between participants may vary significantly over the life course. Such a process model of relationship development and change anchors the VBC model. It is assumed that the individual and collective values and goals of spouses may change over time and that they may face different types and combinations of constraints at different points in the life course in their ability to realize these values and goals (cf. McDonald & Cornille, 1988).

As we have already discussed, it is assumed that spouses may grow more similar in their values and goals for marriage over the marital career. This is likely to be a function of both (1) the mate selection process, which is partially driven by marital homogamy and endogamy, and (2) the process of dispositional convergence, which leads to greater similarity in the values and goals of spouses over time (Borden & Levinger, 1990; Levinger, 1986). In addition, it is likely that spouses who remain married become more collectively oriented in their values and goals for marriage over time and, as interdependency increases, move toward a greater emphasis on maximum joint profit (Scanzoni, 1979a).

It is assumed that there are particular pressure points for couples at points in the marriage and family life cycle that may seriously constrain their ability to realize individual and collective goals in behavior (cf. Voydanoff, 1987). For example, many spouses attempt to begin their careers and start their families simultaneously. The combined responsibilities for meeting the developmental needs of young children together with the pace, high demands, and possible inflexibility of a beginning career may present spouses with a number of constraints to realizing certain values and goals for marriage, such as companionship.

It is important to help spouses understand the dynamic nature of their marital relationship and how attempts to realize certain combinations of values and goals at points in the life cycle may lead to role strain and may increase the probability of marital conflict. Spouses may need assistance at different points in the life course with negotiating arrangements with one another and with planning strategies to overcome personal, relational, and environmental constraints in order to facilitate their ability to achieve higher levels of value-behavior congruency in marriage.

IMPLICATIONS FOR MARITAL ENRICHMENT

From the perspective of marital enrichment, the value-based approach to the definition and conceptualization of marital satisfaction is rich in its implications. First, it is important to help spouses better understand their values and goals regarding marriage. It is particularly important to help them identify areas where they have value differences or incongruities with one another.

For example, the husband and wife may have differing views toward the sharing of household tasks and responsibilities. It is likely that such value discrepancies between spouses that are not recognized or discussed—but where the value in question is more important to one spouse than the other—can create an undercurrent of tension and conflict in the marriage, especially in cases where the discrepancy limits the opportunity of the spouse to realize the value in behavior.

Such a situation is hypothesized to negatively affect the level of marital satisfaction experienced by the spouse by decreasing the level of positive emotion and/or by increasing the level of negative emotion toward the other spouse or toward the relationship or marriage in general. On the other hand, value consensus—or at least value congruity between spouses across those value domains that are defined as important by one or both spouses—is likely to facilitate exchanges in marriage that are defined as rewarding as well as equitable and just (Bowen, 1987).

Second, it is valuable to have spouses compare values and goals for marriage with their actual behavior and patterns of marital interaction. This focus on gaps between marital-related values and behaviors would aid spouses in better understanding their current level of satisfaction with the marriage as well as in identifying aspects of their relationship that they would like to promote or change. The exercise would be especially valuable if spouses were able to jointly examine their ability to behaviorally realize their individual and collective marital-related goals under the guidance of a trained family specialist.

Third, it is possible that spouses may value certain outcomes in their marriage but may face personal, relational, or environmental constraints that hamper their ability to realize these outcomes. For example, spouses may value open and disclosive communication patterns in their relationship but may lack confidence in their ability to develop more effective communication exchanges in their marriage. Practitioners can work with couples to help them confront these barriers and to develop the skills and resources necessary to realize their values for marriage in behavior. Otto (1979) has referred to this type of intervention as helping families to achieve their full "family potential."

Fourth, given the critical role that the process of motivational transformation is hypothesized to play as a causal condition in enabling spouses to negotiate conditions in marriage that are conducive to realizing marital-related values in behavior, couples may benefit from examining their "exchange orientations" in marriage (Murstein, Cerreto, & MacDonald, 1977). For example, in considering different preferences for equity in occupational settings, Huseman, Hatfield, and Miles (1987) present three broad classes of orientations:

(a) Benevolents, those who prefer their outcome/input ratios to be less than the outcome/input ratios of the comparison other; (b) Equity Sensitives, those who, conforming to the traditional norm of equity prefer their outcome/input ratios to equal those of comparison others; and (c) Entitleds, those who prefer their outcome/input ratios to exceed the comparison other's. (p. 223)

It is likely that the level of "equity sensitivity" (Huseman, Hatfield, & Miles, 1987, p. 222) of spouses in marriage may greatly influence their willingness to transform their behaviors in support of one another.

Fifth, through offering marital enrichment opportunities in the workplace, practitioners are in a position to encourage employers to develop policies and programs that are more supportive of marriage. This implication for practice is consistent with the challenge by Curran (1983) for institutions to work in concert with families to better realize their values for family life. Of course, practitioners must be careful not to impose their own paradigms in assuming the role of advocate. However, through policy and program development, work organizations can be made more responsive to marital demands and responsibilities. The aim is to help organizations to remove obstacles that may prevent couples from achieving their full relational power rather than structuring solutions to marital problems.

An important feature of the proposed approach is its relatively value-free position. At a minimum, intervention with couples is geared to assisting them in (1) better understanding their own value positions toward marriage; (2) examining their level of value-behavior congruency in marriage and the implications of this congruency for their level of satisfaction experienced in marriage; (3) developing insight into the causal conditions that promote or restrain their level of value-behavior congruency, including their exchange orientations and patterns in marriage; and (4) developing skills and resources to better realize their individual and collective goals in marriage.

In addition, practitioners are encouraged to work with or advocate on behalf of couples in work organizations to help remove or reduce the interference of system-level constraints that hinder their ability to realize marital-related values in behavior. Consequently, practitioners are not required to assume an explicit value position. The practitioner plays a facilitative and enabling role in working with and on behalf of the couples—a particularly important role given the results of recent studies that suggest some disparity between the marital and family goals of families and the intervention objectives of marital and family practitioners (Fisher, Giblin, & Hoopes, 1982). In addition, because the elements of the approach fit logically together in an integrated whole, practitioners should be able to help couples better understand the dynamics and paradoxes of marital life.

CONCLUSION

This alternative approach to the definition and conceptualization of marital satisfaction has several important advantages for practice. First, it defines marital satisfaction as relative: the ability of spouses to realize their own values and goals for marriage in behavior. The approach leads to an interactional process view of marital dynamics that has significant implications for marital enrichment. Second, it anchors the definition and conceptualization of marital satisfaction within an explicit theoretical perspective—social exchange theory.

Third, it explicitly acknowledges that neither couples nor spouses within the same marriage may necessarily value or want the same things from marriage.

As a consequence, it is important to focus on the values of individual spouses, the level of value congruency between spouses in marriage, and value differences across couples. From this perspective, the marital-related values both within couples as well as across couples are seen as "different from" rather than "better than" or "worse than" those of other spouses or couples. These differing value orientations pose implications for desired marital-related outcomes at the level of the individual and the dyad.

At least three levels of analysis are possible: (1) the effects of values and the level of value congruity between spouses on marital outcomes, (2) the effects of behaviors and the level of behavior congruity between spouses on marital outcomes, and (3) the effects of value-behavior congruency on marital outcomes. An important focus of study will be to examine how spouses cope with value incongruities among themselves as well as with situations in which values and goals are not realized in behavior. It is vital that the utility of this approach to marital satisfaction be examined for couples at different stages of the work and family life cycle, as well as across other demographic parameters, such as racial/ethnic and socioeconomic groups. Such an analytic strategy will provide important data for guiding marital enrichment activities, including information on each of the following subjects: (1) variations in values across different population groups and subgroups, (2) levels of success among various population groups and subgroups in realizing their marital-related values and goals in behavior, and (3) consequences of value congruency between spouses and the level of value-behavior congruency of spouses on marital-related outcomes within different population groups and subgroups.

4

An Empirical Test of the Model: Junior and Mid-Enlisted Army Couples

In Fall 1986, the U.S. Department of Army Office of Chief of Chaplains sponsored a pioneering study entitled "Family Values and Expectations of Ethnic, Lower and Lower Middle Class Families." A major purpose of this study was to assess variations in the marital- and family-related values of junior and mid-enlisted families across racial/ethnic groups and to determine how these values impact on the behavior of the families and their adaptation to life in the army. Caliber Associates, a Washington, D.C.-based consulting firm, working in consultation with the University of North Carolina School of Social Work, was awarded the contract to conduct this study.

After meeting with representatives from the Office of Chief of Chaplains to clarify their expectations for the study and to review the proposed research strategy, the project team worked together to develop a conceptual model to better frame the study questions and to help organize the study effort. As a part of this effort, a comprehensive review of the literature was conducted on marital and family values and their correlates (Bowen & Janofsky, 1987), and experts in the field of marriage and family, including chaplains, were consulted. These efforts culminated in an early version of the model that serves as the conceptual foundation of MAP: the Value-Behavior Congruency Model.

To examine some of the relationships hypothesized in the model, an exploratory survey was conducted at two army posts in the United States as part of a larger study effort. This survey included a purposive sample of 174 married army members and 88 civilian spouses, and it included a number of marital, family, and organizational questionnaire scales and items (see Bowen & Janofsky, 1988).

The data for this chapter were collected under contract MDA903-86-C-0260 for the U.S. Department of Army Office of the Chief of Chaplains. Any opinions, findings, or conclusions expressed in this chapter are those of the author and should not be construed as an official Department of Army position, policy, or decision, unless so designated by other documentation.

Based on a subsample of respondents in which both they and their spouses participated in the survey, this chapter reports the results of a secondary analysis of the data designed to examine several key assumptions of the Value-Behavior Congruency Model of Marital Satisfaction (VBC) that were presented in Chapter 3.

The core assumption of the VBC model is that the level of marital satisfaction is enhanced when spouses are able to realize their collective and individual marital-related values in behavior. Specifically, an asymptotic relationship is hypothesized between the level of value-behavior congruency and marital satisfaction, such that marital satisfaction is highest at the point of perfect congruency and decreases in magnitude as "behavior" begins to fall short of professed "values." No differences are assumed in the level of marital satisfaction between perfect congruency and those points of the continuum where behavior exceeds professed values. Although the survey was designed to assess "family" rather than "marital" values per se, it is possible to explore this assumption or hypothesis in some detail.

Second, it is assumed from the model that a range of personal, relational, and environmental factors may restrict the success of spouses in realizing their individual and collective goals for marriage in behavior. Although this aspect of the model was the most underspecified one in the survey, it is possible to assess several items and scales on the survey that serve as proxy variables for some of the causal conditions discussed in Chapter 3, and to conduct some exploratory analysis of their hypothesized role as mediators of the level of value-behavior congruency experienced by spouses.

For purposes of this secondary analysis, the Family Assessment Profile (FAP) was constructed based on the responses of spouses to 60 parallel value-oriented and behavior-oriented items included on the survey. These survey items were designed to assess various indicators of marital and family functioning that had been identified from a comprehensive literature review as related to several specified marital- and family-related outcomes. Comprised of seven subdimensions, the FAP is described in detail in the following sections, including its development and psychometric properties.

METHOD

Source of Data

Respondents were a purposive sample of 48 couples (96 spouses) with one or both spouses serving in the U.S. Army. These couples had been identified by their unit chaplain to participate in a larger investigation of family strengths and adaptation that was conducted at Fort Bragg, North Carolina and Fort Riley, Kansas in Spring 1987. Couples were proportionally selected at their posts based on racial/ethnic group identification (Hispanic, black, white) and rank (E-1 to E-4, E-5 to E-6). The decision to stratify the sample by rank and racial/ethnic group identification was based on special interests by the sponsor of the study.

Subjects

The modal couple in the sample was dually employed (52%), and 73 percent had children living in the household. Among eight of the 48 couples in the sample (17%), both the husband and the wife were serving on active duty in the U.S. Army. Couples with children in the household most often had either one (41.6%) or two (41.6%), and the youngest child was typically four years of age or younger (69.4%).

Couples in the sample had been married on the average less than five years (M = 4.3), and the majority of husbands (93.5%) and wives (81.3%) were in their first marriage. As a consequence of proportional sampling, more than one-half of husbands and wives reported their racial/ethnic group identification as either Hispanic (28.9% and 25.0%, respectively) or black (26.7% and 27.3%, respectively). On the average, husbands and wives were approximately the same age (M = 27.0 years), and more than four-fifths (84.9%) of all spouses in the sample had either graduated from high school or received a higher level of education.

Among those husbands (97.8%) and wives (19.1%), who were serving in the U.S. Army, 46.3 percent were in the junior enlisted grades (E-1 to E-4); 53.7 percent were in the mid-enlisted grades (E-5 to E-6). On the average, service members in the sample had served approximately six and one-half years on active duty.

Procedures

All respondents completed a structured survey questionnaire and participated in a personal interview with a member of the project team. Husbands and wives completed the survey questionnaire at either a post facility or in their homes under the supervision of project staff. Each husband and wife pair completed the survey in private, at the same time, and without consultation from their partner. Participation in the study was voluntary, and respondents were assured that their responses would be kept confidential and that only the project team would have access to their completed questionnaires. Code numbers were assigned to all questionnaires before they were completed by respondents, and respondents were informed that only the principal investigator would have access to the names associated with these code numbers.

Before the survey was implemented at the two sample posts, a two-day pretest was conducted at Fort Belvoir, Virginia to pilot test the survey instrument and the data collection plans. Based on feedback from pretest respondents and expert reviewers, revisions were made to the survey questionnaire to increase its validity and reliability.

Family Assessment Profile

The Family Assessment Profile (FAP) is a 33-item self-report instrument designed to assess each spouse's perception of the importance of specified marital and family interaction patterns, preferences, and behaviors (Family Values Profile) as well as the degree to which these patterns, preferences, and behaviors are actually evidenced in the family system (Family Behavior Profile) (see Appendices I and II). The level of discrepancy in the ratings of family members on the Family Values Profile (FVP) and the Family Behavior Profile (FBP) provides a second-order profile: the Value-Behavior Congruency Profile (VBC-P). The VBC-P reflects the degree to which spouses succeed in realizing their family-related values in behavior.

Underlying Subdimensions

The FAP identifies seven underlying subdimensions of family interaction and functioning. *Family Integration*, the first subdimension of the FAP, refers to the extent of emotional bonds and cooperativeness between family members, including their level of support of one another and their willingness to invest themselves in the family. The second subdimension is *Achievement Orientation*, which involves the level to which family members have a future and collective orientation toward family life and are instrumentally oriented in their approach to demands and responsibilities. The third subdimension is *Problem-Solving Style*. This subdimension is defined as the degree to which family members confront disagreements and problems in a timely and confident manner and attempt to settle such disagreements and problems through compromise solutions. The fourth subdimension, *Work Orientation*, captures the relative priority that family members assign to family versus work interests and the degree to which they share responsibility for household tasks. The fifth subdimension is *Extended Family*. This subdimension reflects the degree to which family members maintain close and supportive relationships with their extended family system. The sixth subdimension, *Religious Orientation*, refers to the extent to which family members share the same religious beliefs, attend church or synagogue together, and pray together. The final subdimension is *Community Participation*. This subdimension reflects the degree to which family members invest themselves in community events and activities. Table 4.1 lists the 33 items on the FAP organized by its seven underlying subdimensions.

Administration and Scoring

Each spouse takes the FAP twice. It is divided into two components: (1) the Family Values Profile (FVP), and (2) the Family Behavior Profile (FBP). On the FVP, spouses are instructed to evaluate each item based on how important it is to them that members of their family share the specified pattern, preference, or behavior. A response continuum ranges from one to seven, with one representing "Not at all Important" and seven representing "Extremely

Table 4.1
Item Summary Data for the Family Assessment Profile (FAP)

SCALE (Explained Variance) Item	Factor Loading[a]	Mean Value (1-7)	SD	Mean Behavior (1-7)	SD
FAMILY INTEGRATION (36.1%)					
1. Spend free time with one another.	.52	6.0	1.2	6.2	1.2
2. Support one another during difficult times.	.68	6.8	0.4	6.5	0.9
3. Give each other plenty of time and attention.	.76	6.4	0.9	5.8	1.5
4. Share their feelings with one another.	.70	6.5	0.8	6.1	1.2
5. Communicate openly and listen to one another.	.66	6.5	0.8	5.9	1.5
6. Confide in one another.	.67	6.5	0.8	6.2	1.3
7. Respect and appreciate one another.	.87	6.7	0.7	6.4	1.1
8. Feel loved and cared for by one another.	.84	6.8	0.6	6.6	0.9
9. Work together as a team.	.77	6.6	0.8	6.0	1.4
10. Invest much of their time and energy in the family.	.75	5.9	1.2	5.9	1.4
11. Do things together as a family.	.82	6.5	1.0	5.9	1.5
12. Select solutions to problems that are best for everyone.	.51	6.5	0.9	6.0	1.2
13. Trust one another.	.76	6.8	0.8	6.3	1.1
14. Have a sense of play and humor.	.68	6.5	0.8	6.2	1.2
15. Pay compliments and say nice things to one another.	.71	6.2	1.1	5.9	1.2
16. Show commitment to one another.	.79	6.8	0.6	6.4	1.2
ACHIEVEMENT ORIENTATION (7.7%)					
17. Are reliable and dependable.	.67	6.6	0.7	6.3	0.9
18. Plan ahead for future events.	.77	6.2	1.1	5.8	1.4
19. Stick to a job until it is finished.	.73	6.4	0.9	6.1	1.1
20. Try hard to succeed.	.84	6.6	0.7	6.5	0.8
21. Share similar aims and goals for life.	.69	5.8	1.3	5.9	1.3
PROBLEM SOLVING STYLE (5.9%)					
22. Compromise, when problems arise.	.65	6.3	0.9	6.0	1.1
23. Cope well under pressure.	.56	6.0	1.0	5.6	1.3
24. Quickly resolve disagreements when they occur.	.65	6.2	1.1	5.7	1.4
WORK ORIENTATION (4.7%)					
25. Share responsibility for household tasks.	.65	5.8	1.4	5.8	1.4
26. Put family life before work.	.82	5.8	1.5	5.4	1.6
EXTENDED FAMILY (3.9%)					
27. Maintain close ties with extended family members.	.63	5.8	1.4	6.0	1.4
28. Have relatives to turn to when personal or family problems arise.	.80	5.9	1.5	5.8	1.5
RELIGIOUS ORIENTATION (3.5%)					
29. Pray together.	.67	4.5	2.0	3.5	2.3
30. Share the same religious beliefs.	.80	3.9	2.3	4.6	2.2
31. Attend church or synagogue together.	.84	4.5	2.1	4.0	2.6
COMMUNITY PARTICIPATION (3.1%)					
32. Participate in community events and activities.	.85	4.0	1.9	3.4	1.9
33. Become involved in community recreational activities.	.86	4.2	1.8	3.5	1.9

[a]Principal components analysis with varimax rotation was conducted on the behavior items.

Important.'' After rating all 33 items on the FVP, spouses are asked to complete the FBP. On this profile, spouses are instructed to evaluate the same 33 items based on the extent to which they feel that members of their family actually share such patterns, preferences, and behaviors. A response continuum ranges from one to seven, with one representing "Very Little Extent" and seven representing "Very Great Extent.''

Scoring of the FAP is simply a task of addition and division to achieve an average score on each subdimension of the FVP and FBP. First, item scores are summed within each respective subdimension on the FVB and the FBP, and then they are divided by the number of items on that subdimension. This task is completed first for the FVP and then for the FBP. This procedure results in a score ranging from one to seven on each subdimension of the FVP and FBP.

The VBC-P is calculated from corresponding items on each parallel subdimension of the FVP and the FBP. A congruency profile is computed for each of the seven subdimensions by first subtracting the family behavior score from the family value score on each respective item, and then by sum averaging across the items. Although the resulting difference on each subdimension can theoretically range from -6 to +6, negative numbers are converted to a zero because it is assumed from the VBC model that the relationship between value-behavior congruency and marital satisfaction is asymptotic: The level of marital satisfaction remains stable as long as behavior in marriage exceeds or meets values for specified marital and family interaction patterns, preferences, and behavior, and it decreases in a linear fashion the more that behavior falls short of these values. French, Caplan, and Harrison (1982) refer to the simple discrepancy measure as a measure of "Fit;" they label the transformed measure of congruency as a measure of "Deficiency" (see Figure 4.1).

Initial Development

The development of FAP was an attempt to empirically measure the conceptual domains of the VBC model. The initial version of FAP was constructed in 1987 under support of the Office of Chief of Chaplains, U.S. Army, to provide a scale for analyzing variations in family-oriented values across racial/ethnic group and rank as well as to determine how variations in family-related values impacted upon marital- and family-related outcomes (see Bowen & Janofsky, 1988).

The first step in the development of the initial version of FAP was a comprehensive review of the literature on family values, marital and family life satisfaction, family strength and well-being, and family adaptation. From this review, a number of indicators of family interaction and functioning were identified, especially from the literature on family strength and well-being (e.g., Curran, 1983; Hill, 1971; Mace, 1983; Otto, 1962, 1963, 1964; Rekers, 1985; Stinnett & DeFrain, 1985). Although the attributes associated with these outcomes could be conceptualized from a value perspective, for the most part this literature focused more upon family-oriented behaviors

Figure 4.1
Hypothesized Relationship between Value-Behavior Congruency and Marital Satisfaction: Asymptotic versus Linear

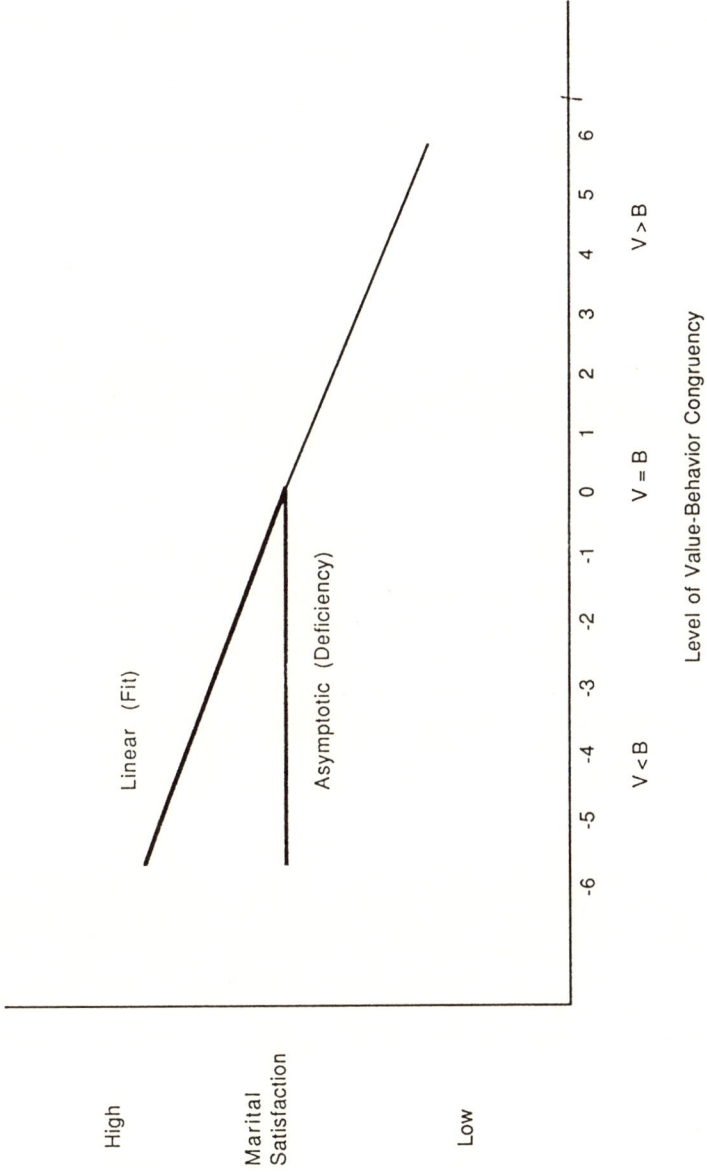

Note. Figure adapted from French, Caplan, and Harrison (1982, p. 29).

rather than family-oriented values per se, including communication, problem solving, respect and appreciation, community participation, religious orientation, and so forth. A number of research instruments designed to assess marital and family interaction and functioning were also reviewed, including those by Beavers, Hampson, and Hulgus (1985); Epstein, Baldwin, and Bishop (1983); Lewis, Beavers, Gossett, and Phillips (1976); Moos and Moos (1986); Olson (1986); Olson and McCubbin (1983); Snyder (1979); and Spanier (1976).

From this review, nine common indicators of family functioning and interaction were identified that could be conceptualized from both a value and a behavior perspective and that were conceptually related to one or more marital- and family-related outcomes: (1) open and direct communication patterns, (2) family integration, (3) spiritual and religious commitment, (4) sense of appreciation and respect for one another, (5) companionship and time together, (6) kinship bonds, including ties with the larger community, (7) shared values between family members, (8) effective problem-solving abilities, and (9) achievement orientation and work commitment. These indicators provided a conceptual framework for selecting and developing items for the FAP. In total, 110 items were either identified from prior instruments or originated to cover each dimension. The sample items were all considered to be at least conceptually related to one of the nine indicators of family functioning and interaction.

These 110 items were then subjected to expert review by a panel of civilian social scientists as well as army social scientists and chaplain leaders. The expert panel was asked to review the items for their responsiveness to study objectives, their relationship to identified marital- and family-related outcomes, their coverage across the nine indicators of family functioning and interaction, as well as for clarity of wording and item duplication. Based on this review, the number of items was reduced from 110 to 60, and two parallel profiles were developed: the Family Values Profile (FVP) and the Family Behavior Profile (FBP). These profiles were included on the survey that was administered to 175 soldiers and 88 civilian spouses at Fort Bragg, North Carolina and at Fort Riley, Kansas in Spring 1987.

Profile Development: Present Analysis

For purposes of the present investigation, 13 of the 60 items on the initial version of FAP were deleted, leaving 47 items for additional analysis. Items deleted were those that concerned the division of parenting responsibilities between spouses (since only a subset of the sample was parents) and those that had been included on the profile largely because of the interest of the client who sponsored its development, such as those concerning impression management and feelings toward military service.

After examining the frequency distributions and descriptive statistics for the remaining 47 items on the FVP and the FBP, items on the FBP were subjected to principal components analysis for the 96 spouses in the sample to determine the presence of underlying subdimensions, and to further screen less cohesive items from the profile. The factor analysis program available in SPSS[x] was used to conduct this analysis (SPSS Inc, 1986). The following program options were in effect: varimax rotation, pairwise deletion of missing data, maximum number of factors equal unspecified, minimum eigen value equal 3.0, and maximum number of iterations equal 25. Because it was expected that the underlying subdimensions of the FBP would be interrelated to some extent, oblique rotation had been originally specified in the analysis. However, this rotation failed to converge in 25 iterations.

The decision to factor analyze items on the FBP rather than those on the FVP was based on the descriptive properties of the items on the respective profiles. Overall, items on the FBP were less skewed and demonstrated more variability than items on the FVP. However, when items on the FVP were subjected to principal components analysis, the analysis yielded similar findings to those found in the analysis of the parallel behavior-oriented items.

Seven underlying subdimensions emerged from the factor analysis that explained at least three percent of the variance in the items, and 33 items remained on the FBP after 14 items were deleted because of low factor loadings (below .50) (see Table 4.1). Of the seven subdimensions, the first factor extracted from the analysis, labeled Family Integration, explained 36.1 percent of the variance in the items. The next factor, labeled Achievement Orientation accounted for 7.7 percent of the variance; the remaining factors explained between 5.9 percent to 3.1 percent of the variance in the items (see Table 4.1).

Reliability was determined for each component subdimension of the FVP and the FBP by using Cronbach's (1951) coefficient alpha, a conservative estimate of internal validity. Ranging from a low of .56 for the value component of the Work Orientation subscale (a two-item subdimension) to a high of .96 for the behavior component of the Family Integration subscale, these coefficients are summarized in Table 4.2. Although alphas tend to be higher on subdimensions of the FBP than the FVP, these results indicate that each subscale on the FVP and the FBP has high enough reliability to support its use.

Descriptive Analysis: FVP and FBP

Table 4.2 presents the means, standard deviations, and other descriptive statistics for each subdimension of the FVP and the FBP. Of the seven subdimensions, Family Integration had the least variance and was the most skewed and peaked in its distribution. Although these characteristics of nonnormality may restrict the robustness of any measure in parametric statistical analysis, such distributions are found in many self-report measures in marital and family research and have not typically posed serious problems in analysis (for example, see Schumm, McCollum, Bugaighis, Jurich, & Bollman, 1986). Religious Orientation and Community Participation had the most variance and were the most normally distributed of the seven subdimensions.

Table 4.2
Family Profile Subdimensions: Sample Summary Data

Subdimension	Mean[a]	SD	SE	Skew	Kurtosis	Alpha
Family Integration						
Value[b]	6.5	0.5	.06	-2.3	7.3	.92
Behavior[c]	6.1	1.0	.11	-2.0	4.5	.96
Achievement Orientation						
Value	6.3	0.7	.07	-1.1	0.6	.80
Behavior	6.1	0.9	.10	-1.4	1.7	.87
Problem-Solving Style						
Value	6.2	0.8	.08	-1.0	0.4	.68
Behavior	5.7	1.0	.11	-0.9	0.3	.78
Work Orientation						
Value	5.8	1.1	.12	-1.4	2.6	.56
Behavior	5.6	1.3	.13	-0.8	-0.8	.60
Extended Family						
Value	5.9	1.2	.12	-1.1	0.7	.58
Behavior	5.9	1.3	.13	-1.3	1.7	.71
Religious Orientation						
Value	4.3	1.9	.20	-0.1	-1.1	.87
Behavior	4.0	1.9	.20	-0.1	-1.3	.76
Community Participation						
Value	4.1	1.7	.18	-0.4	-0.8	.83
Behavior	3.4	1.8	.19	0.2	-1.1	.91

[a]Scores range from 1 to 7.
[b]Range is from "Not at all Important" to "Extremely Important."
[c]Range is from "Very Little Extent" to "Very Great Extent."

When correlational analysis was conducted between subdimensions on both the FVP and the FBP, the results suggested low to moderately high correlations. On the FVP, these correlations ranged from .15 to .72 (see Table 4.3). On the FBP, these correlations ranged from .10 to .55 (see Table 4.4). On the average, these correlations are moderate enough to suggest that the seven subdimensions on each profile are sufficiently independent for purposes of discrimination.

Correlational analysis between respective subdimensions on the FVP and the FBP revealed mid to moderately high levels of association (see Table 4.5). The highest correlation was for Religious Orientation (r = .77); the lowest was for Problem-Solving Style (r = .46). Although each of these correlations was statistically significant ($p < .01$), no more than 60 percent of the variance in the parallel subdimensions was accounted for by the other, suggesting that spouses do make discriminations in their responses to respective value and behavior subdimensions.

Each respective value and behavior subdimension was also correlated with an Index of Social Desirability constructed of six items from Edmonds' (1967) Index of Marital Conventionalization. This abbreviated and slightly modified index of social desirability was developed by Anderson, Russell, and Schumm (1983) and is described in more detail in the following discussion. Although the results demonstrated that responses to the FVP subdimensions had lower correlation with giving socially desirable responses than responses to the behavioral subdimensions, in all cases the correlations were low to moderate (see Table 4.6).

Descriptive Analysis: VBC-P

Table 4.7 presents descriptive statistics on each respective subdimension of the VBC. For purposes of comparison, two calculations of "congruency" are provided: "Fit" and "Deficiency." Fit scores are calculated by taking the sum average of the differences between value and behavior scores on each commensurate item of the FAP by subdimension. This calculation results in a theoretical range on each subdimension from -6 to +6.

Deficiency scores, which serve as the independent variable in the present analysis and whose construction is based on the hypothesized asymptotic relationship between value and behavior congruency and marital satisfaction, are derived from the Fit scores by a simple recode. After the calculation of the level of fit for each subdimension, negative numbers on subdimensions that result from higher average behavioral scores than value scores are recoded to zero. This yields a theoretical range of scores from 0 to +6; the higher the score, the more value scores exceed behavioral scores.

Comparisons of these two calculations across subdimensions suggest that the percentage of scores that equal zero approximately doubles for the Deficiency as compared to the Fit calculation. The means and standard deviations for Deficiency calculations across subdimensions reveal relatively high

Table 4.3
Zero-Order Correlations between Value Subdimensions on the Family Assessment Profile (FAP)

Value Subdimension	Correlations					
	1	2	3	4	5	6
1. Family Integration						
2. Achievement Orientation	.72**					
3. Problem-Solving Style	.52**	.55**				
4. Work Orientation	.36**	.40**	.16			
5. Extended Family	.47**	.46**	.27*	.23*		
6. Religious Orientation	.37**	.45**	.30**	.24*	.28*	
7. Community Participation	.31**	.31*	.17	.15	.46**	.33**

Note.   Two-tailed tests.

*p < .05.
**p < .01.

78

Table 4.4
Zero-Order Correlations between Behavior Subdimensions on the Family Assessment Profile (FAP)

Correlations

Behavior Subdimension	1	2	3	4	5	6
1. Family Integration						
2. Achievement Orientation	.48**					
3. Problem-Solving Style	.55**	.52**				
4. Work Orientation	.41**	.28*	.31**			
5. Extended Family	.45**	.33**	.48**	.14		
6. Religious Orientation	.17	.23*	.20*	.10	.22*	
7. Community Participation	.33**	.25*	.17	.13	.34**	.34**

Note. Two-tailed tests.
*p < .05.
**p < .01.

Table 4.5

Zero-Order Correlations between Corresponding Value and Behavior Profile Subdimensions

	Behavior Subdimension						
	FI	AO	PSS	WO	EF	RO	CP
Value Subdimension							
Family Integration (FI)	.60*						
Achievement Orientation (AO)		.74*					
Problem-Solving Style (PSS)			.46*				
Work Orientation (WO)				.47*			
Extended Family (EF)					.66*		
Religious Orientation (RO)						.77*	
Community Participation (CP)							.57*

Note.   Two-tailed tests.
*p< .01.

average value-behavior congruency among sample respondents and limited variance across subdimensions, characteristics that may restrict their explanatory power in parametric statistical analysis.

Intercorrelational analysis between the seven Deficiency subdimensions suggested high to moderate independence, ranging from .02 to .58 (see Table 4.8). Additional correlational analysis suggested low to mid associations between Deficiency subdimensions and corresponding value subdimensions (ranging from − .02 to .39); correlations between the Deficiency subdimensions and parallel behavioral subdimensions were higher (ranging from − .29 to − .87) (see Table 4.9 and Table 4.10, respectively).

Overall, the correlations between the component value and behavior subdimensions and corresponding Deficiency subdimensions suggest two different patterns. In three of the four cases where the zero-order correlation between the respective value subdimension and the corresponding Deficiency subdimension was significant (p < .05), the higher the assigned importance, the greater the Deficiency. On the other hand, the higher the behavioral response, the lower the Deficiency on the corresponding subdimension (all seven zero-order correlations are significant, p < .01).

Table 4.6

Zero-Order Correlations between Value and Behavior Profile Subdimensions and the Index of Social Desirability

----

Family Assessment Profile Subdimension	Index of Social Desirability
---	
Family Integration	
Value Component	.14
Behavior Component	.45*
Achievement Orientation	
Value Component	.11
Behavior Component	.16
Problem-Solving Style	
Value Component	.18
Behavior Component	.36*
Work Orientation	
Value Component	.08
Behavior Component	.16
Extended Family	
Value Component	.02
Behavior Component	.09
Religious Orientation	
Value Component	.07
Behavior Component	.14
Community Participation	
Value Component	.06
Behavior Component	.13

Note. Two-tailed tests.

*$p < .01$.

Table 4.7

Distribution of Scores on Value-Behavior Congruency Measures across Subdimensions: Fit[a] and Deficiency[b]

Scale Dimension	Perfect Fit%[c]	Mean	Minimum	Maximum	SD	Skew	Kurtosis
Family Integration							
Fit	11.9	0.3	-0.5	4.3	0.8	3.1	12.6
Deficiency	38.1	0.4	0.0	4.3	0.7	3.6	15.5
Achievement Orientation							
Fit	23.1	0.2	-1.0	2.6	0.6	1.2	3.1
Dificiency	53.8	0.3	0.0	2.6	0.5	2.5	7.4
Problem-Solving Style							
Fit	24.7	0.5	-1.0	4.0	1.0	1.9	4.3
Deficiency	44.9	0.6	0.0	4.0	0.9	2.4	5.9
Work Orientation							
Fit	32.6	0.2	-3.0	4.0	1.3	0.7	1.1
Deficiency	65.2	0.5	0.0	4.0	0.9	1.9	3.1
Extended Family							
Fit	37.4	0.1	-3.5	5.0	1.0	0.9	7.3
Deficiency	69.2	0.3	0.0	5.0	0.7	4.2	24.1
Religious Orientation							
Fit	21.6	0.2	-3.0	4.0	1.3	0.3	1.2
Deficiency	53.4	0.6	0.0	4.0	0.9	2.1	4.3
Community Participation							
Fit	27.6	0.6	-2.0	6.0	1.6	1.3	1.7
Deficiency	54.0	0.9	0.0	6.0	1.4	2.0	3.4

[a]Fit = Sum average of Value (V) - Behavior (B) scores on each item by subdimension; Theoretical range = -6 to +6.

[b]Deficiency = Same as "Fit" when sum average of (V - B) scores $\geq$ 0; recoded to 0 when sum average of (V - B) scores < 0; Theoretical range = 0 to +6.

[c]Percentage of responses where V - B = 0 or, in the case of "Deficiency" measures, where (V - B) = 0 or is recoded to equal 0: (V - B) < 0.

Table 4.8
Zero-Order Correlations between Deficiency Subdimensions on the Family Assessment Profile (FAP)

Deficiency Subdimension	Correlations					
	1	**2**	**3**	**4**	**5**	**6**
1. Family Integration						
2. Achievement Orientation	.14					
3. Problem-Solving Style	.36**	.45**				
4. Work Orientation	.25*	.08	.29*			
5. Extended Family	.31**	.23*	.58**	.24*		
6. Religious Orientation	.05	-.16	-.12	.03	-.11	
7. Community Participation	.27*	.14	.16	.02	.22*	.30*

Note. Two-tailed tests.
*$p < .05$.
**$p < .01$.

Table 4.9
Zero-Order Correlations between Corresponding Value and Deficiency
Subdimensions

| | Deficiency Subdimension | | | | | | |
Value Subdimension	FI	AO	PSS	WO	EF	RO	CP
Family Integration (FI)	-.02						
Achievement Orientation (AO)		-.21*					
Problem-Solving Style (PSS)			.22*				
Work Orientation (WO)				.18			
Extended Family (EF)					-.09		
Religious Orientation (RO)						.29*	
Community Participation (CP)							.39**

Note.   Two-tailed tests.
 *$p < .05$.
**$p < .01$.

Despite their conceptual appeal (Holman & Jacquart, 1988; Tiggle, Peters, Kelley, & Vincent, 1982) and their occasional predictive power over and beyond their commensurate components (French, Caplan, & Harrison, 1982; Seashore & Taber, 1976), congruency scores as used in analysis are fraught with potential pitfalls (see Bowen, 1989b). A key consideration is the distribution of the component scores. Special problems may arise when the variances of the component scores are unequivalent, or when the component scores are highly correlated (Althauser, 1971; French, Caplan, & Harrison, 1982; Rosenblatt & Greenberg, 1988). Although the results of analysis presented here suggest some variation in the distributions across the 14 value and behavior subdimensions, in general the commensurate value and behavior subdimensions have similarly shaped distributions, roughly equivalent variability in their component scores, and generally moderate zero-order correlations. These descriptive characteristics increase the level of confidence in the derived Deficiency scores for purposes of analysis.

Marital Satisfaction

The dependent variable, marital satisfaction, was determined by the Kansas Marital Satisfaction Scale (KMS), which was developed by Schumm and associates

Table 4.10
Zero-Order Correlations between Corresponding Behavior and Deficiency
Subdimensions

	Deficiency Subdimension						
Behavior Subdimension	FI	AO	PSS	WO	EF	RO	CP
Family Integration (FI)	-.87**						
Achievement Orientation (AO)		-.72**					
Problem-Solving Style (PSS)			-.70**				
Work Orientation (WO)				-.66**			
Extended Family (EF)					-.55**		
Religious Orientation (RO)						-.29*	
Community Participation (CP)							-.44**

Note. Two-tailed tests.
*p < .05.
**p < .01.

(Schumm, Paff-Bergen, Hatch, Obiorah, Copeland, Meens, & Bugaighis, 1986). Based on Spanier and Cole's (1976) criticism of marital adjustment instruments for failing to conceptually distinguish between units of analysis in their respective items, the KMS is comprised of three items that ask spouses to evaluate level of satisfaction with their partner as a spouse, with their marriage, and with their relationship with their spouse. In a recent review of survey instruments designed to assess marital outcomes, Sabatelli (1988b) summarized a body of research by Schumm and associates that presents considerable evidence for the validity and reliability of the scale.

Although Schumm and associates recommend a seven-point response scale ranging from "Extremely Dissatisfied" to "Extremely Satisfied," an alternate response scale was used in the present research to make it consistent with the response format of other measures in the survey instrument. Spouses responded to each item on a six-point response scale: 1 ("Very Satisfied"), 2 ("Satisfied"), 3 ("Somewhat Satisfied"), 4 ("Somewhat Dissatisfied"), 5 ("Dissatisfied"), and 6 ("Very Dissatisfied"). For purposes of analysis, the response scale was recoded from low to high, and the items were sum averaged to form a scale with a theoretical range between 1 ("Very Dissatisfied") and 6 ("Very Satisfied").

Similar to findings reported by Schumm and associates (Schumm, Paff Bergin et al., 1986), responses to the KMS were heavily skewed toward high levels of satisfaction: M = 5.43; SD = .99; Skewness = -2.63; Kurtosis = 7.94. As concluded by Sabatelli (1988b), this nonnormality seems to be characteristic of such "global" measures of marital outcomes. Despite the tendency of respondents to report toward the high end of satisfaction, Schumm and associates report that the nature of this distribution has not posed significant problems in their parametric statistical analyses (Schumm, McCollum, Bugaighis, Jurich, & Bollman, 1986).

As found by Schumm, Nichols, Schectman, and Grigsby (1983) in their own research using the KMS, its correlation with the Index of Social Desirability was statistically significant but moderate in magnitude (r = .34, p < .01). Despite this rather low correlation, following a strategy mentioned by Schumm and associates (1983) in their review, the level of social desirability was controlled for in the analyses using the KMS as a way to increase the validity of the scale.

The reliability of the KMS was determined by using Cronbach's (1951) coefficient alpha. Supporting previous research by Schumm and associates (see Sabatelli, 1988b), the internal consistency of the scale was high, alpha = .94.

Social Desirability

Based on the work of Anderson, Russell, and Schumm (1983, pp. 130–131), an abbreviated and slightly modified version of Edmond's (1967) Marital Conventionalization Scale was included as a control variable in the survey. Based on the pretest of the survey, several items were slightly modified as compared to the ones suggested by Anderson, Russell, and Schumm (1983)—for example, *spouse* was substituted for *husband*—and item four was worded in a negative rather than a positive direction.

Respondents were asked to respond to each of the following six items that comprised the scale as either 1 "True" or 2 "False": (1) "I have some needs that are not being met by my marriage" (negative wording); (2) "We get angry with each other sometimes" (negative wording); (3) "I don't think any couple could live together with greater harmony than my mate and I" (positive wording); (4) "My marriage is not a perfect success" (negative wording); (5) "Every new thing I have learned about my spouse has pleased me" (positive wording); and (6) "There are times when my mate does things that make me unhappy" (negative wording). Items three and five were recoded so that all items ranged from low social desirability to high social desirability, and responses were summed to calculate a total scale score with a theoretical range of 6 to 12.

Responses to the scale were clustered toward lower levels of social desirability: M = 8.16; SD = 1.39; Skewness = .239; and Kurtosis = -.49. The internal consistency of the scale was low; using Cronbach's (1951) coefficient alpha, alpha was .50.

Causal Conditions

From the perspective of the VBC model, a number of personal, relational, and environmental factors are assumed to influence the goal-directed activities of spouses in marriage. Although the survey was not explicitly designed to examine this aspect of the model, items were included that may serve as proxy measures for three of the factors discussed in Chapter 3: problem-solving skills in marriage, dispositional transformation, and supportiveness of the organizational culture for marriage and family life. Consequently, it is possible to conduct some exploratory analysis of these relationships.

The first variable, problem-solving skills in marriage (SKILLs), was based on the sum average of four items that were evaluated on a five-point response scale: 1 "Very Little Extent," 2 "Little Extent," 3 "Some Extent," 4 "Great Extent," and 5 "Very Great Extent." Using this response scale, respondents were asked to evaluate the extent to which they see themselves as: (1) A Good Listener, (2) An Effective Problem-Solver, (3) A Compromiser in Resolving Family Problems, and (4) Open to the Views of Others.

The unidimensionality of the four items selected for this measure was confirmed by the results of a principal components analysis. All items loaded greater than .50 on the same factor, which explained 49 percent of the variance in the items. Using Cronbach's coefficient alpha, alpha reliability for the scale was .65.

The distribution of scores on the SKILLs scale was close to normal: M = 3.90; SD = .63; Skewness = - .49; and Kurtosis = .81.

The level of dispositional transformation was measured by a single item that also was an item on the Achievement Orientation subdimension of the FBP. Using a seven-point scale from 1 "Very Little Extent" to 7 "Very Great Extent," respondents were asked, "To what extent do members in your family actually share similar aims and goals for life?" Responses to this item (GOALs) was skewed toward more positive responses: M = 5.9; SD = 1.27; Skewness = - 1.40; Kurtosis = 2.17.

The supportiveness of the organizational culture for marriage and family life (ORGCUL) was assessed by the sum average of two items drawn from a larger scale designed to measure family adaptation to army life. These items were both evaluated on a six-point satisfaction scale: 1 "Very Satisfied," 2 "Satisfied," 3 "Somewhat Satisfied," 4 "Somewhat Dissatisfied," 5 "Dissatisfied," 6 "Very Dissatisfied." The first item asked respondents to evaluate how satisfied they were with life for families in the army. The second item asked respondents how satisfied they were with the army's attitude toward families and family problems.

Responses to the ORGCUL scale clustered toward higher levels of overall satisfaction: M = 2.99; SD = 1.09; Skewness = .543; Kurtosis = -.11. The internal consistency between the two items was high; using Cronbach's coefficient alpha, alpha was .75.

Demographic Variables

Several demographic variables were included in the current analysis as control variables: Number of Years Married (0 to 19), Racial/Ethnic Group Identification (Hispanic, Black, White), Gender (Male, Female), and Presence of Children in the Household (No Children, Children). For purposes of analysis, Racial/Ethnic Group Identification was dichotomized into a minority group (Hispanic and Black) and a white group.

DATA ANALYSIS

The analysis strategy involved three stages. To examine the relationship between the Deficiency measure of value-behavior congruency and marital satisfaction, seven hierarchical regression equations were specified and tested in the first stage of the analysis using the regression program in SPSS^X (SPSS, Inc., 1986), one for each subdimension on the VBC-P. The aim of these analyses was to identify the amount of variance explained in the marital satisfaction scores of spouses by each respective Deficiency subdimension over and beyond the variance explained by three blocks of control variables in the models.

In each regression analysis, variables were entered in four steps using the force entry subcommand. Four demographic variables were entered in the first step of the analysis: Years Married—a continuous variable that ranged from less than one year to 19 years; Race—a dichotomous variable with blacks and Hispanics combined as the reference category and whites coded as the other; Gender—a dichotomous variable with males coded as the reference category; and Children—a dichotomous variable with no children in the household coded as the reference category. Each of these variables has been demonstrated in prior research to be associated with variation in the dependent variable or a closely related outcome (Bowen & Henley, 1987; Lewis & Spanier, 1979).

In the second step, the Index of Social Desirability was entered into the equation. The behavior dimension on the FBP corresponding to the Deficiency subdimension of the VBC-P being examined was entered in the next step of each analysis.

Because linear relationships were being assumed and tested in each respective model, the corresponding value subdimension on the FVP was not entered into the equation. Since the Deficiency term in each model was created by a transformation of the Fit score that is a linear function of its corresponding components on the FVP and the FBP, entering both components together with the Deficiency term would possibly confound the linear effects of the three variables in a nonadditive model (see Blalock, 1966, 1967; Bowen, 1989b; Cronbach & Furby, 1970; Glenn, 1988, 1989; Nunnally, 1967). Strictly speaking, this linear dependence is broken by the asymptotic assumption in the hypothesized relationship between Fit and marital satisfaction and by the subsequent transformation of the Fit scores to produce the Deficiency measures. However, the monotonic nature of asymptotic relationships, the restricted range on the negative side of the Fit distribution for each of the congruency measures, and the moderate to high correlations between respective value and behavior subdimensions suggested against including all three variables (Value, Behavior, and Deficiency subdimensions) in the same model. One nonstatistical way to deal with this identification problem is to drop one of the component variables used to construct the second-order term (Blalock, 1967), a solution that was adopted in the present analysis.

In the final step of each analysis, the Deficiency term was entered into the equation. At each step in the analysis, the effects of variables in the model were examined as well as increments in the level of variance explained by the model. Based on a formula suggested by Cohen and Cohen (1975, p. 136), F tests were conducted to evaluate the increment in explained variance associated with the Deficiency term over and beyond the other variables in each equation. This analysis was conducted only following a statistically significant Deficiency term in the last step of the analysis ($p < .05$).

The second stage of analysis was identical to the first with one exception: The behavioral subdimension from the FBP corresponding to the Deficiency subdimension of the VBC-P being examined in the regression analysis was deleted from the respective equation. As will be discussed in more detail, high collinearity between the behavioral and the Deficiency subdimensions presented as an issue in two of the seven models.

In the last stage of analysis, relationships were examined between the three proxy measures of causal conditions—SKILLs, GOALs, and ORGCUL— and each of the seven Deficiency subdimensions on the VBC-P. The Pearson zero-order correlation procedure in SPSS^X was used to examine the hypothesized linear relationship between each of these causal conditions and the dependent variable. One-tailed tests using a .05 level of statistical significance were used to evaluate the results from these analyses.

Precursors to the Analysis Plan

Following the recommendation by Norusis (1986) and others (such as Kerlinger and Pedhazur, 1973 and Lewis-Beck, 1980), as a precursor to conducting the regression analysis, the nature of the relationship between each Deficiency measure on the VBC-P and marital satisfaction was examined to check whether the required assumptions of linearity, normality, and constant variance were met. However, as a first step in these diagnostic analyses, it was necessary to examine an underlying assumption to the construction of the Deficiency measure: that the relationships between Fit, the unrecoded difference score on each subdimension of the VBC-P, and marital satisfaction was asymptotic. In particular, the assumption was examined that increases in marital-and family-related behavior beyond its level of assigned importance by the respondent result in no corresponding increase in the level of reported marital satisfaction beyond that found at the point of perfect value-behavior congruency.

The first step in examining this asymptotic assumption involved running a series of plots using procedures in SPSS^X between the seven Fit subdimensions of the VBC-P and marital satisfaction, including a set of regression statistics. With the exception of the relationship between the Fit measure of religious orientation and marital satisfaction, which appeared random, these plots were generally supportive of the underlying assumption.

To evaluate this assumption more systematically, the breakdown procedure in SPSS^X was used to test for differences in the level of marital satisfaction between Fit scores on each subdimension where either the behavior score exceeded the value score or where there was no difference between the respective behavior and value score—perfect Fit, which is represented by a zero score. Thus, these scores represented points on the Value(V)—Behavior(B) continuum where V minus B was either negative or equal to zero. The results from the one-way analysis of variance that was used to evaluate mean differences by subdimension supported the asymptotic assumption: There were no significant mean differences in the level of marital satisfaction on any of the seven subdimensions ($p > .05$). Consequently, a Deficiency score was constructed by recoding negative scores on each of the seven Fit measures to zero.

The process of evaluating the assumptions necessary to test for a linear relationship between the seven Deficiency measures of value-behavior congruency and marital satisfaction involved a series of steps. First, Pearson zero-order correlations were run between each Deficiency measure and marital satisfaction. The results suggested a significant correlation between the level of marital satisfaction and three of the seven Deficiency measures: Family Integration ($r = -.61$, $p < .01$), Problem-Solving Style ($r = .-27$, $p < .01$), and Work Orientation ($r = -.25$, $p < .05$). As hypothesized, the direction of these correlation coefficients suggested that the less the Deficiency, the higher the level of reported marital satisfaction. Although there are many factors that may explain low and/or statistically nonsignificant correlation coefficients, the results of this correlational analysis brought into question the assumption of a strong and significant linear relationship between each Deficiency measure and marital satisfaction.

To better visualize the nature of the relationship between each Deficiency measure and marital satisfaction, as well as to evaluate the regression assumptions of linearity, normality, and constant variance, a series of plots were run using the regression program in SPSS^X: (1) a plot of the dependent variable by each Deficiency subdimension; (2) histograms of residuals in predicting the dependent variable; (3) plots of observed and predicted values of the dependent variable; (4) plots of residuals against the predicted values of the dependent variable; and (5) a plot of residuals for the dependent variable against the values of each Deficiency subdimension. In addition, a test for linearity and deviation from linearity was conducted between each Deficiency subdimension and the dependent variable using the breakdown procedure in SPSS^X.

The results from these diagnostics generally supported the regression assumptions of linearity, normality, and constant variance between four of the seven Deficiency subdimensions and marital satisfaction: Family Integration, Problem-Solving Style, Work Orientation, and Extended Family. In each of these relationships, marital satisfaction scores appeared to cluster around a straight line (the greater the Deficiency, the lower the marital satisfaction), the distribution of residuals was "approximately" normal (more peaked and negatively skewed than normal), and the spread of residuals was "reasonably" constant (more variance as the level of Deficiency decreased, especially at the point of perfect congruency). In all four relationships, the test for linearity was supported ($p < .05$); in three of the four, the test for deviation from linearity was not supported ($p > .05$). Although both a linear and nonlinear relationship was supported between the Deficiency measure of Family Integration and marital satisfaction, the F-ratio was more supportive of a linear than a nonlinear relationship ($F_{1, 63} = 118.83$ and $F_{19, 63} = 6.09$, respectively). Given these findings combined with the "robustness" of the F and t tests (Kerlinger & Pedhazur, 1973), the use of regression analysis was considered an appropriate strategy to examine these relationships.

The relationship between three of the Deficiency measures and marital satisfaction appeared random: Achievement Orientation, Religious Orientation, and Community Participation. The spread of residuals in two of the three relationships became extreme as the value of the independent variable decreased, and the breakdown procedure suggested neither a linear nor a nonlinear relationship between these Deficiency subdimensions and marital satisfaction. Despite these findings, a regression analysis was also performed to further examine these relationships.

As a final step in the diagnostic process, one additional issue was addressed: the possibility of high collinearity between independent and control variables in each regression analysis, especially between the Deficiency measures and their corresponding behavior subdimension. High collinearity in models can bias parameter estimates and lead to unreliable inferences.

Table 4.11 presents the bivariate correlation matrix between independent and control variables in each equation as well as the correlations between predictor variables in the analysis and the criterion variable: marital satisfaction. With the exception of the relationships between the Deficiency measures and their corresponding behavioral component, these correlations were low to moderate in magnitude. Only the relationship between the Deficiency measure and the behavior component of Family Integration exceeded .80: a frequent cutoff used in social science research to indicate collinearity. However, the zero-order correlations between the behavior component and the Deficiency subdimensions of both Achievement Orientation and Problem-Solving Style were $-.72$ and $-.70$, respectively.

To further examine the potential issue of collinearity between the Deficiency subdimensions and the respective behavior components within each regression

Table 4.11
Correlation Matrix (n = 70)

Correlations

Variable	1	2	3	4	5	6	7	8	9	10	11	12	13	14	15	16	17	18	19
1. Marital Satisfaction																			
2. FI-D[a]	-.74**																		
3. AO-D	-.08																		
4. PSS-D	-.34**																		
5. WO-D	-.16																		
6. EF-D	-.29*																		
7. RO-D	.00																		
8. CP-D	-.11																		
9. FI-B[b]	.67**	-.87**																	
10. AO-B	.16		-.72**																
11. PSS-B	.39**			-.70**															
12. WO-B	.07				-.66**														
13. EF-B	.31**					-.55**													
14. RO-B	.03						-.29*												
15. CP-B	.28*							-.44**											
16. Years Married	.02	-.08	-.01	-.15	-.21*	-.10	.14	-.09	.06	.03	.12	.26*	-.03	.30*	.18				
17. Race	.07	.06	.12	-.02	.09	-.13	-.10	-.19	-.15	-.17	-.13	-.28*	.14	-.18	.07	-.12			
18. Gender	-.09	.05	-.01	-.23*	.15	-.18	.20	-.04	-.06	-.10	.07	-.16	.02	-.04	-.12	-.07	.17		
19. Number Children	-.08	.01	.01	-.23*	-.08	.27*	.09	-.04	-.02	-.08	.13	.09	-.02	.13	.13	.68**	-.19	.08	
20. Social Desirability	.47**	-.47**	-.08	-.25*	-.24*	-.03	-.06	-.07	.47**	.12	.37**	.18	.03	.07	.09	-.08	-.17	-.13	-.11

Note. FI = Family Integration; AO = Achievement Orientation; PSS = Problem-Solving Style; WO = Work Orientation; EF = Extended Family; RO = Religious Orientation; CO = Community Participation.

Note. Two-tailed tests.

*p < .05.
**p < .01.

[a] Deficiency Subdimension.
[b] Behavior Subdimension.

equation, each Deficiency measure was regressed on the other predictor variables in each respective model. Although Lewis-Beck (1980, p. 60) refers to the practice of regressing each independent variable on all the other predictor variables in the model as the "preferred method" for assessing multicollinearity, in the present analysis only the Deficiency measure in each model was examined as a criterion variable. This decision was based on both the results of the bivariate analysis and the central focus of the Deficiency variable in the analyses.

The amount of variance accounted for in each of the Deficiency measures by the other predictor variables in each respective model ranged from a low of .23 to a high of .77: Family Integration (R^2 = .77); Achievement Orientation (R^2 = .53); Problem-Solving Style (R^2 = .56); Work Orientation (R^2 = .47); Extended Family (R^2 = .43); Religious Orientation (R^2 = .23); and Community Participation (R^2 = .23). In each model, the corresponding behavior component was the strongest and most statistically significant predictor of variation in the respective Deficiency measure. In five of the seven models, it was the only significant predictor of variation in the criterion variable. When the behavior component was removed from the analysis and the level of multicollinearity was recalculated, the amount of shared variance was reduced dramatically between the Deficiency measure and the other predictors in each model: Family Integration (R^2 = .24); Achievement Orientation (R^2 = .03); Problem-Solving Style (R^2 = .20); Work Orientation (R^2 = .13); Extended Family (R^2 = .20); Religious Orientation (R^2 = .10); and Community Participation (R^2 = .06).

Given the results of this diagnostic analysis, in conjunction with correlational analysis already reported, a decision was made to evaluate two explanatory models in each regression analysis: one with the behavior subdimension entered as a control variable, and another with the behavior subdimension discarded from the model. This analysis strategy permitted some assessment of the implications of including both subdimensions together in the same model.

RESULTS

Regression Analysis: Model 1

The results of the seven hierarchical regressions predicting marital satisfaction that included the behavior component in the respective models are presented in Table 4.12. These models explained from 27 percent to 47 percent of the variance in marital satisfaction when they were fully specified. However, only partial support for the hypothesized relationship between the Deficiency measures of value-behavior congruency and marital satisfaction was found.

In two of the seven models, the Deficiency measure was statistically significant beyond the control variables in the analysis: Family Integration (b = − .39, p < .05) and Extended Family (b = − .41, p < .05). In both

Table 4.12
Hierarchical Multiple Regression Predicting Marital Satisfaction[a] (n = 67)

Variable	Family Integration		Achievement Orientation		Problem-Solving Style		Work Orientation		Extended Family		Religious Orientation		Community Participation	
	B	Beta	B	Beta	B	Beta	B	Beta	B	Beta	B	Beta	B	Beta
Years Married	-.00	-.03	.00	.00	-.00	-.02	.00	.01	.01	.04	-.00	-.03	-.00	-.02
Race[b]	.22	.19	.27	.23*	.27	.24*	.25	.22	.24	.20	.26	.23	.24	.20
Gender[c]	-.04	-.03	.05	.04	-.04	-.03	.05	.05	-.01	-.01	.04	.03	.06	.05
Children[d]	.10	.08	.17	.12	.08	.06	.13	.10	-.03	-.02	.17	.13	.17	.12
Social Desirability	.10	.22*	.20	.47**	.15	.36**	.20	.46**	.19	.45**	.20	.47**	.20	.47**
Behavior[e]	.13	.17	.09	.15	.11	.20	.00	.01	.02	-.03	.04	.12	.07	.21
R²: Step 3	.42		.28		.34		.27		.30		.28		.30	
Deficiency[f]	-.39	-.37*	.08	.06	-.10	-.15	-.04	-.06	-.41	-.30*	.01	.02	.02	.06
Multiple R	.68		.53		.59		.52		.60		.53		.55	
R²	.47		.28		.35		.27		.35		.28		.30	
R² Change[g]	.05*		.00		.01		.00		.05*		.00		.00	

[a] Range on marital satisfaction scale: 1 = "Very Dissatisfied" to 6 = "Very Satisfied."
[b] Dummy variable with minority (i.e., Black and Hispanic) as the reference category.
[c] Dummy variable with male as the reference category.
[d] Dummy variable with no children as the reference category.
[e] Respective behavioral subdimension.
[f] Deficiency = Value (V) Score - Behavior Score for (V - B) ≥ 0 and Deficiency = 0 for (V - B) < 0.
[g] Percent of total explained variance that the respective "Deficiency" measure explains beyond other variables in the model.
Note. The unstandardized and standardized regression coefficients shown are from the fully specified model in Step 4.
* p < .05; ** p < .01.

cases, the inclusion of these variables in the model in step four produced a small but significant increase in the amount of variance explained in the level of marital satisfaction: Family Integration (R^2 change = .05, $F_{1,\ 60}$ = 4.85, $p <$ .05) and Extended Family (R^2 change = .05, $F_{1,\ 60}$ = 4.46, $p <$ .05). As hypothesized, the greater the Deficiency on these two subdimensions of the VBC-P, the lower the level of reported marital satisfaction. As discussed previously, because of the high collinearity between the behavior and Deficiency measures of Family Integration, caution should be exercised in extrapolating parameter estimates from the model including these variables.

Several additional caveats are important to mention in these analyses. First, the Index of Social Desirability had a strong and statistically significant impact in each analysis ($p <$ .05). This finding supports the importance of controlling for the effects of this variable in examining variation in reported levels of marital satisfaction. Second, the respective behavior subdimension in each model did not explain a significant amount of variation in the level of marital satisfaction beyond the other variables in the fully specified models. Third, although the behavior subdimension was statistically significant in two of the seven models after the third step of the analysis (Family Integration, b = .34, $p <$ .01, R^2 step 3 = .42, $p <$ .01; and Problem-Solving Style, b = .17, $p <$ .05, R^2 step 3 = .34, $p <$ .01), its effect in each of these models disappeared once the Deficiency variable was entered in step four. This finding supports the results from the correlational analysis that showed (1) a moderate to high level of overlapping variance between the behavior and Deficiency measures on these two subdimensions, and (2) in the analysis including the Family Integration subdimension, the greater relative influence of the Deficiency measure to the behavior measure as a predictor of marital satisfaction.

Regression Analysis: Model 2

Table 4.13 presents the results from the seven hierarchical multiple regressions predicting marital satisfaction that excluded the behavior measure from each respective model. With the exception of the model including the Deficiency measure of Family Integration that explained 60 percent as compared to 47 percent of variance in the dependent variable, these fully specified models explained a similar level of variance in marital satisfaction as their model one counterparts.

However, compared to the regression analyses conducted in the first stage of analysis, the Deficiency measure was statistically significant beyond the control variables in the analysis in three of the seven models: Family Integration (b = −.63, $p <$ .01); Problem-Solving Style (b = −.24, $p <$ .05); and Extended Family (b = −.52, $p <$ .05). In each case, the inclusion of these variables in the model in step three produced a significant increase in the amount of variance explained in the level of marital satisfaction—especially in the model including the Deficiency measure of Family Integration, where the amount of explained variance increased substantially: Family Integration (R^2 change = .33,

Table 4.13

Hierarchical Multiple Regression Predicting Marital Satisfaction: Behavior Subdimension Removed[a] ($n = 67$)

Variable	Family Integration B	Beta	Achievement Orientation B	Beta	Problem-Solving Style B	Beta	Work Orientation B	Beta	Extended Family B	Beta	Religious Orientation B	Beta	Community Participation B	Beta
Years Married	-.01	-.03	.01	.03	.00	.01	.01	.03	.01	.06	.01	.03	.01	.03
Race[b]	.25	.18*	.32	.22	.31	.22*	.31	.21	.28	.20	.32	.22*	.29	.20
Gender[c]	-.10	-.06	-.09	-.06	-.19	-.13	-.08	-.06	-.14	-.10	-.11	-.08	-.08	-.06
Children[d]	.05	.03	.07	.04	-.03	-.02	.06	.03	-.15	-.09	.06	.03	.07	.04
Social Desirability	.09	.17	.25	.48**	.21	.41**	.25	.48**	.24	.46**	.26	.49**	.25	.49**
R^2: Step 2	.27		.27		.27		.27		.27		.27		.27	
Deficiency[e]	.63	-.66**	-.10	-.06	-.24	-.27*	-.03	-.04	-.52	-.30*	.05	.07	.02	.03
Multiple R	.77		.53		.57		.52		.59		.53		.52	
R^2	.60		.27		.33		.27		.34		.28		.27	
R^2 Change[f]	.33**		.00		.06*		.00		.07*		.01		.00	

[a] Range on marital satisfaction scale: 1 = "Very Dissatisfied" to 6 = "Very Satisfied."
[b] Dummy variable with minority (i.e., Black and Hispanic) as the reference category.
[c] Dummy variable with male as the reference category..
[d] Dummy variable with no children as the reference category.
[e] Deficiency = Value (V) Score - Behavior Score for (V - B) $\geq$ 0 and Deficiency = 0 for (V - B) < 0.
[f] Percent of total explained variance that the respective "Deficiency" measure explains beyond other variables in the model. Note. The unstandardized and standardized regression coefficients shown are from the fully specified model in Step 3.
*$p < .05$; **$p < .01$.

$F_{1, 61}$ = 50.17, $p < .01$); Problem-Solving Style (R^2 change = .06, $F_{1, 61}$ = 5.18, $p < .05$); and Extended Family (R^2 change = .07, $F_{1, 61}$ = 6.70, $p < .05$). As hypothesized, the greater the Deficiency on these subdimensions of the VBC-P, the lower the marital satisfaction score.

In general, these findings suggest that the more parsimonious models in the stage two analysis fit better with the data than the stage one models that included the behavioral measure. Comparing the unstandardized regression coefficients for the Deficiency measures that were significant in either or both stages of analysis as well as the amount of explained variance for the models including these measures between the two stages of analysis, the behavior measure seemed to suppress the effect of the Deficiency variables in the analysis. However, it failed to yield sufficient unique variance beyond that explained by other variables in the analysis to emerge as a significant predictor of variation in marital satisfaction.

Causal Conditions and Value-Behavior Congruency

Although a total of 21 Pearson zero-order correlations were run in an exploratory analysis between three proxy measures of causal conditions and each of the seven Deficiency subdimensions, few statistically significant correlations emerged from the analysis. The first proxy variable, Problem-Solving Skills in Marriage, did not demonstrate a statistically significant linear relationship with any of the seven Deficiency subdimensions ($p > .05$). However, the proxy measure for Dispositional Transformation, GOALs, was significantly correlated with three of the seven Deficiency subdimensions: Family Integration ($r = -.25$, $p < .05$); Achievement Orientation ($r = -.62$, $p < .01$); and Problem-Solving Style ($r = -.25$, $p < .05$). The direction of each of these correlation coefficients supported the hypothesized relationship: The more spouses said that members in their family actually shared similar aims and goals for life, the lower the level of Deficiency. Because the independent variable in this analysis was also used to construct the behavioral subdimension of Achievement Orientation, some common method variance may help explain the moderately high correlation between these two variables.

Only one significant relationship emerged between the proxy measure for organizational culture and the seven Deficiency subdimensions. As hypothesized, the more respondents were satisfied with life for families in the army and the level of support the army gives its families, the more congruent was their behavior for Family Integration with their values ($r = .35$, $p < .01$).

CONCLUSION

The results from the analysis suggested partial support for the two key assumptions of the VBC model of marital satisfaction that have been examined in this chapter. First, as hypothesized and as supported in the second stage of analysis, the more spouses were able to achieve their marital- and family-related values toward Family Integration, Problem-Solving Style, and Extended Family in behavior, the higher their reported level of marital satisfaction. The Deficiency variable in these three models explained a significant amount of variation in marital satisfaction beyond the influence of four demographic variables and a measure of social desirability, which were entered as control variables in the analysis. In addition, the entry of the Deficiency variable in these models produced a significant increase in explained variance over the control variables alone. Combined with the results from the diagnostic precursors to the regression analyses, these findings lend support to the hypothesized asymptotic relationship between value-behavior congruency among spouses in marriage and their level of marital satisfaction.

In two of these three models, Family Integration and Extended Family, the Deficiency variable remained statistically significant and continued to produce a statistically significant increase in explained variance, even when the corresponding behavior component of the FAP was added to the combination of other control variables in the analysis. As we have discussed, however, problems of collinearity between the behavior and the Deficiency measure of Family Integration limit confidence in the parameter estimates for this model when both components are simultaneously entered into the regression model.

Although these findings were supportive of the VBC model, no significant relationship was found between the Deficiency measure and marital satisfaction in either the first or the second stage analysis for four of the seven subdimensions on the FAP: Achievement Orientation, Work Orientation, Religious Orientation, and Community Participation. However, in some of these analyses, the results of the diagnostic procedures brought into question the assumptions necessary for parametric statistical analysis, presenting issues in the application of regression analysis to study covariation between the Deficiency measures and the dependent variable.

A major issue in each of these analyses, whether statistically significant or not, was the restricted range and the limited variance in both the measure of marital satisfaction and the Deficiency terms. The nature of the sample, which was limited to generally young married couples, probably contributed in part to the restricted amount of variance in these measures. Such restricted distributions in the Deficiency measures not only limited opportunities to study their covariation with the dependent variable in the first two stages of the analysis, but also their covariation with several proxy measures of causal conditions that was examined in the third stage of analysis. As in the first stages of analysis, only partial support was found for the moderating influence that causal conditions may have in limiting the opportunities of spouses to realize their values for family life in behavior. However, in each case where statistically significant correlations were found, they were in the expected direction.

Based on these findings, several recommendations are offered for continued research. First, the conceptual appeal of congruency scores to examine key assumptions of the VBC model of marital satisfaction must be matched by improved measures of value-behavior congruency. A key issue that is addressed by French, Caplan, and Harrison (1982) in their discussion of person-environment fit measures, and which is supported by correlational analysis in the present study, is the conceptual dependence between the value and behavior components and the constructed measures of congruency that are based on these components. For example, to what extent are the responses by spouses to the value and behavior subdimensions on the FAP independent of their perception toward value and behavior congruency?

Based on the work of Sabatelli (1984) in the development of the marital comparison level index, it is suggested that an analysis of value-behavior congruency may be built into the response format to survey items instead of being constructed after the fact from parallel items on two components. For example, after conceptually distinguishing "values" from "behavior," respondents could be asked to evaluate a set of items based on whether their experiences are less than desired, about the same as desired, or greater than desired. It may also be necessary to augment traditional survey techniques with more intensive interview protocols—including the use of Q-sorts, which are more capable of capturing the dynamic, process-level aspects of value-behavior congruency in marriage.

Second, it is suggested that the relationship between value-behavior congruency and marital satisfaction be re-examined with both larger and more diversified samples. Such samples are likely to result in greater variance in both independent and dependent variables, providing an opportunity to better understand their covariation—as well as possible variations in the nature of the covariation within different population subgroups.

5

An Empirical Test of the Model: Corporate Couples

The Value-Behavior Congruency Model of Marital Satisfaction (VBC) is based on a key assumption from the person-environment (P-E) fit perspective: that "goodness of fit" between person and environment components may explain variance in dependent outcomes beyond that accounted for by its component effects (Caplan, 1987; French, Caplan, & Harrison, 1982; Harrison, 1978). From the VBC model, it is assumed that the level of marital satisfaction is influenced by the level of fit between values and goals for marriage and opportunities to realize these values and goals behaviorally, and that this goodness of fit will account for variance in marital satisfaction not accounted for by its component variables, either singly or together.

As calculated in Chapter 4, the level of value-behavior congruency is based on a simple discrepancy score between parallel value and behavioral components across various aspects of marital and family functioning and interaction. Based on this calculation, value-behavior congruency scores can range from negative to positive. When behavior scores exceed value scores, a negative score is generated. A zero score (perfect fit) occurs when the value and behavior scores are equal. A positive score occurs when value scores exceed behavior scores. In Chapter 4, negative VBC scores were recomputed to zero based on an asymptotic assumption between value-behavior congruency in marriage and marital satisfaction, creating a "Deficiency" measure of value-behavior congruency in marriage.

Compared to Chapter 4, in which we evaluated the asymptotic hypothesis between value-behavior congruency in marriage and marital satisfaction following a set of diagnostic procedures, this chapter assumes more of an exploratory stance. Based on the work of French, Caplan, and Harrison (1982), who have studied the relationship between level of person-environment fit and job strain, the nature of relationship between value and behavior congruency in marriage and marital satisfaction may be asymptotic, as hypothesized, or it may follow one or more other shapes. Several of these other possible relationships are considered here.

First, the relationship may be linear. Generally consistent with the VBC model, for example, it may be hypothesized that the more positive the value-behavior congruency score, the lower the marital satisfaction. To test this hypothesis, it is necessary to calculate a simple discrepancy score between value and behavior components (V – B) that may range from negative (behavior exceeds values) to positive scores (values exceed behavior). French, Caplan, and Harrison (1982) refer to this measure as ''Fit.''

Because the calculation of Fit is a linear function of the respective value and behavior components, which are assumed to be linearly associated with variation in the dependent variable, their linear effects are confounded with one another and there is no statistical solution available to unconfound their effects when they are included in the same analysis (Glenn, 1988, 1989). Consequently, when only linear relationships are specified, interaction terms such as *Fit* offer no analytical advantage to the simpler component terms and they should not be included in the same analytical model with these lower-order formulations (Harrison, 1978; Cronbach and Furby, 1970).

Second, the nature of this relationship may be curvilinear. Research on the relationship between person-environment fit in the workplace and job strain (French, Caplan, & Harrison, 1982) leads us to suggest that the relationship between value-behavior congruency in marriage and marital satisfaction may assume an inverted U shape, with increasing discrepancy between value and behavior scores on either side of the Fit continuum producing lower marital satisfaction. In this case, the highest reported levels of marital satisfaction would be from spouses with minimal value-behavior congruency. To test this relationship with linear statistics it is necessary to simply take the absolute value of Fit, which results in a measure that French and associates refer to as ''Poor Fit.''

Unlike Fit, because a nonlinear relationship is assumed between Poor Fit and the marital satisfaction, its linear dependence with its component value and behavior variables is broken (see Blalock, 1967; Glenn, 1989). As a consequence, these variables may be included in the analysis together, and the variance in marital satisfaction that the interaction term explains beyond the linear component variables can be assessed directly (Harrison, 1978).

Third, two types of asymptotic relationships may be assumed between value-behavior congruency and marital satisfaction. The first is a Deficiency relationship as discussed previously, where only positive discrepancies are related to marital satisfaction (values exceed behavior). In this case, all negative discrepancies are recoded to zero to produce a linear relationship between congruency and marital satisfaction. In the second relationship, only negative discrepancies may be related to marital satisfaction (behavior exceeds values).

In this case, all positive discrepancies are assigned a zero to transform the congruency measure to have a linear relationship with the dependent variable. French and associates refer to such measures as "Excess."

Although a nonlinear relationship is hypothesized between marital satisfaction and both Deficiency and Excess, the linear dependence of these interaction variables with their component value and behavior variables may not be totally broken. While asymptotic relationships are nonlinear in shape, the relationship between the independent and dependent variable is monotonic (Harrison, 1978). Consequently, the interaction term and the component variables may overlap significantly in the variance they share with the dependent variable, decreasing the potential of the interaction term to explain additional variance beyond the component effects (Harrison, 1978; Nunnally, 1967). Because their linear effects may be confounded, special caution is advised in interpreting the parameter estimates from models that include these first- and second-order terms together in the same model—a practice that is neither recommended nor pursued in the present analysis.

This chapter comparatively evaluates the hypothesized Deficiency relationship between value-behavior congruency and marital satisfaction from the Value-Behavior Congruency Model with these other possible patterns: Fit, Poor Fit, and Excess. It also evaluates these second-order effects, which are based on the calculation of Fit, with the component value and behavior measures: first-order effects that may be assumed from the Deficiency hypothesis to have a negative and a positive relationship with marital satisfaction, respectively. This comparison of first- and second-order effects is consistent with a scientific position stated by Cronbach (1958) more than three decades ago:

Parsimony is not the only criterion of explanation, but we should not set forth a complicated explanation unless we gain something thereby. . . . An interaction hypothesis, i.e., a second-degree relationship, is justified only if it improves significantly upon these simpler predictions. (p. 356)

An analysis plan is developed that allows for a comparative test of these first- and second-order effects. It is based on survey data collected in Spring and Fall 1988 from two groups of respondents who participated in the original pilot testing of MAP.

For purposes of this secondary analysis, the Marital Assessment Profile (MAP) was developed based on the responses of these spouses to 36 parallel value-oriented and behavior-oriented items included on the survey. The survey items were selected from the original version of the Family Assessment Profile (FAP) that was presented in Chapter 4. However, the items were reworded to assume a couple rather than a family perspective, and a slight modification was made to the response continuum on the Marital Value Profile. Consisting of four subdimensions, the MAP is described in detail here, including its development and psychometric properties.

METHOD

Source of Data

Respondents were a self-selected sample of 34 couples (67 spouses) who had volunteered to participate in a corporate-sponsored marital enrichment seminar (MAP) during either Spring 1988 or Fall 1988. Either the husband or the wife worked within a small market-oriented work group of approximately 50 employees. This work group was part of a larger corporate division within a multinational, Fortune 500 corporation with corporate headquarters in the northeastern United States. This corporation has had a traditional focus on product development.

Subjects

Couples in the sample had been married an average of 16 years, and approximately three-quarters of the husbands and wives were in their first marriage. The modal couple was dually employed (63%), and sixty-eight percent had one or more children living in the home. For those couples with children living in the home, the average age of the youngest child was nearly 13 years old (M = 12.75 years).

Ninety-two percent of the spouses were white, and more than three-quarters had a four-year (49.3%) or graduate (26.9%) college degree. On the average, spouses were approximately 44 years of age.

In four of the 34 couples in the sample (11.8%), both the husband and the wife worked for the corporation. However, none of these spouses worked in the same work group. On the average, employees had worked 19 years for the corporation, and the majority were male (73%) and held management-level positions (81%).

Procedures

Before participating in the marital enrichment seminar, spouses were asked to complete a self-administered, structured survey questionnaire. This questionnaire was designed to take no longer than 20 minutes to complete, and it included a number of work, family, and stress-related items and scales, including MAP.

To help coordinate the survey effort, a point of contact within the corporation was appointed by senior management. Survey packets were prepared for each spouse, including a letter of introduction and instructions from the consulting team, a letter of support from senior management about the survey, a blank survey, and an envelope for sealing and returning the completed survey. Each survey respondent had been assigned a survey control number by the point of contact to help ensure confidentiality, and respondents were assured in the cover letter that their responses would be kept confidential and that only the consulting team would have access to the completed survey. The telephone number of the consulting team was provided to all survey respondents to address any questions or concerns about the survey.

Spouses were requested to complete the survey without consultation from their partner, and to either return the sealed survey to the point of contact or to mail it to the consulting team directly. All but one spouse completed and returned the survey. This spouse had some special concerns about the sensitivity of information that was being requested.

Marital Assessment Profile

The Marital Assessment Profile (MAP) is a 26-item, self-report instrument designed to assess each spouse's perception of the importance of specified marital interaction patterns, preferences, and behaviors (Marital Values Profile), as well as the degree to which these patterns, preferences, and behaviors are actually evidenced in the marriage (Marital Behavior Profile). (See Appendices III and IV to review these profiles.) The level of discrepancy in item ratings by spouses on the Marital Values Profile (MVP) and the Marital Behavior Profile (MBP) produces a second-order profile: the Value-Behavior Congruency Profile (VBC-P). The VBC-P reflects the degree to which spouses succeed in realizing their marital-related values in behavior.

Underlying Subdimensions

Four underlying subdimensions of marital functioning and interaction are identified on the MAP. The first, *Marital Integration*, refers to the extent of emotional bonds and cooperation between spouses in marriage, including their level of support for one another and their commitment to the relationship. *Achievement Orientation*, the second subdimension of the MAP, involves the degree to which spouses stress personal responsibility, success, and reaching one's full potential. The third subdimension, *Active-Religious Orientation*, captures two aspects. First, it reflects the priority that spouses give to involvement in community events and activities, including providing help to those outside the family. Second, it refers to the extent to which spouses share the same religious beliefs, attend church or synagogue together, and pray together. The final subdimension is *Extended Family*. This subdimension reflects the degree to which spouses maintain close and supportive relationships with their extended family system. Table 5.1 identifies the 26 items on the MAP organized by its four underlying subdimensions.

Administration and Scoring

Each spouse takes the MAP twice. It is divided into two components: (1) the Marital Values Profile (MVP), and (2) the Marital Behavior Profile (MBP).

Table 5.1

Item Summary Data for the Marital Assessment Profile (MAP)

SCALE (Explained Variance) Item	Factor Loading[a]	Mean Value (1-7)	SD	Mean Behavior (1-7)	SD
MARITAL INTEGRATION (42.3%)					
1. Spend your free time with each other.	.73	5.9	1.0	5.8	1.1
2. Support each other during difficult times.	.74	6.8	0.5	6.3	0.9
3. Give each other plenty of time and attention.	.82	5.9	1.1	5.5	1.2
4. Share your feelings with each other.	.81	6.4	0.8	5.7	1.0
5. Communicate openly and listen to each other.	.84	6.7	0.5	5.5	1.2
6. Confide in each other.	.70	6.3	0.8	5.9	1.1
7. Respect and appreciate each other.	.80	6.7	0.5	6.1	0.9
8. Feel loved and cared for by each other.	.84	6.7	0.5	6.1	1.2
9. Select solutions to problems that are best for both of you.	.71	6.3	0.8	5.6	1.2
10. Trust each other.	.59	6.7	0.5	6.4	0.9
11. Show commitment to each other.	.80	6.5	0.7	6.1	1.0
12. Compromise when problems arise.	.62	6.2	1.0	5.6	1.1
13. Quickly resolve disagreements when they occur.	.60	5.9	1.3	5.1	1.4
ACHIEVEMENT ORIENTATION (12.8%)					
14. Are reliable and dependable.	.59	6.4	0.8	6.3	0.7
15. Take responsibility for your own actions.	.74	6.5	0.7	6.3	0.9
16. Strive to be the best at whatever you do.	.80	5.8	1.2	5.8	1.3
17. Try hard to succeed.	.66	5.9	1.2	6.0	1.0
18. Cope well under pressure.	.64	5.9	1.1	5.4	1.1
ACTIVE-RELIGIOUS ORIENTATION (6.5%)					
19. Participate in community events and activities.	.87	4.2	1.7	3.5	1.6
20. Become involved in community recreational activities.	.77	3.5	1.5	3.4	1.7
21. Provide help to those outside the family.	.56	4.9	1.4	4.5	1.5
22. Pray together.	.85	4.1	2.0	3.2	2.1
23. Share the same religious beliefs.	.68	4.4	2.0	5.3	1.9
24. Attend church or synagogue together.	.83	4.5	2.1	4.1	2.4
EXTENDED FAMILY (4.7%)					
25. Maintain close ties with extended family members.	.78	5.8	1.1	5.6	1.4
26. Have relatives you can turn to when personal or family problems arise.	.84	4.6	1.6	5.0	1.8

[a]Principal components analysis with varimax rotation was conducted on the behavior items.

On the MVP, spouses are instructed to evaluate each item based on how important it is to them that they and their spouse share the specified pattern, preference, or behavior. A response continuum ranges from one to seven, with one representing "Not Important" and seven representing "Extremely Important." After rating all 26 items on the MVP, spouses are asked to complete the MBP. On this profile, spouses are instructed to evaluate the same 26 items on the MVP based on the extent to which they feel they and their spouse actually share such patterns, preferences, and behaviors. A response continuum ranges from one to seven, with one representing "Very Little Extent" and seven representing "Very Great Extent."

The scoring of the MAP is simply a task of addition and division to achieve an average score on each subdimension of the MVP and the MBP. First, item scores are summed within each respective subdimension on the MVB and the MBP, and then they are divided by the number of items on that subdimension. This task is completed first for the MVP and then for the MBP. This procedure results in a score ranging from one to seven on each subdimension of the MVP and the MBP.

The VBC-P is calculated from corresponding items on each parallel subdimension of the MVP and the MBP. As defined previously, four separate measures of value and behavior congruency may be constructed to examine the relationship between value-behavior congruency in marriage and the level of marital satisfaction reported by spouses. The first measure is Fit. It is computed for each of the four subdimensions by first subtracting the behavior score from the value score on each respective item on the MAP, and then by sum averaging across the items by subdimension. The resulting difference can theoretically range from -6 to +6, providing an opportunity to test for a linear relationship between value-behavior congruency and marital satisfaction.

The other three measures of value-behavior congruency are derived from this measure of Fit. A measure of Poor Fit is calculated by taking the absolute value of Fit. This results in a theoretical distribution from 0 to 6, with scores increasing as the discrepancy between values and behavior increases in either a positive or a negative direction. This transformation of Fit provides an opportunity to test for a curvilinear relationship between value-behavior congruency and marital satisfaction using linear-based statistical procedures.

To examine the possibility of an asymptotic relationship between value-behavior congruency and marital satisfaction, two additional transformations of Fit are calculated based on either recoding negative discrepancies to zero (Deficiency) or recoding positive discrepancies to zero (Excess). These transformations result in a theoretical distribution of 0 to 6 and −6 to 0, respectively. Both Deficiency and Excess transformations allow for the testing of asymptotic hypotheses with linear-based statistics.

Each of these measures of value-behavior congruency—as well as their descriptive labels, Fit, Poor Fit, Deficiency, and Excess—was adapted from the work of French, Caplan, and Harrison (1982).

Initial Development

The development of MAP was based on earlier research in the U.S. Army to develop a measure for analyzing variations in family-oriented values and how variations in these values impacted upon marital- and family-related outcomes (see Chapter 4). From this research, which included a comprehensive review of marital and family interactional and outcome measures and extensive consultation with an expert panel, 60 parallel value and behavior items were identified or developed to assess a number of different aspects of marital and family interaction and functioning. These items were included on a survey that was administered to a sample of soldiers and spouses at two army posts in Spring 1987. Several versions of a value and behavior assessment profile have since been developed from this dataset to examine hypotheses from the Value-Behavior Congruency Model of Marital Satisfaction (Bowen & Janofsky, 1988; see Chapter 4).

Based on various statistical analyses of the earlier profile combined with more extensive reviews of the literature, 36 items were selected from the original profile of 60 items, and two parallel profiles were developed for inclusion on the present survey: the Marital Values Profile (MVP) and the Marital Behavior Profile (MBP). Each of the 36 items was considered to have conceptual relevance to one of 12 subdimensions that were hypothesized as underlying components of marital interaction and functioning: (1) Respect and Appreciation, (2) Communication Openness, (3) Problem Solving, (4) Role Equity, (5) Achievement Orientation, (6) Impression Management, (7) Religious Orientation, (8) Community Participation and Support, (9) Extended Family, (10) Companionship, (11) Commitment, and (12) Autonomy. Because these items had originally focused on family rather than marital interaction per se, each item was reworded, if necessary, to focus only on the couple system.

Profile Development: Present Analysis

For purposes of the present investigation, four of the 36 MAP items that were included on the survey were deleted, leaving 32 items for additional analysis. The deleted items included two that concerned the sharing of parenting responsibilities between spouses (only a subset of the sample was parents) and two that were related to impression management. The items concerning impression management had been included on MAP because of their earlier use on the Family Assessment Profile (FAP); however, they were considered less cohesive with the other items in the present analysis.

After examining the frequency distributions and descriptive statistics for the remaining 32 items on the MVP and the MBP, items on the MBP were factor analyzed using principal components analysis for the 67 spouses in the sample. The purpose of the factor analysis was to determine the presence of underlying subdimensions and to further screen less cohesive items from the profile. The factor analysis program in SPSS^X was used to conduct this analysis. The following program options were in effect: varimax rotation, pairwise deletion of missing data, maximum number of factors equal unspecified, minimum eigen value equal 1.0, and maximum number of iterations equal 25. Because it was expected that the underlying subdimensions of MAP would be correlated to some extent, an oblique rotation was attempted. However, this rotation failed to converge in 25 iterations.

The decision to factor analyze items on the MBP rather than the MVP was based on the descriptive properties of the items on the respective profiles. Overall, items on the MBP were more normally distributed than items on the MVP.

Four underlying subdimensions emerged from the factor analysis that loaded with more than one item and that were interpretable. As the first four factors that emerged from the principal components analysis, each explained four or more percent of the variance in the items. Twenty-six items remained on the MBP after six items were deleted because of low factor loadings (.55). (See Table 5.1.)

The first factor extracted from the analysis, Marital Integration, explained 42.3 percent of the variance in the items. Half of the 26 items loaded on this factor. The next factor, Achievement Orientation, accounted for 12.8 percent of the variance. Five items loaded on this factor. Two additional factors, Active-Religious Orientation and Extended Family, explained 6.5 percent and 4.7 percent of the variance in the items, respectively. Five items loaded on the Active-Religious factor; two items loaded on the Extended Family factor. In general, the results of the factor analysis were supportive of the earlier FAP analysis that was presented in Chapter 4.

Reliability was determined for each component subdimension on the MVP and the MBP by using Cronbach's coefficient alpha (1951), a conservative estimate of internal validity. These coefficients ranged from a low of .56 for the value component of the Extended Family subdimension to .96 for the behavior component of the Marital Integration subdimension (see Table 5.2). Coefficients on the remaining value and behavior subdimensions were .80 or higher. These results are generally supportive of the internal consistency of each subdimension on the MVP and the MBP.

Descriptive Analysis: MVP and MBP

Table 5.2 presents the means, standard deviations, and other descriptive statistics for each subdimension of the MVP and the MBP. Of the four subdimensions, Marital Integration and Achievement Orientation had the highest mean values and the least variance on both their value and behavior components. In all cases, the distributions were skewed with a higher proportion of responses toward larger values—not uncharacteristic of self-report measures in marital and family research. In general, although characteristics of nonnormality may restrict the robustness of any measure in parametric statistical analysis, such distributions have not been found to pose serious problems

Table 5.2
Marital Profile Subdimensions: Sample Summary Data

Subdimension	Mean[a]	SD	SE	Skew	Kurtosis	Alpha
Marital Integration						
Value[b]	6.4	0.5	.07	-0.6	-0.7	.90
Behavior[c]	5.8	0.9	.11	-0.9	0.8	.96
Achievement Orientation						
Value	6.1	0.8	.10	-0.8	-0.2	.89
Behavior	5.9	0.8	.10	-0.8	0.3	.89
Active-Religious Orientation						
Value	4.3	1.5	.18	-0.4	-0.7	.89
Behavior	4.0	1.5	.18	-0.4	-1.0	.89
Extended Family						
Value	5.2	1.2	.14	-0.3	-0.5	.56
Behavior	5.3	1.5	.18	-0.9	0.3	.80

[a]Scores range from 1 to 7.
[b]Range is from "Not Important" to "Extremely Important."
[c]Range is from "Very Little Extent" to "Very Great Extent."

in analysis (for example, see Schumm, McCollum, Bugaighis, Jurich, & Bollman, 1986).

When correlational analysis was conducted between subdimensions on both the MVP and the MBP, the results suggested low to moderately high correlations. On the MVP, these correlations ranged from .36 between Active-Religious Orientation and Marital Integration to .75 between Achievement Orientation and Marital Integration (see Table 5.3). Overall, although correlations between subdimensions on the two profiles followed a similar pattern, those on the MBP were more modest than those on the MVP. These correlations ranged from a low of .21 between Active-Religious Orientation and Marital Integration to a high of .71 between Achievement Orientation and Marital Integration (see Table 5.4). On the average, these correlations were moderate enough to consider the four subdimensions on each profile as sufficiently independent for purposes of discrimination.

Correlational analysis between respective subdimensions on the MVP and the MBP revealed mid to moderately high levels of association (see Table 5.5). Three of the four correlation coefficients ranged from .70 to .74. The lowest correlation was for Marital Integration ($r = .56$). Although each of these correlations was statistically significant ($p < .01$), no more than 55 percent of the variance in the respective subdimensions was accounted for by the other. These findings suggest that spouses do make discriminations in their responses to respective value and behavior subdimensions.

Each respective value and behavior subdimension was also correlated with an index of social desirability based on six items from Edmonds' (1967) Index of Marital Conventionalization. This abbreviated and slightly modified index of social desirability was developed by Anderson, Russell, and Schumm (1983) and is described in more detail here. In all but one case, these correlation coefficients were low (less than ± .14): The behavior component of the

Table 5.3
Zero-Order Correlations between Value Subdimensions on the Marital Assessment Profile (MAP)

Value Subdimension	Correlations		
1. Marital Integration	1		
2. Achievement Orientation	.75*	2	
3. Active-Religious Orientation	.36*	.45*	3
4. Extended Family	.37*	.37*	.50*

Note.   Two-tailed tests.
*$p < .01$.

Table 5.4
Zero-Order Correlations between Behavior Subdimensions on the Martial Assessment Profile (MAP)

Behavior Subdimension	Correlations			
1. Marital Integration	1			
2. Achievement Orientation	.71**	2		
3. Active-Religious Orientation	.21*	.27*	3	
4. Extended Family	.36**	.38**	.40**	

Note. Two-tailed tests.
* $p < .05$.
** $p < .01$.

Table 5.5
Zero-Order Correlations between Corresponding Value and Behavior Profile Subdimensions

	Behavior Subdimension			
	MI	AO	ARO	EF
Value Subdimension				
Marital Integration (MI)	.56*			
Achievement Orientation (AO)		.73*		
Active-Religious Orientation (ARO)			.70*	
Extended Family (EF)				.74*

Note. Two-tailed tests.
* $p < .01$.

Table 5.6

Zero-Order Correlations between Value and Behavior Profile Subdimensions and the Index of Social Desirability

----

Marital Assessment Profile Subdimension	Index of Social Desirability
Marital Integration	
Value Component	.09
Behavior Component	.40*
Achievement Orientation	
Value Component	-.06
Behavior Component	.13
Active-Religious Orientation	
Value Component	.01
Behavior Component	.04
Extended Family	
Value Component	-.08
Behavior Component	.02

Note.   Two-tailed tests.
*$p < .01$.

Marital Integration subdimension was moderately correlated with the index of social desirability ($r = .40$, $p < .01$). (See Table 5.6.)

Descriptive Analysis: VBC-P

Table 5.7 provides descriptive statistics by subdimension for each of the four measures of value and behavior congruency: Fit, Poor Fit, Deficiency, and Excess. The similarly skewed distributions of the value and behavior components used to construct these congruency measures yielded some interesting patterns in the distributions of these measures that potentially constrain (1) their explanatory power beyond their component value and behavior measures in parametric statistical analysis and (2) their degree of independence from one another in predicting variation in marital satisfaction.

First, partly as an artifact of their construction, both the Deficiency and Excess measures revealed a high proportion of congruency scores equal to zero.

Table 5.7
Distribution of Scores on Value-Behavior Congruency Measures across Subdimensions

Scale Dimension	Perfect Fit%[a]	Mean	Minimum	Maximum	SD	Skew	Kurtosis
Marital Integration							
Fit[b]	15.4	0.6	-0.3	3.1	0.7	1.6	2.6
Poor Fit[c]	15.4	0.6	0.0	3.1	0.7	1.8	3.2
Deficiency[d]	27.7	0.6	0.0	3.1	0.7	1.7	2.9
Excess[e]	87.7	-0.0	-0.3	0.0	0.7	-3.2	9.6
Achievement Orientation							
Fit	19.7	0.2	-1.4	2.0	0.6	0.2	1.1
Poor Fit	19.7	0.5	0.0	2.0	0.4	1.3	1.8
Deficiency	50.0	0.3	0.0	2.0	0.4	1.8	3.4
Excess	69.7	-0.2	-1.4	0.0	0.3	-2.4	5.8
Active-Religious Orientation							
Fit	13.6	0.3	-4.0	3.0	1.3	-0.2	2.7
Poor Fit	13.6	0.8	0.0	4.0	0.8	1.7	3.2
Deficiency	47.0	0.5	0.0	3.0	0.8	1.7	2.3
Excess	66.7	-0.3	-4.0	0.0	0.6	-4.0	21.7
Extended Family							
Fit	22.7	-0.2	-2.0	3.0	1.0	0.6	0.4
Poor Fit	22.7	0.7	0.0	3.0	0.6	1.0	0.9
Deficiency	66.7	0.4	0.0	3.0	0.7	2.0	3.9
Excess	56.1	-0.4	-2.0	0.0	0.5	-1.3	0.8

[a]Percentage of responses where congruency score is equal to zero.
[b]Fit = Sum average of Value (V) - Behavior (B) scores on each item by subdimension; Theoretical range = -6 to +6.
[c]Poor Fit = Absolute value of "Fit"; Theoretical range = 0 to +6.
[d]Deficiency = Same as "Fit" when sum average of (V - B) scores $\geq$ 0; recoded to 0 when sum average of (V - B) scores < 0;
   Theoretical range = 0 to +6.
[e]Excess = Same as "Fit" when sum average of (V - B) scores $\leq$ 0; recoded to 0 when sum average of (V - B) scores > 0;
   Theoretical range = -6 to 0.

Perhaps the exception to this generality was the Deficiency measure on the Marital Integration subdimension, where the congruency score was equal to zero for only 27 percent of respondents. However, this was especially the case for the measures of Excess, which demonstrated highly skewed distributions across three of the four subdimensions (Marital Integration, Achievement Orientation, and Active-Religious Orientation), but particularly on the Marital Integration subdimension. In each case, a higher proportion of respondents reported their values as exceeding their behavior than the converse.

Because of both the restricted range and the small proportion of cases with negative value-behavior discrepancies on these three subdimensions, the descriptive properties of the Fit, Poor Fit, and Deficiency measures were more similar than different. This was especially the case for the Marital Integration subdimension. In fact, the correlations between these measures were nearly perfect on the Marital Integration subdimension (.99), and they ranged from .35 to .88 on the Achievement Orientation subdimension and from .26 to .86 on the Active-Religious subdimension. In each case, the correlation between Fit and Deficiency exceeded .85. Moreover, the relationship between Fit and Deficiency demonstrated a high correlation even on the Extended Family subdimension (r = .87), and on three of the four subdimensions (Achievement Orientation, Active-Religious Orientation, and Extended Family), the correlations between Fit and Excess ranged from .75 to .80 (see Table 5.8).

Table 5.9 presents the correlations and multiple correlations between each congruency measure and its respective value, behavior, and combined value and behavior components by subdimension. In general, with the exception of Excess, the findings suggest a higher level of association between behavior components and the respective congruency components than between value components and the respective congruency components. However, it is not surprising that the highest overall associations are between the combined value and behavior components and the respective congruency measures. Because Fit is a perfect linear function of its respective value and behavior components, these coefficients are not entered in the table.

Supporting the discussion in the introduction of the potential issue of linear dependence between transformed congruency measures and their components, the size of some of the multiple correlations between combined value and behavior components and congruency measures, especially Deficiency and Excess, suggests the presence of high multicollinearity in most cases between these measures and their components. It is not surprising, given the high association between Poor Fit and both Fit and Deficiency measures on the Marital Integration subdimension, that even the multiple correlation between the combined value and behavior components on this subdimension and the measure of Poor Fit suggests almost perfect multicollinearity. Such high correlations cast doubt on the predictive validity of congruency measures to explain variation in marital satisfaction beyond their component value and behavior measures.

Table 5.8
Correlations between Value-Behavior Congruency Measures by Marital Assessment Profile (MAP) Subdimension

			Subdimension	
Measures	Marital Integration	Achievement Orientation	Active-Religious Orientation	Extended Family
Fit & Poor Fit	.99**	.35**	.26*	.22
Fit & Deficiency	.99**	.88**	.86**	.87**
Fit & Excess	.36**	.75**	.75**	.80**
Poor Fit & Deficiency	.99**	.74**	.72**	.67**
Poor Fit & Excess	.20	-.35**	-.44**	-.40**
Deficiency & Excess	.28*	.35**	.31**	.41**

Note. Two-tailed tests.
*p < .05.
**p < .01.

Table 5.9

Correlations and Multiple Correlations between Value, Behavior, and Respective Value-Behavior Congruency Measures by Marital Assessment Profile (MAP) Subdimension

		Respective Congruency Measure		
	Fit[a]	Poor Fit[b]	Deficiency[c]	Excess[d]
Value[e]				
Marital Integration	.05	-.00	.02	.29*
Achievement Orientation	.37**	-.22	.15	.52**
Active-Religious Orientation	.37**	.02	.28*	.33**
Extended Family	.07	-.30*	-.09	.25*
Behavior[e]				
Marital Integration	-.80**	-.82**	-.82**	-.13
Achievement Orientation	-.37**	-.49**	-.50**	-.03
Active-Religious Orientation	-.40**	-.18	-.38**	-.25*
Extended Family	-.61**	-.39**	-.66**	-.34**
Value and Behavior				
Marital Integration	.NA	.99**	.99**	.45**
Achievement Orientation	.NA	.51**	.91**	.81**
Active-Religious Orientation	.NA	.27*	.86**	.75**
Extended Family	.NA	.36**	.89**	.82**

[a] Fit = (V - B).
[b] Poor Fit = IV - Bl..
[c] Deficiency = Value (V) Score - Behavior Score for (V - B) $\geq$ 0 and Deficiency = 0 for (V - B) < 0.
[d] Excess = Value (V) Score - Behavior Score for (V - B) $\leq$ 0 and Excess = 0 for (V - B) > 0.
[e] Range is from one to seven. Value: 1 = Not Important, 7 = Extremely Important;
   Behavior: 1 = Very Little Extent, 7 = Very Great Extent.
Note. NA = Not Applicable because Fit is a perfect linear function of value and behavior components.
Note. Two-tailed tests.
*p < .05.
**p < .01.

These findings support an analytical strategy that does not combine congruency measures with their respective value and behavior components in the same predictive model. Although no multicollinearity problems were found between the combined value and behavior components and several measures of Poor Fit and one measure of Excess, in general, including both congruency measures and their components together in multiple regression models would seriously violate the regression assumption of independence among predictor variables and would produce highly unreliable parameter estimates.

Marital Satisfaction

The dependent variable, marital satisfaction, was determined by the Kansas Marital Satisfaction Scale (KMS), which was developed by Schumm and associates (Schumm, Paff-Bergen, Hatch, Obiorah, Copeland, Meens, & Bugaighis, 1986). Based on Spanier and Cole's (1976) criticism of marital adjustment instruments for failing to conceptually distinguish between units of analysis in their respective items, the KMS is comprised of three items that ask spouses to evaluate their level of satisfaction with their partner as a spouse, with their marriage, and with their relationship with their spouse. In a recent review of survey instruments designed to assess marital outcomes, Sabatelli (1988b) summarized a body of research by Schumm and associates that presents considerable evidence for the validity and reliability of the scale.

Although Schumm and associates recommend a seven-point response scale ranging from "Extremely Dissatisfied" to "Extremely Satisfied," an alternate response scale was used in the present research to make it consistent with the format of other measures in the survey instrument. Spouses responded to each item on a six-point response scale: 1 ("Very Satisfied"), 2 ("Satisfied"), 3 ("Somewhat Satisfied"), 4 ("Somewhat Dissatisfied"), 5 ("Dissatisfied"), and 6 ("Very Dissatisfied"). For purposes of analysis, the response scale was recoded from low to high, and the items were sum averaged to form a scale with a theoretical range between 1 ("Very Dissatisfied") and 6 ("Very Satisfied").

Similar to findings reported by Schumm and associates (Schumm, Paff-Bergen, et al., 1986), responses to the KMS were skewed toward high levels of satisfaction: $M = 5.12$; $SD = 1.13$; Skewness = -1.99; Kurtosis = 4.43. As concluded by Sabatelli (1988b), this nonnormality seems to be characteristic of such "global" measures of marital outcomes. Despite the tendency of respondents to report toward the high end of satisfaction, Schumm and associates report that the nature of this distribution has not posed significant problems in their parametric statistical analyses (Schumm, McCollum, Bugaighis, Jurich, & Bollman, 1986).

Contrary to findings by Schumm and associates (Schumm, Nichols, Schectman, & Grigsby, 1983) in their own research using the KMS, its correlation with the Index of Social Desirability (see detailed description in the next section) was low ($r = .04, p > .05$). Despite this low correlation, social desirability was used as a control variable in the analyses reported in the following section to increase the validity of the KMS (see Schumm et al., 1983, who comment on this strategy).

The reliability of the KMS was determined by using Cronbach's (1951) coefficient alpha. Supporting previous research by Schumm and associates (see Sabatelli, 1988b), the internal consistency of the scale was high, alpha = .95.

Social Desirability

Based on the work of Anderson, Russell, and Schumm (1983, pp. 130–131), an abbreviated and slightly modified version of Edmond's (1967) Marital Conventionalization Scale was included as a control variable in the survey. Based on the pretest of the survey, several items were slightly modified as compared to the ones suggested by Anderson, Russell, and Schumm (1983)—for example, *spouse* for *husband*—and item four was worded in a negative rather than a positive direction.

Respondents were asked to respond to each of the following six items that comprised the scale as either 1 "True" or 2 "False": (1) "I have some needs that are not being met by my marriage" (negative wording); (2) "We get angry with each other sometimes" (negative wording); (3) "I don't think any couple could live together with greater harmony than my mate and I" (positive wording); (4) "My marriage is not a perfect success" (negative wording); (5) "Every new thing I have learned about my spouse has pleased me" (positive wording); and (6) "There are times when my mate does things that make me unhappy" (negative wording). Items three and five were reverse coded so that all items ranged from low social desirability to high social desirability, and responses were recoded as either 0 "Not Socially Desirable" or 1 "Socially Desirable." The recoded responses were summed to create a total scale score with a theoretical range of 0 "No Socially Desirable Responses" to 6 "All Socially Desirable Responses."

Responses to the scale were clustered toward lower levels of social desirability: $M = 1.39$; $SD = 1.49$; Skewness = .908; and Kurtosis = .03. The internal consistency of the scale was moderate; using Cronbach's (1951) coefficient alpha, alpha was .65.

Demographic Variables

Several demographic variables were included in the analysis as control variables based on their past association with variation in the dependent variable (Lewis & Spanier, 1979): Number of Years Married—a continuous variable that ranged from 1 to 36 years; Gender—a dichotomous variable with males coded as the reference category; and Children—a dichotomous variable with no children in the household coded as the reference variable.

DATA ANALYSIS

Two stages of analysis were conducted to explore the ability of the four congruency measures to account for variance in marital satisfaction beyond their component value and behavior measures, either singly or in combination. In the first stage, either Pearson zero-order or multiple correlations were run between the dependent variable, marital satisfaction, and each congruency measure (Fit, Poor Fit, Deficiency, Excess) and their component value and behavior measures (Value, Behavior, Value and Behavior) by the four Marital Assessment Profile subdimensions. Two-tailed tests using a .05 level of probability were used to determine statistical significance.

Paralleling the correlational analysis, 28 hierarchical regression equations were specified in the second stage of analysis: seven for each of the four MAP subdimensions. Each equation included a single congruency measure or a component value, behavior, or combined value and behavior entry: Value, Behavior, Value and Behavior, Fit, Poor Fit, Deficiency, or Excess. Because of the generally high correlations between the congruency measures and their component value and behavior measures that have already been reported, congruency measures were not combined with their respective value and behavior components, either singly or together, in the same model.

The aim of these analyses was to compare the amount of variance in marital satisfaction explained by each of the four congruency measures and their value and behavior components, both singly and together, beyond a single block of control variables. In each regression analysis, four control variables were entered in the first step of analysis using a force entry subcommand: Number of Years Married, Gender, Children, and Social Desirability. Based on a formula suggested by Cohen and Cohen (1975, p. 136), F tests were conducted to evaluate the increment in explained variance associated with the respective congruency or component measure in the equation beyond that explained by the block of control variables entered on the first step. This analysis was conducted only following a statistically significant entry in the second step of the analysis. A .05 level of significance was used to determine statistical significance, and both the correlational and the regression analysis were conducted using routines in SPSS^X (SPSS, Inc., 1986).

Precursors to the Analysis

To better visualize the nature of the relationship between value-behavior congruency and marital satisfaction, both descriptive and diagnostic procedures were performed as precursors to the analysis. Because the construction of the Poor Fit, Deficiency, and Excess measures of congruency were simple transformations of Fit, a decision was made to focus only on the relationship between Fit and marital satisfaction.

The first step in these procedures involved running a series of plots using procedures in SPSS^X between the Fit measure for each MAP subdimension and marital satisfaction. With the exception of the relationship between the Fit measure of Extended Family and marital satisfaction, which appeared random, these plots suggested a negative linear relationship between each Fit subdimension and marital satisfaction: Marital satisfaction tended to decrease as Fit moved from negative scores (Behavior exceeds Values) to positive scores (Values exceed Behavior). In general, these plots were more supportive of a linear rather than either a curvilinear or asymptotic relationship between Fit and marital satisfaction.

However, when a residual analysis was performed on the relationship between each Fit subdimension and marital satisfaction, the results brought into question the fit of a linear model with the data. This residual analysis was based on the results from running a series of additional plots using the regression program in SPSS^X: (1) histograms of residuals in predicting the dependent variable; (2) plots of observed and predicted values of the dependent variable; (3) plots of residuals against the predicted values of the dependent variable; and (4) a plot of residuals for the dependent variable against the values of each Fit subdimension. In the relationship between each Fit subdimension and marital satisfaction, the distribution of residuals was more peaked and negatively skewed than normal and the variance in the residuals tended to be highest near or at the point of perfect congruency and lowest at points of negative discrepancy (where behavior exceeds values).

To explore the nature of these relationships more systematically, tests of linearity and deviation from linearity were performed using the breakdown procedure in SPSS^X. These results were mixed. In the relationship between marital satisfaction and the Fit subdimensions of Marital Integration and Achievement Orientation, the test for linearity was supported ($p < .05$); the test for deviation from linearity was not supported ($p > .05$). In the relationship between marital satisfaction and the Fit subdimension of Active-Religious Orientation, neither linearity nor deviation from linearity was supported ($p > .05$). Last, in the relationship between marital satisfaction and the Fit subdimension of Extended Family, the test for deviation from linearity was supported ($p < .05$); the test for linearity was not supported ($p > .05$). However, even upon further visual scrutiny, no discernible pattern could be seen in the nonlinear relationship between the Fit subdimension of Extended Family and marital satisfaction. In general, these findings are supportive of the exploratory strategy proposed in the present analysis between measures of value-behavior congruency and marital satisfaction.

RESULTS

Correlational Analysis

The results of correlational analysis generally supported previous patterns between variables in both the descriptive and diagnostic analyses. Although none of the correlation coefficients were statistically significant ($p > .05$) on two of the four subdimensions (Active-Religious Orientation and Extended Family), six out of seven of the correlations were statistically significant on the Marital Integration subdimension and five out of seven were statistically significant on the Achievement Orientation subdimension. The value component was not statistically significant on either of these two subdimensions,

Table 5.10

Correlations and Multiple Correlations between Marital Satisfaction and Value, Behavior, and Value-Behavior Congruency Measures by Marital Assessment Profile (MAP) Subdimension[a]

	MAP Subdimension			
	Marital Integration	Achievement Orientation	Active-Religious Orientation	Extended Family
Value[b]	.07	.07	-.12	.12
Behavior[b]	.36**	.29*	.03	.07
Value and Behavior	.37**	.33**	.19	.08
Fit[c]	-.39**	-.28*	-.20	.03
Poor Fit[d]	-.37**	-.21*	-.02	-.19
Deficiency[e]	-.38**	-.31**	-.15	-.07
Excess[f]	-.21*	-.13	-.16	.15

[a] Range on marital satisfaction scale: 1 = "Very Dissatisfied" to 6 = "Very Satisfied."
[b] Range is from one to seven. Value: 1 = Not Important, 7 = Extremely Important; Behavior: 1 = Very Little Extent, 7 = Very Great Extent.
[c] Fit = (V - B).
[d] Poor Fit = |V - B|.
[e] Deficiency = Value (V) Score - Behavior Score for (V - B) $\geq$ 0 and Deficiency = 0 for (V - B) < 0.
[f] Excess = Value (V) Score - Behavior Score for (V - B) $\leq$ 0 and Excess = 0 for (V - B) > 0.
Note. Two-tailed tests.
*p < .05.
**p < .01.

and the Excess measure failed to achieve statistical significance on the Achievement Orientation subdimension (see Table 5.10).

In general, the correlation coefficients that achieved statistical significance on the Marital Integration and Achievement Orientation subdimensions were similarly modest in magnitude. None of the coefficients exceeded ±.40, and they ranged in size from -.21 to -.39. Most important, the size of the multiple correlations between the combined value and behavior components and marital satisfaction were as large as, if not larger than, the correlation coefficients between the various congruency measures and marital satisfaction. In fact, the behavior component alone on these two subdimensions shared a similar degree of common variance with the dependent variance as either the composite value and behavior component or the congruency measures. In the context of the generally high correlations between congruency measures and their component value and behavior measures, these findings cast doubt on the ability of the congruency measures to explain a significantly greater amount of variance in marital satisfaction across the four subdimensions in a multivariate analysis than the simpler first-order effects.

Regression Analysis

The results of the hierarchical regressions by the respective MAP subdimensions are presented in Tables 5.11 through 5.14. In terms of the amount of variance explained by each model beyond the control variables entered in the first step of the analysis (R^2 = .03), these results provided no support for an interaction hypothesis. In each of the four analyses, the composite first-order effects explained a similar or greater amount of variation in marital satisfaction than either of the four congruency measures, including the Deficiency measure.

On two of the four subdimensions (Active-Religious Orientation and Extended Family), the regression results paralleled the previous correlational analysis. Neither the first- nor the second-order terms explained a significant amount of variation in marital satisfaction beyond the control variables in the equations.

On the Marital Integration subdimension, all but the Values and the Excess terms explained a significant proportion of variation in marital satisfaction beyond the control variables in the analysis: Behavior (R^2 change = .13, $F_{1, 61}$ = 9.44, p < .01); Composite Value and Behavior (R^2 change = .19, $F_{2, 60}$ = 7.20, p < .01); Fit (R^2 change = .19, $F_{1, 61}$ = 14.61, p < .01); Poor Fit (R^2 change = .17, $F_{1, 61}$ = 12.96, p < .01); and Deficiency (R^2 change = .18, $F_{1, 61}$ = 13.90, p < .01). Based on the high correlations between these terms shown in Tables 5.8 and 5.9, these findings are not surprising.

Although the Value term was not significant in the model when it was included alone in the second step of the regression (b = − .03, p > .05), it did emerge as a significant predictor of marital satisfaction when included in the model together with the Behavior term (b = − .73, p < .05). Even the Behavior term became a stronger predictor of marital satisfaction when it was included in the same model with the Value term (b = .78, p < .01). This finding suggests some level of interaction between the two terms that, based on the correlational analysis, is seemingly captured by the congruency terms.

On the Achievement Orientation subdimension, four of the seven respective models explained a significant amount of variation in marital satisfaction in the second step of the analysis beyond that explained in the first step: Behavior (R^2 change = .09, $F_{1, 61}$ = 4.02, p < .05); Composite Value and Behavior (R^2 change = .16, $F_{2, 60}$ = 5.93, p < .01); Fit (R^2 change = .11, $F_{1, 61}$ = 7.80,

Table 5.11

Hierarchical Multiple Regression Predicting Marital Satisfaction[a]: Marital Integration Subdimension

Model Variable	Values		Behavior		Value/Behavior Components		Fit		Poor Fit		Deficiency		Excess	
	B	Beta	B	Beta	B	Beta	B	Beta	B	Beta	B	Beta	B	Beta
R^2: Step 1[b]	.03		.03		.03		.03		.03		.03		.03	
Value[c]	-.03	-.01			-.73*	-.34								
Behavior[c]			.53**	.40	.78**	.59								
Fit[d]							-.77**	-.50						
Poor Fit[e]									-.75**	-.46				
Deficiency[f]											-.77**	-.48		
Excess[g]													-4.47	-.26
Multiple R	.16		.39		.47		.47		.45		.46		.29	
R^2	.03		.16		.22		.22		.20		.21		.08	
F	.30		2.11		2.66*		3.24*		2.79*		3.04*		1.02	
df	5, 56		5, 56		6, 55		5, 56		5, 56		5, 56		5, 56	
R^2 Change[h]	.00		.13**		.19**		.19**		.17**		.18**		.05	

[a] Range on marital satisfaction scale: 1 = "Very Dissatisfied" to 6 = "Very Satisfied."
[b] Five control variables were entered in the first step of analysis: Years Married, Race, Gender, Children, and Social Desirability.
[c] Range is from one to seven. Value: 1 = Not Important, 7 = Extremely Important; Behavior: 1 = Very Little Extent, 7 = Very Great Extent.
[d] Fit = (V - B).
[e] Poor Fit = |V - B|.
[f] Deficiency = Value (V) Score - Behavior Score for (V - B) $\geq$ 0 and Deficiency = 0 for (V - B) < 0.
[g] Excess = Value (V) Score - Behavior Score for (V - B) $\leq$ 0 and Excess = 0 for (V - B) > 0.
[h] Percent of total variance explained by the Step 2 entry or entries beyond that explained by the Step 1 entries.
Note. The unstandardized and standardized regression coefficients shown are from the fully specified model in Step 2.
* $p < .05$.
** $p < .01$.

Table 5.12

Hierarchical Multiple Regression Predicting Marital Satisfaction[a]: Achievement Orientation Subdimension

Model Variable	Values		Behavior		Value/Behavior Components		Fit		Poor Fit		Deficiency		Excess	
	B	Beta	B	Beta	B	Beta	B	Beta	B	Beta	B	Beta	B	Beta
R^2: Step 1[b]	.03		.03		.03		.03		.03		.03		.03	
Value[c]	.07	.05			-.57*	-.42								
Behavior[c]			.43*	.31	.89**	.64								
Fit[d]							-.70**	-.38						
Poor Fit[e]									-.65	-.24				
Deficiency[f]											-1.05**	-.40		
Excess[g]													-.65	-.18
Multiple R	.17		.34		.43		.38		.28		.40		.23	
R^2	.03		.12		.19		.14		.08		.16		.05	
F	.33		1.46		2.13		1.89		.98		2.12		.63	
df	5, 56		5, 56		6, 55		5, 56		5, 56		5, 56		5, 56	
R^2 Change[h]	.00		.09*		.16**		.11**		.05		.13**		.02	

[a] Range on marital satisfaction scale: 1 = "Very Dissatisfied" to 6 = "Very Satisfied."
[b] Five control variables were entered in the first step of analysis: Years Married, Race, Gender, Children, and Social Desirability.
[c] Range is from one to seven. Value: 1 = Not Important, 7 = Extremely Important; Behavior: 1 = Very Little Extent, 7 = Very Great Extent.
[d] Fit = (V - B).
[e] Poor Fit = |V - B|.
[f] Deficiency = Value (V) Score - Behavior Score for (V - B) $\geq$ 0 and Deficiency = 0 for (V - B) < 0.
[g] Excess = Value (V) Score - Behavior Score for (V - B) $\leq$ 0 and Excess = 0 for (V - B) > 0.
[h] Percent of total variance explained by the Step 2 entry or entries beyond that explained by the Step 1 entries.
Note. The unstandardized and standardized regression coefficients shown are from the fully specified model in Step 2.
* $p < .05$.
** $p < .01$.

Table 5.13

Hierarchical Multiple Regression Predicting Marital Satisfaction[a]: Active-Religious Orientation Subdimension

Model Variable	Values B	Values Beta	Behavior B	Behavior Beta	Value/Behavior Components B	Value/Behavior Components Beta	Fit B	Fit Beta	Poor Fit B	Poor Fit Beta	Deficiency B	Deficiency Beta	Excess B	Excess Beta
R^2: Step 1[b]	.03		.03		.03		.03		.03		.03		.03	
Value[c]	-.14	-.18			-.22	-.29								
Behavior[c]			-.03	-.04	.13	.16								
Fit[d]							-.18	-.18						
Poor Fit[e]									-.04	-.03				
Deficiency[f]											-.21	-.14		
Excess[g]													-.28	-.15
Multiple R	.24		.17		.26		.24		.16		.21		.22	
R^2	.06		.03		.07		.06		.03		.05		.05	
F	.67		.32		.68		.67		.31		.54		.56	
df	5, 56		5, 56		6, 55		5, 56		5, 56		5, 56		5, 56	
R^2 Change[h]	.03		.00		.04		.03		.00		.02		.02	

[a] Range on marital satisfaction scale: 1 = "Very Dissatisfied" to 6 = "Very Satisfied."

[b] Five control variables were entered in the first step of analysis: Years Married, Race, Gender, Children, and Social Desirability. Range is from one to seven. Value: 1 = Not Important, 7 = Extremely Important; Behavior: 1 = Very Little Extent, 7 = Very Great Extent.

[c] Range is from one to seven. Value: 1 = Not Important, 7 = Extremely Important; Behavior: 1 = Very Little Extent, 7 = Very Great Extent.

[d] Fit = (V - B).

[e] Poor Fit = |V - B|.

[f] Deficiency = Value (V) Score - Behavior Score for (V - B) ≥ 0 and Deficiency = 0 for (V - B) < 0.

[g] Excess = Value (V) Score - Behavior Score for (V - B) ≤ 0 and Excess = 0 for (V - B) > 0.

[h] Percent of total variance explained by the Step 2 entry or entries beyond that explained by the Step 1 entries.

Note. The unstandardized and standardized regression coefficients shown are from the fully specified model in Step 2.

* p < .05.

** p < .01.

Table 5.14
Hierarchical Multiple Regression Predicting Marital Satisfaction[a]: Extended Family Subdimension

Model Variable	Values B	Values Beta	Behavior B	Behavior Beta	Value/Behavior Components B	Value/Behavior Components Beta	Fit B	Fit Beta	Poor Fit B	Poor Fit Beta	Deficiency B	Deficiency Beta	Excess B	Excess Beta
R^2: Step 1[b]	.03		.03		.03		.03		.03		.03		.03	
Value[c]	.09	.09			.09	.09								
Behavior[c]			.05	.06	-.00	-.00								
Fit[d]							.01	.01						
Poor Fit[e]									-.43	-.24				
Deficiency[f]											-.18	-.10		
Excess[g]													.32	.14
Multiple R	.18		.17		.18		.16		.28		.19		.21	
R^2	.03		.03		.03		.03		.08		.04		.05	
F	.39		.44		.32		.30		.93		.42		.54	
df	5, 56		5, 56		6, 55		5, 56		5, 56		5, 56		5, 56	
R^2 Change[h]	.00		.00		.00		.00		.05		.01		.02	

[a] Range on marital satisfaction scale: 1 = "Very Dissatisfied" to 6 = "Very Satisfied."
[b] Five control variables were entered in the first step of analysis: Years Married, Race, Gender, Children, and Social Desirability.
[c] Range is from one to seven. Value: 1 = Not Important, 7 = Extremely Important; Behavior: 1 = Very Little Extent, 7 = Very Great Extent.
[d] Fit = (V - B).
[e] Poor Fit = IV - Bl.
[f] Deficiency = Value (V) Score - Behavior Score for (V - B) ≥ 0 and Deficiency = 0 for (V - B) < 0.
[g] Excess = Value (V) Score - Behavior Score for (V - B) ≤ 0 and Excess = 0 for (V - B) > 0.
[h] Percent of total variance explained by the Step 2 entry or entries beyond that explained by the Step 1 entries.
Note. The unstandardized and standardized regression coefficients shown are from the fully specified model in Step 2.
* $p < .05$.
** $p < .01$.

$p < .01$); and Deficiency (R^2 change $= .13$, $F_{1, 61} = 9.40$, $p < .01$). As found on the Marital Integration subdimension, although the Value term was not significant in the model when it was included alone in the second step of the regression ($b = .07$, $p > .05$), it did emerge as a significant predictor of marital satisfaction when included in the model together with the Behavior term ($b = -.57$, $p < .05$). Also paralleling previous findings, even the Behavior term became a stronger predictor of marital satisfaction when it was included in the same model with the Value term ($b = .89$, $p < .01$). Again, this finding suggests some level of interaction between the two terms that, based on the correlational analysis, is seemingly captured by the congruency terms.

CONCLUSION

These findings suggest that value-behavior congruency measures (second-order effects) offer no significant empirical advantage over simpler value and behavior component measures (first-order effects) in accounting for variation in levels of marital satisfaction. Based on discussions by Harrison (1978) of unexpected findings from examinations of person-environment fit and job stress, at least two interpretations of these findings are possible.

One interpretation is to accept the findings as they are reported: the Value-Behavior Congruency Model of Marital Satisfaction has little to offer beyond a theory of main effects of value and behavior components. The second interpretation advances a methodological argument. As Harrison (1978) points out in discussing measures of person and environment and as supported by correlational analyses in the present chapter, the component value and behavior measures are "contaminated" by each other. Each reflects to some degree an underlying value-behavior congruency assessment such that respondents take into account the level of value-behavior congruency as they respond to value- and behavior-oriented survey items. Consequently, according to logic presented by Harrison, the variance accounted for in marital satisfaction by the main effects will be "inflated"; the variance accounted for by the congruency measures will be "underestimated" to the extent that their component measures are contaminated.

Additional research should be conducted to compare the predictive validity of these first- and second-order effects. As we concluded in Chapter 4, more sophisticated measurement instruments of value-behavior congruency are needed. In addition, the present congruency assessment represents constructed "snapshots" at a single point in time. More dynamic and process-oriented measures of value-behavior congruency are needed to capture the reciprocal interaction of value and behavior components over time (Pervin, 1987; Spokane, 1987). Harrison (1978) suggests the potential utility of more "idiographic" approaches, where the individual defines those dimensions of person-environment fit that are most relevant for purposes of assessment.

In the present analysis, various relationships between value and behavior congruency and marital satisfaction were explored. Although the Value-Behavior Congruency Model assumes an asymptotic relationship where marital satisfaction is highest at points of perfect congruency and where behavior exceeds values, this assumption requires additional evaluation. For example, Harrison (1978) reviews research that suggests that some deficiency between values and behavior may have positive implications. Consistent with a growth perspective, it may also be possible that individuals continue to strive to enhance those aspects of their marital relationship that they value, never being completely satisfied with their outcomes (cf. Hobfoll, 1988, cited in Shirom, 1989).

As we concluded in Chapter 4, the Value-Behavior Congruency Model of Marital Satisfaction must be tested with larger and more diversified samples. However, additional evaluations of the model must be preceded by the development of assessment tools that match its complexity and that yield unbiased estimates of its components.

Marital Enrichment in the
Workplace: Rationale

In recent years there has been a significant increase in the level of employer support for the family lives of employees. Employees today are much more likely than a decade ago to work for an employer that has developed initiatives to help employees better balance work and family responsibilities and demands (Bureau of National Affairs, Inc. (BNA), 1986; Galinsky, 1986, Galinsky & Stein, 1990; Kamerman & Kahn, 1987; Kamerman & Kingston, 1982; McNeely & Fogarty, 1988). Such initiatives include flexible alternatives in the scheduling and hours of work, extended maternity leave provisions and benefits, paid personal days for child and family responsibilities, information and referral services, expanded relocation assistance, marriage and family counseling services, and even on-site child care. Although relatively few employers have offered marital and family enrichment programs, like MAP, for both employees and their spouses in the workplace, work and family seminars for employees are becoming increasingly common (Catalyst, 1984; Voydanoff, 1980a).

Despite these trends in corporate America, employers have been slow to respond to the "changing dynamic between work and family" (BNA, 1986, p. 4). In addition, despite the fact that nearly half the workers in the United States are employed by organizations with less than 100 employees, the development of comprehensive family-oriented initiatives has been mostly limited to large corporations with more than 1,000 employees (Galinsky, 1986). Many employers, both large and small, remain skeptical of the benefit/cost ratio for expanded supports (BNA, 1986; Bohen, 1984; Bowen, 1988c; Orthner & Pittman, 1986; Stillman & Bowen, 1985). Others lack sensitivity to the work and family dilemmas of employees or are concerned about overstepping their boundaries and becoming too involved in the marital and family lives of their employees (D. E. Friedman, 1987, Stillman & Bowen, 1985). The incorporation of programs like MAP in the workplace depends on helping corporate decision-makers to frame the growing tension between work and family and to justify their potential value to the corporate "bottom line" (Bohen, 1984; Bowen, 1988c).

This chapter reviews the rationale for the expansion of marital support programs like MAP to employees and their families. Including a discussion of the context for expanded family supports in the workplace, it is based on a briefing that was developed for senior managers in the corporation in which MAP was first developed and pilot tested. The aim of this briefing was to help management develop a better appreciation of the changing nature of work and family dynamics in the workplace and the need for a coherent set of policies, practices, and programs—including marital enrichment opportunities—for enhancing the ability of employees to respond to organizational and family demands. Although it is intended as a broad overview, this chapter should be particularly helpful to human resource managers who are faced with such a task and who must defend their initiatives for employees on more than humanitarian grounds.

THE CONTEXT

The morale, productivity, and retention of employees are key aspects of organizational effectiveness. As a consequence, understanding individual and work group variations in these outcomes has been an important focus of attention by organizational researchers.

Historically, this research has drawn upon two rich traditions in social and behavioral science research: the "human factors" approach and the "situational" approach. From a human factors approach, the key to understanding variations in the attitudes and behavior of employees lies in the study of their values, expectations, motives, traits, feelings, and aptitudes—more or less stable and enduring features of individuals (Chatman, 1989). From a situational perspective, variations in the attitudes and behaviors of employees are best understood through the study of the social context in which individuals live and work—typically viewed as more dynamic and changing than individual-level features (Chatman, 1989).

Although organizational researchers have traditionally recognized the importance and interaction of human factors and situational influences on variations in individual attitudes and behavior (cf. Moos, 1986a; Shouksmith, 1987), at least historically, the study of situational components has been largely limited to physical and social environmental features of the work setting (Blegen, Mueller, & Price, 1988). However, in recent years the modeling of situational influences has evolved beyond the confines of the work setting to the broader ecosystem of the employee (French & Bell, 1984; Moos, 1986a; Rice, McFarlin, Hunt, & Near, 1985). This expanded focus not only parallels developments in ecological and systems theory in the social and behavioral sciences (Bronfenbrenner, 1979; Buckley, 1967; Miller, 1978; Schwartzman, 1985) and their application to the study of organizational effectiveness (Bedeian, 1987; Katz & Kahn, 1978), but it also accompanies increasing attention to the study of organization-environment relations in industrial and organizational psychology (cf. Bedeian, 1987; Kahn, 1981; Moos, 1986a).

Within this broader ecosystem, the nature of the interface between work and family life has become an important area of investigation in social and behavioral science. This interest has been stimulated by both demographic and social changes in American society, by established linkages between marital status and physical and psychological well-being, and by growing recognition by both academicians and members of the business community of the linkages between organizational effectiveness and attention to the family responsibilities and satisfactions of employees (Bowen, 1988c).

DEMOGRAPHIC AND SOCIAL TRENDS

Paralleling the rise of industry in the United States, the boundaries between work and family life became more demarcated. No competition between work and family life was assumed: roles were clearly separated between the sexes, with men assuming the economic role and women being responsible for home and family management. As long as roles between the sexes remained fixed and normatively constrained, little negotiation of work and family responsibilities was required. Consequently, although it often relied on the family to provide instrumental and expressive support to the worker, the corporate world assumed little responsibility for the internal relationship between spouses in marriage beyond its wage and benefit structure.

However, recent demographic and social trends have shattered traditional marital and family life patterns and have challenged corporations to become more responsive to the work-family interface. Among the most significant of these forces has been the substantial influx of married women into the labor force, especially married mothers with preschool children (Hayghe, 1986), less traditional gender-role patterns among men and women in marriage (Bowen, 1987; McBroom, 1984; Scanzoni & Fox, 1980; Thornton, 1989), and contemporary lifestyles that place greater emphasis on personal fulfillment (Bellah, Madsen, Sullivan, Swidler, & Tipton, 1985; Shouksmith, 1987; Yankelovich, 1981) and balancing work and family priorities (Orthner, Bowen, & Beare, 1990; Yankelovich, 1979).

No longer can it be assumed that a spouse is available to provide instrumental and expressive support to the employee. Although estimates are often subject to distortion and exaggeration (Blankenhorn, 1989), the traditional family of an employed husband and a homemaker wife with dependent children has declined substantially as a proportion of family households in recent years (Merrick & Tordella, 1988, cited by Bielby & Bielby, 1989). Based on March 1987 statistics from the Bureau of Labor Statistics, this "Ozzie and Harriet" family type comprised only two-fifths (41.3 percent) of all married households with preschoolers (Blankenhorn, 1989). Like their husbands, the majority of wives today are employed outside the home (Teachman, Polonko, & Scanzoni, 1987), including those with preschool children (Glick, 1989); there has also been a significant increase in the number of women in more prestigious and higher-paying positions that have been traditionally occupied by men (Glick, 1989; Powell, 1988; Reubens & Reubens, 1979). In an increasing number of households, spouses are renegotiating their marital relationship to accommodate their new employment patterns.

In addition, it can no longer be assumed that the work role is primary for men; an increasing number of men want to become husbands and fathers of presence, both physically and psychologically (Bowen & Orthner, 1991; Lamb, 1987; LaRossa, 1988). Although women in married households, whether employed or not employed, continue to perform a disproportionate share of household and child care tasks and to hold more egalitarian gender-role preferences about work and family roles than men (Atkinson, 1987; Berk & Berk, 1979; Bowen, 1987; Coverman & Sheley, 1986; England & Farkas, 1986; Farkas, 1976; Hertz, 1986; Pleck, 1985; Thornton, 1989), the division of labor in families and the nature of the relationship between spouses in marriage is less normatively constrained today than it has been historically (Orthner, 1989; Pleck, 1985; Scanzoni, Polonko, Teachman, & Thompson, 1989; Thornton, 1989). In a recent commentary, David Popenoe (1989) discussed the changing character of the contemporary family:

Today's societal trends are bringing to an end the cultural dominance of what historians call the modern (I will use the term "traditional") nuclear family. By traditional family I mean: a family situated apart from both the larger kin group and the workplace, focused on the procreation of children, and consisting of a legal, lifelong, sexually exclusive, heterosexual, monogamous marriage, based on affection and companionship, in which there is a sharp division of labor (separate spheres) with the female as full-time housewife and the male as primary provider and ultimate authority. Lasting for only a little more than a century, this family form emphasized the male as a "good provider," the female as "a good wife and mother" and the paramount importance of the family for childrearing. . . . The psychological character of the marital relationship has also changed dramatically. Traditionally, marriage has been understood as a social obligation—an institution designed mainly for economic security and childrearing. Today marriage is understood mainly as a path toward self-fulfillment. (pp. 1–2)

In the context of these societal trends and cultural shifts so eloquently described by David Popenoe, an increasing number of men and women in marriage are struggling to negotiate a relationship that reflects a more equitable balance of rewards and costs in work and family life. However, as concluded by Scanzoni et al. (1989), as compared to men, women face a particularly difficult set of structural constraints and relational barriers in their attempts to balance work and family roles:

It is important to keep in mind that for men, pursuing their occupational and economic achievements has been compatible with a traditional family. . . . Historically, they have not had to choose between individualistic achievement and relationship stability, though the opposite is true for women. (pp. 191–192)

Scanzoni et al. (1989) stress the importance of both a supportive husband and a supportive employer in helping women more successfully combine work and family roles. As the economic well-being of the family becomes increasingly co-determined by husbands and wives in marriage, it is likely that a greater number of couples may need help in developing patterns of interaction and mutual support that enable both spouses to realize their collective and individual ambitions for work and family life in marriage.

MARITAL STATUS AND PERSONAL WELL-BEING

Despite the high divorce rate in contemporary society (Glick, 1989), research suggests that both men and women highly value the institution of marriage (Campbell, Converse, & Rogers, 1976; Glick, 1989; Thornton, 1989), derive high levels of satisfaction and support from their relationships (Gove, Hughes, & Style, 1983), and experience marital termination as being extremely traumatic and difficult (Bloom, Asher, & Whyte, 1978; Gove, Style, & Hughes, 1990). In addition, as compared with their single counterparts—including those that live with other adults, especially the divorced and separated—married men and women experience higher levels of physical and psychological well-being, including lower mortality rates, better physical health, lower rates of institutionalization (e.g., in hospitals, or correctional facilities), lower rates of mental illness, less depression and anxiety, and higher levels of reported happiness and life satisfaction (see Gove, Style, & Hughes, 1990 for a review of the literature on this subject).

Taken together, these findings suggest that despite its greater fragility, marriage remains a viable institution in contemporary society, enhancing both personal performance and social stability through its positive and protective effects. Based on their study of the relationship between marital status, life strains, and depression, Pearlin & Johnson (1977) drew a similar conclusion:

What we have learned suggests that marriage can function as a protective barrier against the distressful consequences of external threats. Marriage does not prevent economic and social problems from invading life, but it apparently can help people fend off the psychological assaults that such problems otherwise create. Even in an era when marriage is often a fragile arrangement between couples, its capacity to protect people from the full impact of external strains makes it a surprisingly stable institution, at least in the absence of alternative relations providing similar functions. (p. 714)

Recent research by Gove, Hughes, and Style (1983) provides an important qualification to the established link between marital status and well-being. Their research suggests that the relationship between marital status and well-being is conditional, mediated by the quality of the relationship between marital partners. Supported by research by Renne (1971) in the early 1970s, which they cite, Gove et al. report that although most married individuals are "very happy" with their marital relationships and experience high levels of well-being as a consequence, spouses in "unhappy" marriages experience extremely low levels of well-being, even lower than divorced individuals.

Summarizing the results from their earlier reviews and research, Gove, Style, and Hughes (1990) conclude that "it appears that at any particular point in time most marriages are 'good marriages' and that such marriages have a strong positive effect on well-being and that 'bad marriages' have a strong negative effect on well-being" (p. 14). According to additional research cited by Gove, Style, and Hughes (1990), so-called good marriages have styles of interaction that evidence features such as high levels of intimacy and affection, communication and sharing, and mutual supportiveness. These features are consistent with descriptions of marriage as a therapeutic resource for its participants and as a "mediator" between the individual and society and its social institutions (Bellah et al., 1985; Blood & Wolfe, 1960; Pearlin & Johnson, 1977; Pollak, 1967; Vincent, 1966).

Given the attractiveness of marriage and its benefits to both its participants and society, it is somewhat surprising that investigators have only recently begun to explore its implications on work. This is especially true given the growing number of studies that document the prevalence of physical and psychological dysfunction in the workplace and the link between emotional well-being and both organizational effectiveness and health care costs (Byers, 1987; Donatelle & Hawkins, 1989). It is likely that the nature of the marriage relationship has a strong indirect link to work outcomes by influencing the physical and psychological well-being of its participants (Burke & Weir, 1982; Byers, 1987; House, 1981; Kahn, Hein, House, Kasl, & McLean, 1982; Kessler & Essex, 1982; Lavee, McCubbin, & Patterson, 1985; Mobley, Griffeth, Hand, & Meglino, 1979; Revicki & May, 1985; Savery, 1988; Sekaran, 1983; Shinn, Wong, Simko, & Ortiz-Torres, 1989; Shirom, 1989; Statuto, Ooms, Brand, & Pittman, 1984). In *Work Stress and Social Support*, House (1981) captures the dynamic between work and nonwork and the importance of such supportive relationships to overall well-being and stress:

the boundary between work and nonwork is highly flexible and permeable. Nonwork stress and support can affect workers' functioning and health on the job while work-related stress and support can affect people's functioning and health outside of work. People often carry their problems from home with them to work, while their occupational stresses often go home with them in one form or another. Similarly, support from family, friends, and relatives can and sometimes does help people to adapt to occupational stress, and their social supports at work may similarly help them deal with stress outside of work. (p. 57)

Despite the benefits of positive affective relationships between husbands and wives to individual outcomes, commentaries on marriage in contemporary society show an increasing concern about the institution (see Glenn, 1987a, 1987b; Glenn & Weaver, 1988; Popenoe, 1989). These commentaries suggest that the "internal fabric" of marital relationships is weakening, paralleling trends in individualism and priorities toward self-fulfillment (Bellah et al., 1985; Glenn, 1987a; Pankhurst & Houseknecht, 1983). In one such commentary, David Popenoe (1989) drew the following conclusions about the "transformed" family of today:

> marriage is becoming deinstitutionalized. No longer comprising a set of norms and obligations that are widely enforced, marriage today is a voluntary relationship which individuals can make and break at will. . . .
> Fundamentally, what emerges from these cultural shifts is an ethos of radical individualism in which personal autonomy, individual rights, and social equality have gained supremacy as cultural ideals. In keeping with these ideals, the main goals of personal behavior have shifted—from obligation and commitment to social units (families, communities, religions, nations) to personal choices, lifestyle options, self-fulfillment, and personal pleasure. (pp. 2–3)

Glenn (1987a) contends that, rather than increasing individual happiness and satisfaction, the pursuit of individual goals at the expense of group welfare is likely to be counterproductive, eroding the bonds of trust and commitment under which marital partners are willing to invest themselves in the relationship and to develop patterns of mutual support and reciprocal obligation. These developments are also likely to have negative consequences for social institutions external to the family, such as work, that depend upon the family as an emotional refuge and social support system for the individual (Pollak, 1967).

Rather than lamenting these trends or becoming "nostalgic" about family patterns of the past, Schwartz (1987) suggests dealing with the reality of modern relationships. This reality suggests that the norms governing marriage have become less scripted and are more open to redefinition and negotiation by spouses in marriage, who are likely to be more "equity sensitive" than in the past in their dealings with one another (Orthner, 1989). It also suggests that an increasing number of couples may need assistance in understanding the complexity of contemporary relationships and may require help in negotiating a marital arrangement that balances individual priorities and interests with collective needs and expectations.

WORK AND FAMILY LINKAGES

Individuals occupy a number of social positions in life, such as workers, spouses, and parents. These social positions are associated with a variety of roles (i.e., expectations for behavior) that create demands on the time, energy, and resources of individuals (Burr, Leigh, Day & Constantine, 1979). Of these roles, those associated with work and family life are among the most salient for men and women in American society (Burke & Greenglass, 1987). For example, the work career involves a number of potential role and lifestyle demands that vary in their intensity and duration over the life course. These may include long work hours, high stress assignments, frequent travel and family separations, relocations, and job advancement.

At the same time, families make a number of demands on spouses and parents over time. Not only do basic household and child care tasks have to be accomplished by spouses and parents, but also family members need time for companionship and intimacy. Coser's (1974) notion of the "greedy institution" captures the essence of the great demands that institutions like work and family may impose on the time, energy, and commitments of many men and women in marriage:

Their demands on the person are omnivorous. . . . Greedy institutions are characterized by the fact that they exercise pressures on component individuals to weaken their ties, or not to form any ties, with other institutions or persons that might make claims that conflict with their own demands. (Coser, 1974, cited by Segal, 1989, p. 8)

The demands from work and family roles often vary in type, number, intensity, and interrelationship over the family and career life cycle (Rapoport & Rapoport, 1965; Voydanoff, 1980c, 1987). There are certain "pressure" or "squeeze" points at certain intersections of the work and family career cycles that may have consequences for both work and family role performance (Greenhaus & Beutell, 1985; Oppenheimer, 1974, 1982; Voydanoff, 1987). For example, many couples start their families at the same time one or both spouses are facing high demands and time requirements from a beginning career. Often these families—especially if the spouses are young in age—face these demands with inadequate financial resources and social support. As a consequence, they must shoulder the total burden of work and family demands themselves, unable to purchase services or mobilize social support systems that would ease the demands on their time and energy.

A second critical life cycle pressure point seems to occur when couples' children are in the adolescent stage of development. The middle career phase for many men and women combined with the presence of adolescents in the home poses special challenges for parents who are attempting to coordinate high work demands and special job requirements with the normal issues that accompany the adolescent stage of development. For example, job relocations may become much more emotional issues for families with adolescents than for families with younger children. In addition, adolescents are likely to draw heavily on the emotional resources of the family at a time that may make or break the promotion opportunities of the mother or father. Families at such critical juncture points in the work and family life cycles may need special supports and assistance that are tailored to their individual needs and issues.

The "Conflict" and "Spillover" Perspectives

A number of different models have been proposed to capture the complex relationship between events and demands in the work and family arenas (Burke & Bradshaw, 1981; Burke & Greenglass, 1987; Mortimer & London, 1984; Wilensky, 1960). Although it is unlikely that any single model is sufficient to capture the nature of this relationship under all circumstances (Evans & Bartolome, 1986; Kabanoff, 1980; Lambert, 1990), research exploring the interplay between work and family life in recent years has most often hypothesized either a "conflict" or a "spillover" effect.

The Conflict Perspective

From the conflict perspective, role demands from work and family life are seen as being in "opposition" or "incompatible" in some respect (Burke & Greenglass, 1987; Greenhaus & Beutell, 1985; Piotrkowski, 1979; Voydanoff, 1980b), ranging on a continuum from a low to a high degree of interference (Pleck, 1977). In discussing interrole conflict as applied to work and family roles, Greenhaus and Beutell (1985, p. 301) cite a passage from Kahn, Wolfe, Quinn, Snoek, and Rosenthal (1964):

In such cases of interrole conflict, the role pressures associated with membership in one organization are in conflict with pressures stemming from membership in other groups. Demands from role senders on the job for overtime or take-home work may conflict with pressures from one's wife to give attention to family affairs during the evening hours. The conflict arises between the role of the focal person as worker and his role as husband and father. (Kahn et al., p. 20)

This specific description of interrole conflict is consistent with the definition of work-family conflict that is subsequently offered by Greenhaus and Beutell (1985):

a form of interrole conflict in which the role pressures from the work and family domains are mutually incompatible in some respect. That is, participation in the work role is made more difficult by virtue of participation in the family role, and vice versa. (p. 301)

Drawn from role theory (Biddle, 1986; Goode, 1960), discussion and research from this perspective (cf. Burr, Leigh, Day, & Constantine, 1979; Voydanoff 1980c) have often included situations of both role interference and role overload (i.e., excessive role demands from one or more roles that exceed the ability of the individual to manage) as causal links between role accumulation and role strain. Goode (1960, p. 483) defines role strain as "the felt difficulty in fulfilling role obligations."

As contrasted to an expansion approach to human energy (Marks, 1977; Sieber, 1974), it is assumed from the conflict perspective that individuals have a finite amount of time and energy available to meet role demands (Coser & Coser, 1974; Goode, 1960; Merton, 1957). As a consequence, when the demands from work and family roles become too taxing on the time, energy, and resources of the individual or in situations where role demands are contradictory, the person may not be able to successfully meet expectations for role enactment in either or both spheres (Voydanoff, 1980b, 1987).

Such failure or "felt difficulty" in meeting role demands may lead to lower levels of role performance and success in both work and family arenas (Burden & Googins, 1987; Rudd & McKenry, 1986). It may also have negative emotional consequences for the individual, including psychological distress, life dissatisfaction, marital and family tension and dissatisfaction, and job strain and dissatisfaction (Aneshensel, 1986; Burden & Googins, 1987; Burr, 1973; Devilbiss & Perrucci, 1982; Fowlkes, 1987; Voydanoff, 1987; Voydanoff & Donnelly, 1989).

On the other hand, individuals may negotiate their roles in a way that reduces discrepancy between demands and enactment (Thoits, 1987), thereby enhancing role performance and promoting more positive emotional consequences for the individual. The success of such negotiation often depends upon the level of fit between the nature and extent of the role demands and the internal and external resources that are available to the individual to meet these demands, including the level of teamwork and mutual support given by spouses in marriage (Bowen, 1990).

In investigating the level and consequences of role demands for spouses in marriage, Hall and Hall (1980) stress the importance of focusing not only on the role demands of individual spouses in marriage, but also on the particular pattern of role demands between spouses. Although they restrict their attention to the pattern of work and home roles of dual career couples, they have developed a typology of family role structure based on the respective role involvements of the husband and wife. Four general role patterns were identified: (1) accommodators, (2) adversaries, (3) allies, and (4) acrobats. Handy (1978) presents a similar typology based on the respective attitudes of husbands and wives toward achievement/dominance and affiliation/nurturance. Such typologies are useful in broadening the focus of attention from the individual to couple qua unit.

The Spillover Perspective

The negative and positive emotional outcomes that result from work and family role performance are most often conceptualized from a spillover perspective (Gutek, Repetti, & Silver, 1988). From this perspective, the level of satisfaction and strain that is experienced in the work or family setting can either facilitate or undermine a person's ability to discharge responsibilities in the other setting (Bergermaier, Borg, & Champoux, 1984; Kanter, 1977b).

Although spillover is not limited to just the emotional aspects of work and family life (Marshall, 1988), this aspect is the most relevant in the present review.

Research to date supports both the conflict and the spillover models of work and family linkages (Belsky, Perry-Jenkins, & Crouter, 1985; Draughn, 1989; Greenhaus & Beutell, 1985; Near, Rice, & Hunt, 1980; Renshaw, 1976; Small & Riley, 1990; Voydanoff & Kelly, 1984). Based on their comprehensive review of the literature, Burke and Greenglass (1987) succinctly describe the nature of the reciprocal and dynamic relationship between work and family that is assumed by both models: "There is an integral relationship between one's work and family such that experiences in one cannot help but influence the other" (p. 275).

However, although it is increasingly evident that employees neither necessarily leave their job concerns at work nor their family concerns at home, research to date has focused more on how work intrudes into family life than vice versa (Burke & Greenglass, 1987; Crouter, 1984; Lambert, 1990). For example, research has emphasized the effects on marriage and family life from work-related events and phenomena including time and schedules (Kingston & Nock, 1987; Pleck, 1977; Pleck & Staines, 1985; Presser, 1988; White & Keith, 1990), family separations and travel (Culbert & Renshaw, 1972), relocation (Anderson & Stark, 1988; Bowen, 1989d; Brett & Werbel, 1980), job demands and gratifications (Piotrkowski, 1979); job tensions and strains (Bartolome & Evans, 1979; Evans & Bartolome, 1980, 1984, 1986; Jackson & Maslach, 1982; Piotrkowski & Crits-Christoph, 1981), job competence (Draughn, 1989), occupational commitment (Ladewig & McGee, 1986), wives' employment (Booth, Johnson, White, & Edwards, 1984; Hofferth & Moore, 1979; Rallings & Nye, 1979; Simpson & England, 1981; Smith, 1985), social climate at work (Repetti, 1987), and occupational setting and resources (Aldous, 1969; Aldous, Osmond, & Hicks, 1979; Kohn, 1963, 1969; Miller & Swanson, 1958; Scanzoni, 1970, 1975). Studies have also examined the implications of family-oriented support services in the workplace on the well-being and satisfaction of employees and their families (e.g., Bowen & Neenan, 1989; Orthner & Pittman, 1986). In discussing the greater attention to the effects of work on family than vice versa, Crouter (1984, p. 426) quotes Kanter (1977b):

Most analyses of work and family life in the modern American context have settled into a comfortable economic determinism—the centrality of work in setting the conditions for family life. No equally compelling and tested framework exists for reversing the relationship and looking at the effects of family patterns on work systems. (Kanter, p. 53)

Because MAP is focused on the couple subsystem, and given that programs like MAP often depend on demonstrating how employer costs associated with such programs are balanced by benefits to the organization, this review focuses on what Crouter (1984, p. 425) refers to as "the neglected side of the work-family interface'': the influence of family variables on the work experience. Specifically, attention is given to the direct and indirect effects of husband and wife team-work, spouse support, and marital satisfaction on job satisfaction and organizational commitment, work-related outcomes that are themselves highly interrelated (cf. Lofquist & Davis, 1984; Orthner & Pittman, 1986) as well as correlated with various indicators of work performance and stability such as absenteeism and turnover (Blegen, Mueller, & Price, 1988; Mobley, Griffeth, Hand, & Meglino, 1979).

As compared with other more tangible types of social support (e.g., advice, information, service) that may be provided by formal organizations or informal groups, it is these ''emotional'' aspects of social support (e.g., caring, love, empathy, encouragement, confidence, acceptance, trust) that Litwak et al. (1989) contend primary groups like the family are perhaps best able to provide to the individual. As concluded by Burke and Weir (1982) in their discussion of the spouse as a viable source of social support for both men and women, ''there are very few dyadic relationships in our society that provide individuals with the degree of proximity, accessibility, commitment, interdependence, and opportunity for intimacy that marriage does'' (p. 221).

The Influence of Marital Teamwork and Support on Work

Study of the influence of family characteristics and dynamics on work life was given considerable impetus by Rosabeth Moss Kanter's (1977b) pioneering delineation of four distinct ways in which the family system may impact upon the world of work. First, she described the family system as a potentially powerful socialization and control agent by means of cultural traditions that may have considerable influence on the work decisions and behaviors of its members, especially in particular ethnic groups. Second, she discussed situations (such as in family-owned or -controlled businesses) in which the boundaries between work and family life overlap substantially and in which family relations define work involvement and opportunities. Kanter next discussed situations in which family members, typically the wife, are co-opted by the work organization through the work commitments of one of its members, most often the husband. Fourth, she noted the interrelationship between ''demands'' and ''emotional climates'' in the work and family spheres, such that the nature of the family environment can have as compelling influences on work life as the work environment has on family life. According to Kanter, ''Family situations can define work orientations, motivations, abilities, emotional energy, and the demands people bring to the workplace'' (p. 57).

Of the four broad ways in which Kanter described families as potentially influencing work systems, it is the effects of the family through its demands (structural aspects) and emotional climate (psychological and relational aspects) that may have received the most consideration since the date of her publication. Within the broad framework of the family's demands and emotional climate, the direct and indirect influence of husband and wife teamwork, marital satisfaction, and spouse support—primarily aspects of emotional and social support (House, 1981)—on the work outcomes of spouses in marriage has been an important, yet somewhat limited, focus of attention. The research that is available provides important empirical support for the potential benefit to employers of incorporating programs like MAP in the workplace.

Closely tied to the central tenets of MAP and underscoring the link between the qualitative aspects of marriage and outcomes at work is the research by Ronald Burke and Tamara Weir. In a series of studies (1977a, 1977b, 1982), these researchers have examined the nature of the "husband-wife helping relationship and its relationship to the personal, family-related, and work-related outcomes of spouses. Citing (1) literature that discusses the important role of social support in times of stress and difficulty and (2) research that shows the spouse of married men and women to be the most important source of such support, Burke and Weir propose three potential effects of the helping relationship between spouses. The first is a "preventive" effect, where the nature of the husband and wife relationship is hypothesized to attenuate the job and life stresses experienced by spouses. The second is a "therapeutic" effect. From this perspective, the helping relationship between spouses is depicted as directly impacting upon the personal, marital, and work-related outcomes of spouses. Third, a "buffering" effect is proposed, wherein the nature of the husband and wife helping relationship is hypothesized to mediate the impact of stress on the personal, marital, and work-related outcomes of spouses.

Measuring the nature of the husband-wife helping relationship by several different measures across studies, including nine Likert-type questionnaire items that assessed both instrumental and expressive support (Burke & Weir, 1977a, 1977b), Burke and Weir have found support for each proposed effect. Specific to the focus of the present review, the series of studies by Burke and Weir provides strong support for the direct and indirect contribution of a supportive helping relationship in marriage to the level of job satisfaction reported by married men and women. Specifically, their research shows that the quality of the husband and wife relationship not only directly and positively impacts on the level of reported job satisfaction, but also reduces job stress and buffers the negative impacts of job and life stress on job satisfaction. Based on their research, Burke and Weir (1982) draw the following conclusion:

The marital helping interaction by giving explicit recognition to the personal distress of one or other spouse sets the process in motion of dealing with stressful events as they arise and interrupts the building up of tensions. It can provide for the comfort, support, and validation of the distressed spouse through selected environmental manipulations and/or through personal attention and understanding. It can offer the individual short-term relief by giving him an opportunity to ventilate his feelings in an atmosphere of concern and caring. It can hold out the promise of long-term relief by providing the occasion for him to clarify his perceptions of the problem areas and to consider appropriate behavioral strategies for resolving these. Thus, the marital helping process by minimizing and resolving the stressful experiences of husbands and wives can increase the likelihood that their perceptions of their life's experiences will be more positive and reduce the potential that accumulated tensions will be translated into pathology. (pp. 236–237)

An interesting finding in the research by Burke and Weir was the central role of the wife in defining the nature of the husband-wife helping relationship. Compared to husbands, wives both gave and received a greater degree of help; they relied more on their husbands as a primary source of social support than husbands relied on their wives. However, Burke and Weir present evidence suggesting that the nature of the helping process in marriage for both husbands and wives declines across the family life cycle. This finding suggests that older couples may be in special need of relational invigoration and support.

Despite variations by gender and stage of the family life cycle, the research by Burke and Weir underscores a consistent finding in the literature: the critical role that spouses play as support systems for married men and women (Burke & Weir, 1975; Burden & Googins, 1987; Caplan, Cobb, French, Harrison, & Pinneau, 1975; House & Wells, 1978; Savery, 1988; Shinn, Wong, Simko, & Ortiz-Torres, 1989). For example, in a recent study by Shinn et al. (1989) of 208 married fathers and 287 married mothers from eight firms and state agencies in New York City, respondents were asked about the level of social support that they received from various sources based on their "experiences as a working parent over the last two months" (p. 37): the supervisor, friends/neighbors/relatives, co-workers, and spouse. Multiple items were used to assess the level of social support from each source. Of the four sources of social support, both male and female respondents reported most often receiving support from their spouse.

Given the role of spouses as important resources for one another, it is not surprising that the presence of a supportive spouse has been correlated with a number of work-related outcomes, especially higher job satisfaction (Andrisani & Shapiro, 1978; House & Wells, 1978; Rudd & McKenry, 1986; Savery, 1988; Sekaran, 1983) and greater levels of organizational commitment (Arnott, 1972; Bowen, 1986, 1988d; Orthner & Pittman, 1986). In her study of dual career couples, Sekaran (1983) referred to the level of support that spouses provided to one another in pursuing their work and family roles as an "enabling process." This enabling process has been found by Sekaran (1983) and others to be highly related to the level of job satisfaction experienced by men and women. For example, research by Rudd and McKenry (1986) based on a sample of 237 rural and urban mothers in Ohio who were employed outside the home found that the more "helpful" and "supportive" husbands were evaluated by wives to be concerning their employment, the greater their job satisfaction. In a stepwise multiple regression, the level of husband support was a significant predictor beyond the entry of a set of demographic control variables and additional family-oriented variables that concerned other aspects of family support and the degree of work and family conflict.

The presence of a supportive spouse has also been correlated with higher levels of organizational commitment by men and women. For example, in the corporation in which MAP was first developed and field-tested, the results of a survey with a sample of employees and spouses from the target work group suggested a direct and positive relationship between level of support by spouses for the employee to continue with the organization and level of organizational commitment reported by the employee (Bowen, 1988d).

Closely related to the concept of organizational commitment are the concepts of employee retention and turnover. Given past issues in the retention of personnel in the military services that paralleled the advent of the all-volunteer force in 1973 and the transition from a single to a predominantly married force since World War II, the link between spouse support and employee retention and turnover has been a special focus of attention in the U.S. military (see Bowen, 1989c for a review of this literature). Of the many factors associated with the retention intentions and behavior of military personnel, the level of spouse support for the career ambitions of both military men and women has been consistently identified in the research literature as a strong and direct predictor of these outcomes (Bowen, 1989c). Given the many similarities between the military services and other large bureaucratic employers, including other forms of government service (Orthner, Bowen, & Beare, 1990), it is likely that these findings have high levels of generalizability to civilian employment settings. However, greater attention to the nature of this linkage in civilian organizations is needed.

The link between dimensions of marital and family life satisfaction/adjustment and work-related outcomes has been more equivocal than the nature of the linkages previously discussed. For example, although several studies report a significant correlation between job satisfaction and qualitative aspects of the husband and wife relationship such as marital adjustment (Barling & Rosenbaum, 1986) and family satisfaction (Kopelman, Greenhouse & Connolly, 1983, study 1), research by Neenan (1989) found no support for the relationship between five aspects of marital quality, including marital satisfaction, and job satisfaction among a random sample of 865 married men serving in the U.S. Air Force. Although it was limited to the military sector, Neenan's research is noteworthy in its incorporation of demographic, work-related, and marital-related variables in a multivariate analysis.

Although the relationship between job satisfaction and satisfaction and adjustment dimensions of marriage has received mixed support in the literature, research with military samples suggests an important link between these aspects of marriage and family life and job commitment. Perhaps the most noteworthy of this research is that conducted by Orthner and Pittman (1986) and Pittman and Orthner (1988) using large random samples of men and women serving in the U.S. Air Force. Drawing upon a sample of 751 married air force members with less than ten years of service, Orthner and Pittman (1986) used structural equations analysis to examine the relationship between family support and job commitment. The latent variable, family support, was defined by two characteristics related to the respondent's marital relationship: (1) marital satisfaction and (2) perceived level of spousal support for the member's military career. Job commitment, also a latent variable, was defined by three characteristics: (1) job morale, (2) intent to pursue air force career, and (3) perceived quality of job performance. As hypothesized, Orthner and Pittman found family support to be a strong and direct predictor of job commitment.

In a second study with a sample of 851 men and 186 women serving in the U.S. Air Force, Pittman and Orthner offer some gender-related qualifications to their earlier study. Defining job commitment with two of three indicators used in the earlier study (job morale and career intent), Pittman and Orthner used path analytic procedures to examine the relationship between marital satisfaction, one of several variables in the model, and job commitment. For men, the level of marital satisfaction was a positive indirect predictor of job commitment through its positive and direct influence on the level of fit between the work organization and the self/family. A multidimensional construct, the fit dimension was a composite measure of five personal, organizational, and familial variables, including the level of perceived spousal support for the member's career. On the other hand, for women, the level of marital satisfaction had a direct and negative effect on job commitment, but a positive indirect effect on job commitment through its positive and direct effect on the fit dimension. In interpreting these findings for the women members, Pittman and Orthner conclude: "While more satisfying marriages may be associated with lower job commitment, they also result in a more comfortable fit between organization and self/family, which, in turn, has an enhancing effect on job commitment" (1988, p. 241).

The research by Pittman and Orthner underscores the potential complexity in the impact of marital influences on the work lives of men and women. To date, research on work and family linkages has too often been restricted to simple bivariate analysis. Additional research is needed to examine the direct and indirect pathways of influence of family-oriented variables on outcomes in the workplace, especially longitudinal research that is designed to capture the complex and reciprocal interplay of work and family dynamics over time.

It is important not only to study a broader range of work-related outcomes such as direct indicators of work performance, but also to examine variations in the nature of the relationship between relational dynamics in the home and work-related outcomes by gender and across the work and family life cycle. For example, the work of Crouter (1984) suggests that the level of spillover between work and family life varies for women over the family life cycle.

In addition, most studies to date have examined the influence of marital dynamics on work outcomes using linear-based statistics. As suggested by Evans and Bartolome (1986), the nature of the relationship between work and family life follows no single pattern or path. Research is required that not only examines different models of work and family linkages, but also that tests both linear and nonlinear relationships in examining these linkages. Such refinements will improve the baseline of knowledge that employers have to defend and target an expanded network of family-oriented supports, like MAP, for employees and their families.

CONCLUSION

From an open systems perspective, organizational effectiveness depends upon innovation and adaptation to a changing environmental context (Bedeian, 1987). It is assumed from this perspective that organizations are involved in continuous interplay with their environments in an attempt to turn ''scarce resources'' into desired ''outputs'' (Bedeian, 1987). Of these scarce resources, the productive capacity of any organization is perhaps most dependent on its employees and their ability to devote themselves to the task at hand. When these employees face constraints and problems on the home front, it is doubtful that they are able to perform to their optimal capacity.

Based on reciprocal interaction between the work and family life of employees, MAP focuses on helping married couples forge a more supportive marital team for realizing both marital and occupational objectives. By focusing on the dynamics of the marital relationship of employees and by directly involving the spouse in the enrichment opportunity, programs like MAP are an important extension of work and family life seminars that are now offered by a number of corporations. Despite the considerable justification in the literature for expanding corporate initiatives to include such programs, marital enrichment in the workplace has far more potential than has been realized to date. As concluded by Evans and Bartolome (1986) in a recent discussion of the relationship between the personal and professional lives of managers, there appears to be at least a baseline of interest in offering such programs in the workplace:

Millions of dollars are invested in professional training and development. By contrast, no formal training concerns itself specifically with preparing people to be better husbands or parents or to manage creatively their leisure lives. People are supposed to learn those things by trial and error. Imagine society taking the same attitude with respect to the training of surgeons, engineers, or accountants!

What about managing the relationship between professional and private lives? In this respect the individual is left to exchange anecdotes with friends and struggle through, and if things get out of hand he may be advised to consult with a therapist. Yet in discussions with thousands of managers, the authors know of no other topic that arouses in them such depth of interest, concern, and feeling. (p. 314)

It is especially critical that spouses have the same opportunities for personal growth and development as employees. Too often, spouses in marriage have differential opportunities for growth in marriage, which may lead to marital incompatibility, conflict, and dissolution (Aldous, 1969; Voydanoff, 1980a).

By extending opportunities for relational growth to both employees and their spouses, employers are making an investment in the marriage that, according to the literature reviewed in this chapter, should produce handsome dividends to the corporate "bottom line" through increased physical and psychological well-being, job satisfaction, and commitment.

Postscript

There have been two parallel movements in recent years that have rich potential for increasing intersection as we move toward the next century. First, there has been a tremendous growth in marital enrichment activities, both in the number of programs and in the number of participants (Denton, 1986; L'Abate, 1990; Mace & Mace, 1986). In general, these programs have been shown to be effective in improving the relational skills of spouses and in producing positive marital outcomes (Giblin, Sprenkle, & Sheehan, 1985; Guerney & Maxson, 1990). Moreover, these programs have been shown to have positive implications not only for couples who wish to make an already "good" marriage better, but also for couples experiencing marital distress (Guerney & Maxson, 1990). In a recent decade review of marital and family enrichment research, Guerney and Maxson (1990) concluded: "On the whole, enrichment programs work and the field is an entirely legitimate one. No more research or interpretative energy needs to be devoted to that basic concern" (p. 1133).

Second, paralleling demographic and social trends, which include increases in the proportion of married women in the workforce and less gender-specific roles for men and women, there has been increased interest and activity in corporate America toward creating a more family-responsive workplace (Galinsky & Stein, 1990). Over the last decade, there has been both increased sensitivity by private employers to work and family linkages and substantial growth in family-oriented policies and services that are designed to help employees manage better work and family demands and responsibilities (Bowen, 1988c; Galinsky, Hughes, & David, 1990; Raabe & Gessner, 1988).

Still, despite recent corporate initiatives to promote the ability of employees to better balance work and family life, employers have been slow to expand the organizational boundary to recognize and encompass the spouses of employees as legitimate and contributing members of the corporate team. Consequently, although corporations are increasingly including the family variable as a component in the corporate success equation, spouses are seldom included in the informational loop of the company and are rarely provided opportunities to participate directly in corporate-sponsored educational and enrichment activities. Although considerable theoretical and empirical justification exist for corporations to sponsor marital enrichment opportunities for employees and their spouses, relatively few corporations have offered such programs.

One obstacle to increasing the intersection between these parallel movements has been the lack of enrichment programs that are specifically tailored to the corporate environment. MAP is presented as a starting point to removing this obstacle. As a theoretically derived and field-tested marital enrichment program that incorporates the interdependency of work and family dynamics as a key component, MAP builds upon the assumptions that are the basis for both the marital enrichment movement and the trends in corporate America that are designed to enhance employer and family partnerships. First, not only is marriage highly valued in our society (Thornton, 1989), but also having a happy marriage is an important personal value in this country (Mellman, Lazarus, & Rivlin, 1990). Second, spouses in marriages are a viable source of social support for one another (Burke & Weir, 1982; Litwak et al., 1989); they play an instrumental role in promoting each other's physical and emotional well-being, which is essential to successful performance in both work and non-work roles (cf. Burke & Weir, 1977a, 1977b, 1982; Gove, Style, & Hughes, 1990). Third, many couples need assistance both in understanding relational dynamics, especially within a larger ecological context, and in negotiating a relationship that has the potential to respond to changing individual and collective interests and goals over the life span (Orthner, 1990). Fourth, marriages can be strengthened through interventions that are designed to increase the capabilities of spouses and to provide them with resources and opportunities that address their collective and individual needs and goals (Giblin, Sprenkle, & Sheehan, 1985; Guerney & Maxson, 1990). Last, because of the centrality of marriage as a social institution, efforts to enrich marriage have the capability to pay rich dividends in enhanced societal well-being and welfare (Blankenhorn, 1990).

MAP is considered to have a great deal of potential in the corporate marketplace. A key strength lies in its flexibility. Although the VBC model provides the program with a defined structure, the program itself, including the type and sequencing of activities to accomplish its objectives, can be tailored to particular situations and groups.

Enrichment specialists are encouraged to experiment with different formats and activities. For example, in one workshop conducted by the author, the priority values of each spouse were defined by having each spouse record his or her five most important marital goals (this was done as an alternative to using a structured survey instrument, as was discussed in Chapter 2). The manual for workshop leaders, which is currently under development, will include optional formats, activities, and assessment tools for accomplishing workshop objectives. Plans also call for the development of a workbook for participants that will include a similar level of flexibility.

To date, MAP has been well received by both sponsors and participants. Yet the program requires additional field-testing with different population groups of employees in various types of industry. For example, it would be interesting to implement MAP as presented in Chapter 2 with a group of blue-collar workers and their spouses in a rural textile community. The program also may be adapted for testing with public sector clients—including the U.S. military, which played an instrumental role in its development.

A major shortcoming in the implementation of family support initiatives in the private sector has been the lack of well-designed evaluation studies (Aldous, 1990; Kingston, 1990). Without a firm empirical foundation, the continuation of programs like MAP may become extremely vulnerable to changes in corporate leadership and market conditions. Whoever the client may be, evaluation should be a key component in the design and implementation of MAP. Such evaluation should assess (1) the responses of participants and sponsors to the program itself and (2) its short- and long-term implications for marital team building, relational satisfaction, and the sponsor's bottom line.

In addition to evaluation research, continued basic research as presented in Chapters 4 and 5 is required. This research should examine the assumptions undergirding the VBC model, the conceptual framework for the program. A combined program of basic and applied research will provide a sound theoretical and empirical foundation upon which to refine, extend, and market MAP.

Effective marketing is an important component of the success of any marital enrichment program. In large part, the stage of corporate development in creating a family-responsive workplace and the culture of the organization itself will influence the manner in which the program is introduced into the company. For some companies, the sponsoring of marital enrichment opportunities is a logical extension of their already comprehensive family support system. Called "Stage 2" companies by Galinsky and Stein (1990, p. 380), these companies are likely to be especially receptive to programs like MAP that are responsive to the needs of the organization and its employees. These companies also are likely to have an infrastructure for implementing such programs, including a person who is identified as being responsible for family support initiatives. Given the lack of marital enrichment programs in the marketplace that are tailored to the corporate environment, MAP is likely to be well received in Stage 2 companies.

However, as concluded by Galinsky and Stein (1990), few companies in the United States have reached Stage 2 status. Most have more modest family support systems in operation. In these "Stage 1" companies (Galinsky & Stein, 1990, p. 379), there is often an unevenness in and lack of coordination of family support initiatives across organizational divisions or departments, and there may be a general insecurity in the corporate culture about the wisdom of stepping "too far" into the family lives of employees. Marital enrichment programs for employees and their spouses may be viewed with some degree of skepticism by corporate players, especially those who have had limited exposure to them.

In marketing MAP in these Stage 1 companies, it is critical to identify an influential person in the corporate chain of command who is supportive of the idea of sponsoring marital enrichment opportunities for employees and their spouses. This person is a critical resource to the interventionist in devising a marketing and evaluation strategy that is congruent with the corporate culture. For example, some companies may readily see the bottom-line implications of programs like MAP from a briefing presentation and may make a decision to implement the program with little or no employee and spouse input. Other companies may want first to better understand the support needs of employees and their spouses, including their interest in marital enrichment activities; this may be achieved by conducting a survey or by organizing focus groups. A solid foundation of basic and applied research regarding MAP, combined with supportive rationale for corporate sponsorship of programs like MAP in the workplace (see Chapter 6), may be especially critical to marketing the program in Stage 1 companies.

In closing, this book has been an ambitious attempt to introduce MAP and to provide a beginning scientific foundation for the program and its justification through integration of theory, research, and practice. Consistent with a critical theory perspective (Constantine, 1986), and in agreement with House (1981), it represents the author's belief that (1) explanatory theory and basic research and (2) practice theory and evaluation research can complement and extend one another, advancing both the theory and the development of scientifically derived and empirically validated practice models. It is hoped that this book will foster the increasing incorporation of marital enrichment activities like MAP in corporate America. It also is hoped that it will stimulate increased attention to theory development and basic and applied research in the marital enrichment field.

Appendixes

Appendix I: Family Value Profile (FVP)
Gary L. Bowen and Barbara J. Janofsky

Below is a list of 33 statements that describe possible patterns, preferences, and behaviors in families. For each one indicate how important it is to you that members in your family share such patterns, preferences, and behaviors. Circle the NUMBER on the line from one to seven that best represents your feelings: 1 = NOT AT ALL IMPORTANT AND 7 = EXTREMELY IMPORTANT.

How important is it to you that members in your family:	Not at all Important					Extremely Important	
1. Share responsibility for household tasks.	1	2	3	4	5	6	7
2. Spend their free time with one another.	1	2	3	4	5	6	7
3. Support one another during difficult times.	1	2	3	4	5	6	7
4. Compromise, when problems arise.	1	2	3	4	5	6	7
5. Pray together.	1	2	3	4	5	6	7
6. Share the same religious beliefs.	1	2	3	4	5	6	7
7. Attend church or synagogue together.	1	2	3	4	5	6	7
8. Give each other plenty of time and attention.	1	2	3	4	5	6	7
9. Share their feelings with one another.	1	2	3	4	5	6	7
10. Put family life before work.	1	2	3	4	5	6	7
11. Participate in community events and activities.	1	2	3	4	5	6	7
12. Maintain close ties with extended family members.	1	2	3	4	5	6	7
13. Communicate openly and listen to one another.	1	2	3	4	5	6	7
14. Confide in one another.	1	2	3	4	5	6	7

How important is it to you that members in your family:	Not at all Important					Extremely Important	
15. Have relatives to turn to when personal or family problems arise.	1	2	3	4	5	6	7
16. Respect and appreciate one another.	1	2	3	4	5	6	7
17. Feel loved and cared for by one another.	1	2	3	4	5	6	7
18. Work together as a team.	1	2	3	4	5	6	7
19. Invest much of their time and energy in the family.	1	2	3	4	5	6	7
20. Do things together as a family.	1	2	3	4	5	6	7
21. Select solutions to problems that are best for everyone.	1	2	3	4	5	6	7
22. Trust one another.	1	2	3	4	5	6	7
23. Have a sense of play and humor.	1	2	3	4	5	6	7
24. Become involved in community recreational activities.	1	2	3	4	5	6	7
25. Are reliable and dependable.	1	2	3	4	5	6	7
26. Plan ahead for future events.	1	2	3	4	5	6	7
27. Cope well under pressure.	1	2	3	4	5	6	7
28. Stick to a job until it is finished.	1	2	3	4	5	6	7
29. Try hard to succeed.	1	2	3	4	5	6	7
30. Share similar aims and goals for life.	1	2	3	4	5	6	7
31. Quickly resolve disagreements when they occur.	1	2	3	4	5	6	7
32. Pay compliments and say nice things to one another.	1	2	3	4	5	6	7
33. Show commitment to one another.	1	2	3	4	5	6	7

Appendix II: Family Behavior Profile (FBP)
Gary L. Bowen and Barbara J. Janofsky

Below is a list of 33 statements that describe possible patterns, preferences, and behaviors in families. For each one indicate to what extent you feel that members in your family actually share such patterns, preferences, and behaviors. Circle the NUMBER on the line from one to seven that best represents your feelings: 1 = VERY LITTLE EXTENT AND 7 = VERY GREAT EXTENT.

To what extent do members in your family actually:	Very Little Extent					Very Great Extent	
1. Share responsibility for household tasks.	1	2	3	4	5	6	7
2. Spend their free time with one another.	1	2	3	4	5	6	7
3. Support one another during difficult times.	1	2	3	4	5	6	7
4. Compromise, when problems arise.	1	2	3	4	5	6	7
5. Pray together.	1	2	3	4	5	6	7
6. Share the same religious beliefs.	1	2	3	4	5	6	7
7. Attend church or synagogue together.	1	2	3	4	5	6	7
8. Give each other plenty of time and attention.	1	2	3	4	5	6	7
9. Share their feelings with one another.	1	2	3	4	5	6	7
10. Put family life before work.	1	2	3	4	5	6	7
11. Participate in community events and activities.	1	2	3	4	5	6	7
12. Maintain close ties with extended family members.	1	2	3	4	5	6	7
13. Communicate openly and listen to one another.	1	2	3	4	5	6	7
14. Confide in one another.	1	2	3	4	5	6	7

To what extent do members in your family actually:	Very Little Extent						Very Great Extent
15. Have relatives to turn to when personal or family problems arise.	1	2	3	4	5	6	7
16. Respect and appreciate one another.	1	2	3	4	5	6	7
17. Feel loved and cared for by one another.	1	2	3	4	5	6	7
18. Work together as a team.	1	2	3	4	5	6	7
19. Invest much of their time and energy in the family.	1	2	3	4	5	6	7
20. Do things together as a family.	1	2	3	4	5	6	7
21. Select solutions to problems that are best for everyone.	1	2	3	4	5	6	7
22. Trust one another.	1	2	3	4	5	6	7
23. Have a sense of play and humor.	1	2	3	4	5	6	7
24. Become involved in community recreational activities.	1	2	3	4	5	6	7
25. Are reliable and dependable.	1	2	3	4	5	6	7
26. Plan ahead for future events.	1	2	3	4	5	6	7
27. Cope well under pressure.	1	2	3	4	5	6	7
28. Stick to a job until it is finished.	1	2	3	4	5	6	7
29. Try hard to succeed.	1	2	3	4	5	6	7
30. Share similar aims and goals for life.	1	2	3	4	5	6	7
31. Quickly resolve disagreements when they occur.	1	2	3	4	5	6	7
32. Pay compliments and say nice things to one another.	1	2	3	4	5	6	7
33. Show commitment to one another.	1	2	3	4	5	6	7

Appendix III: Marital Value Profile (MVP)
Gary L. Bowen

How important is it to you that you and your spouse:	Not Important					Extremely Important	
1. Respect and appreciate each other.	1	2	3	4	5	6	7
2. Share your feelings with each other.	1	2	3	4	5	6	7
3. Compromise, when problems arise.	1	2	3	4	5	6	7
4. Try hard to succeed.	1	2	3	4	5	6	7
5. Pray together.	1	2	3	4	5	6	7
6. Participate in community events and activities.	1	2	3	4	5	6	7
7. Maintain close ties with extended family members.	1	2	3	4	5	6	7
8. Spend your free time with each other.	1	2	3	4	5	6	7
9. Show commitment to each other.	1	2	3	4	5	6	7
10. Feel loved and cared for by each other.	1	2	3	4	5	6	7
11. Communicate openly and listen to each other.	1	2	3	4	5	6	7
12. Select solutions to problems that are best for both of you.	1	2	3	4	5	6	7
13. Share the same religious beliefs.	1	2	3	4	5	6	7

How important is it to you that you and your spouse:	Not Important						Extremely Important
14. Become involved in community recreational activities.	1	2	3	4	5	6	7
15. Have relatives you can turn to when personal or family problems arise.	1	2	3	4	5	6	7
16. Give each other plenty of time and attention.	1	2	3	4	5	6	7
17. Support each other during difficult times.	1	2	3	4	5	6	7
18. Trust each other.	1	2	3	4	5	6	7
19. Confide in each other.	1	2	3	4	5	6	7
20. Quickly resolve disagreements when they occur.	1	2	3	4	5	6	7
21. Strive to be the best at whatever you do.	1	2	3	4	5	6	7
22. Cope well under pressure.	1	2	3	4	5	6	7
23. Attend church or synagogue together.	1	2	3	4	5	6	7
24. Provide help to those outside the family.	1	2	3	4	5	6	7
25. Are reliable and dependable.	1	2	3	4	5	6	7
26. Take responsibility for your own actions.	1	2	3	4	5	6	7

Appendix IV: Marital Behavior Profile (MBP)
Gary L. Bowen

Below is a list of 26 statements that describe possible patterns, preferences, and behaviors in families. For each one indicate to what extent you feel that you and your spouse actually share such patterns, preferences, and behaviors. Circle the NUMBER on the line from one to seven that best represents your feelings: 1 = VERY LITTLE EXTENT AND 7 = VERY GREAT EXTENT.

To what extent do you and your spouse actually:	Very Little Extent					Very Great Extent	
1. Respect and appreciate each other.	1	2	3	4	5	6	7
2. Share your feelings with each other.	1	2	3	4	5	6	7
3. Compromise, when problems arise.	1	2	3	4	5	6	7
4. Try hard to succeed.	1	2	3	4	5	6	7
5. Pray together.	1	2	3	4	5	6	7
6. Participate in community events and activities.	1	2	3	4	5	6	7
7. Maintain close ties with extended family members.	1	2	3	4	5	6	7
8. Spend your free time with each other.	1	2	3	4	5	6	7
9. Show commitment to each other.	1	2	3	4	5	6	7
10. Feel loved and cared for by each other.	1	2	3	4	5	6	7
11. Communicate openly and listen to each other.	1	2	3	4	5	6	7
12. Select solutions to problems that are best for both of you.	1	2	3	4	5	6	7
13. Share the same religious beliefs.	1	2	3	4	5	6	7

<u>To what extent do you and your spouse actually</u>:	Very Little Extent					Very Great Extent	
14. Become involved in community recreational activities.	1	2	3	4	5	6	7
15. Have relatives you can turn to when personal or family problems arise.	1	2	3	4	5	6	7
16. Give each other plenty of time and attention.	1	2	3	4	5	6	7
17. Support each other during difficult times.	1	2	3	4	5	6	7
18. Trust each other.	1	2	3	4	5	6	7
19. Confide in each other.	1	2	3	4	5	6	7
20. Quickly resolve disagreements when they occur.	1	2	3	4	5	6	7
21. Strive to be the best at whatever you do.	1	2	3	4	5	6	7
22. Cope well under pressure.	1	2	3	4	5	6	7
23. Attend church or synagogue together.	1	2	3	4	5	6	7
24. Provide help to those outside the family.	1	2	3	4	5	6	7
25. Are reliable and dependable.	1	2	3	4	5	6	7
26. Take responsibility for your own actions.	1	2	3	4	5	6	7

References

Adams, B. N. (1979). Mate selection in the United States: A theoretical integration. In W. R. Burr, R. Hill, F. I. Nye, & I. L. Reiss (Eds.), *Contemporary theories about the family* (Vol. 1, pp. 259-267). New York: Free Press.

———. (1988). Fifty years of family research: What does it mean? *Journal of Marriage and the Family, 50*, 5-17.

Aldous, J. (1969). Occupational characteristics and males' role performance in the family. *Journal of Marriage and the Family, 31*, 707-712.

———. (1990). Specification and speculation concerning the politics of workplace family policies. *Journal of Family Issues, 11,*, 355-367.

Aldous, J., Osmond, M. W., & Hicks, M. W. (1979). Men's work and men's families. In W. R. Burr, R. Hill, F. I. Nye, & I. L. Reiss (Eds.), *Contemporary theories about the family* (Vol. 1, pp. 227-256). New York: Free Press.

Althauser, R. P. (1971). Multicollinearity and non-additive regression models. In H. M. Blalock, Jr. (Ed.), *Causal models in the social sciences* (2nd ed., pp. 453-472). Chicago, IL: Aldine.

Anderson, C., & Stark, C. (1988). Psychosocial problems of job relocation: Preventive roles in industry. *Social Work, 33*, 38-41.

Anderson, S. A., Russell, C. S., & Schumm, W. R. (1983). Perceived marital quality and family life-cycle categories: A further analysis. *Journal of Marriage and the Family, 45*, 127-139.

Andreyeva, G. M., & Gozman, L. J. (1981). Interpersonal relationships and social context. In S. Duck & R. Gilmour (Eds.), *Personal Relationships 1: Studying personal relationships* (pp. 47-66). London: Academic Press.

Andrisani, P. J., & Shapiro, M. B. (1978). Women's attitudes toward their jobs: Some longitudinal data on a national sample. *Personnel Psychology, 31*, 15-35.

Aneshensel, C. S. (1986). Marital and employment role-strain, social support, and depression among adult women. In S. E. Hobfall (Ed.), *Stress, social support, and women* (pp. 99-114). New York: Hemisphere.

Angell, R. C. (1936). *The family encounters the Depression.* New York: Charles Scribner.

Antonovsky, A. (1979). *Health, stress and coping.* San Francisco: Jossey-Bass.

———. (1987). *Unraveling the mystery of health.* San Francisco: Jossey-Bass.

Antonovsky, A., & Sourani, T. (1988). Family sense of coherence and family adaptation. *Journal of Marriage and the Family, 50,* 79–92.

Arnott, C. (1972). Husbands' attitude and wives' commitment to employment. *Journal of Marriage and the Family, 34,* 673–684.

Atkinson, A. M. (1987). Father's participation and evaluation of family day care. *Family Relations, 36,* 146–151.

Bagorozzi, D. A., & Wodarski, J. S. (1977). A social exchange typology of conjugal relationships and conflict development. *Journal of Marital and Family Counseling, 3*(4), 53–60.

Barlett, H. (1970). *The common base of social work practice.* New York: National Association of Social Workers.

Barling, J., & Rosenbaum, A. (1986). Work stressors and wife abuse. *Journal of Applied Psychology, 71,* 346–348.

Bartolome, F., & Evans, P. A. L. (1979). Professional lives versus private lives: Shifting patterns of managerial commitment. *Organizational Dynamics, 3,* 3–29.

Baucom, D. H., & Epstein, N. (1990). *Cognitive-behavioral marital therapy.* New York: Brunner/Mazel.

Beavers, W. R., Hampson, R. B., & Hulgus, Y. F. (1985). Commentary: The Beavers systems approach to family assessment. *Family Process, 24,* 398–405.

Beavers, W. R., & Voeller, M. N. (1983). Comparing and contrasting the Olson circumplex model with the Beavers system model. *Family Process, 22,* 85–98.

Beck, A. T. (1970). Cognitive therapy: Nature and relation to behavior therapy. *Behavior Therapy, 1,* 184–200.

———. (1976). *Cognitive therapy and the emotional disorders.* New York: International Universities Press.

Bedeian, A. G. (1987). Organization theory: Current controversies, issues, and directions. In C. L. Cooper & I. T. Robertson (Eds.), *International review of industrial and organizational psychology* (pp. 1–33). New York: John Wiley & Sons.

Bellah, R. N., Madsen, R., Sullivan, W. M., Swidler, A., & Tipton, S. M. (1985). *Habits of the heart.* New York: Harper & Row.

Belsky, J., Perry-Jenkins, M., & Crouter, A. C. (1985). The work-family interface and marital change across the transition to parenthood. *Journal of Family Issues, 6,* 205–220.

Bem, D. J. (1970). *Beliefs, attitudes and human affairs.* Belmont, CA: Brooks/Cole.

Bergermaier, R., Borg, I., & Champoux, J. E. (1984). Structural relationships among facets of work, nonwork, and general well-being. *Work and Occupations, 11,* 163–181.

Berk, R., & Berk, S. F. (1979). *Labor and leisure at home.* Beverly Hills, CA: Sage.

Berkowitz, A. D., & Perkins, H. W. (1984). Stress among farm women: Work and family as interacting systems. *Journal of Marriage and the Family, 46,* 161–166.

Berscheid, E. (1983). Emotion. In H. H. Kelley, E. Berscheid, A. Christensen, J. H. Harvey, T. L. Huston, G. Levinger, E. McClintock, L. A. Peplau, & D. R. Peterson (Eds.), *Close relationships* (pp. 110–168). New York: W. H. Freeman and Company.

———. (1985). Compatibility, interdependence, and emotion. In W. Ickes (Ed.), *Compatible and incompatible relationships* (pp. 143–161). New York: Springer-Verlag.

Berscheid, E., Gangestad, S. W., & Kulakowski, D. (1984). Emotion in close relationships: Implications for relationship counseling. In S. D. Brown & R. W. Lent (Eds.), *Handbook of counseling psychology* (pp. 435–476). New York: John Wiley & Sons.

Biddle, B. J. (1986). Recent developments in role theory. *Annual Review of Sociology, 12,* 67–92.

Bielby, W. T., & Bielby, D. D. (1989). Family ties: Balancing commitments to work and family in dual earner households. *American Sociological Review, 54,* 776–789.

Blalock, H. M., Jr. (1966). The identification problem and theory building: The case of status inconsistency. *American Sociological Review, 31,* 52–61.

———. (1967). Status inconsistency, social mobility, status integration and structural effects. *American Sociological Review, 32,* 790–801.

Blankenhorn, D. (1986). A pro-family workplace. *Youth Policy, 10*(8), 20–21.

———. (1989). Ozzie and Harriet: Have reports of their death been greatly exaggerated? *Family Affairs, 2*(2–3), 10–11.

———. (1990). Introduction. In D. Blankenhorn, S. Bayme, & J. B. Elshtain (Eds.), *Rebuilding the nest: A new commitment to the American family* (pp. xi–xv). Milwaukee, WI: Family Service America.

Blau, P. (1964). *Exchange and power in social life.* New York: Wiley.

Blegen, M. A., Mueller, C. W., & Price, J. L. (1988). Measurement of kinship responsibility for organizational research. *Journal of Applied Psychology, 73,* 402–409.

Blood, R. O., Jr., & Wolfe, D. M. (1960). *Husbands and wives: The dynamics of married living.* Glencoe, IL: Free Press.

Bloom, B. L., Asher, S. J., & White, S. W. (1978). Marital disruption as a stressor: A review and analysis. *Psychological Bulletin, 85,* 867–894.

Bohen, H. H. (1984). Gender equality in work and family: An elusive goal. *Journal of Family Issues, 5,* 254–272.

Booth, A., Johnson, D. E., White, L., & Edwards, J. (1984). Women, outside employment, and marital instability. *American Journal of Sociology, 90,* 567–583.

Borden, V. M. H., & Levinger, G. (1990). Interpersonal transformations in intimate relationships. In W. H. Jones & D. Perlman (Eds.), *Advances in personal relationships* (Vol. 2). London: J. Kingsley Publishers.

Boss, P. (1988). *Family stress management.* Newbury Park, CA: Sage.

Bowen, G. L. (1986). Spouse support and the retention intentions of air force members: A basis for program development. *Evaluation and Program Planning, 9,* 209–220.

———. (1987). Changing gender-role preferences and marital adjustment: Implications for clinical practice. *Family Therapy, 14,* 17–33.

———. (1988a). Family life satisfaction: A value-based approach. *Family Relations, 37,* 458–462.

———. (1988b). The value-behavior congruency model of family life satisfaction: Implications for clinical practice. *Family Therapy, 15,* 7–21.

———. (1988c). Corporate supports for the family lives of employees: A conceptual model for program planning and evaluation. *Family Relations, 37,* 183–188.

———. (1988d). *A model of work and family partnership: Executive briefing.* Chapel Hill, NC: University of North Carolina.

———. (1989a). Toward conceptual refinement of operational outcome variables: The case of family life satisfaction. In G. L. Bowen & D. K. Orthner (Eds.), *The organization family: Work and family linkages in the U.S. military* (pp. 142-162). New York: Praeger.

——— . (1989b). Marital sex role incongruence and marital adjustment: A comment of Li and Caldwell. *Journal of Family Issues, 10,* 409-415.

——— . (1989c). Family factors and member retention: A key relationship in the work and family equation. In G. L. Bowen & D. K. Orthner (Eds.), *The organization family: Work and family linkages in the U.S. military* (pp. 37-57). New York: Praeger.

——— . (1989d). *Family adaptation to relocation: An empirical analysis of family stressors, adaptive resources, and sense of coherence* (Technical Report No. 856). Alexandria, VA: U.S. Army Research Institute for the Behavioral and Social Sciences.

——— . (1990). *The family adaptation model: A life course perspective* (Technical Report No. 880). Alexandria, VA: U.S. Army Research Institute for the Behavioral and Social Sciences.

Bowen, G. L, & Henley, H. C. (1987). Asian-wife marriages in the U.S. military: A comparative analysis with white-wife and black-wife marriages. *Family Perspective, 21*(1), 23-37.

Bowen, G. L., & Janofsky, B. J. (1987). *Family strength and adaptation to army life.* Washington, DC: Department of the Army, Office of the Chief of Chaplains.

——— . (1988). *Family strength and adaptation to army life: A focus on variations in family values and expectations across racial/ethnic group and rank.* Washington, DC: Department of the Army, Office of the Chief of Chaplains.

Bowen, G. L., & Neenan, P. (1988). Sex-role orientations among married men in the military: The generational factor. *Psychological Reports, 62,* 523-526.

——— . (1989). Organizational attitude toward families and satisfaction with the military way of life: Perceptions of civilian spouses of U.S. Army members. *Family Perspective, 23,* 3-13.

Bowen, G. L., & Orthner, D. K. (1983). Sex-role congruency and marital quality. *Journal of Marriage and the Family, 45,* 223-230.

——— . (Eds.). (1989). *The organization family: Work and family linkages in the U.S. military.* New York: Praeger.

——— . (1991). Effects of organizational culture on fatherhood. In F. W. Bozett & S. M. H. Hanson (Eds.), *Fatherhood and families in cultural context* (pp. 182-217). New York: Springer Press.

Bradbury, T. N., & Fincham, F. D. (1987). Assessment of affect in marriage. In K. Daniel O'Leary (Ed.), *Assessment of marital discord* (pp. 59-108). Hillsdale, NJ: Lawrence Erlbaum Associates.

——— . (1990). Attributions in marriage: Review and critique. *Psychological Bulletin, 107*(1), 3-33.

Brett, J. M., & Werbel, J. D. (1980). *The effects of transfer on employees and their families.* Washington, DC: Employee Relocation Council.

Bronfenbrenner, U. (1979). *The ecology of human development.* Cambridge, MA: Harvard University Press.

Brown, R. C. (1985). Family and marital counseling in industry. In D. W. Myers (Ed.), *Employee problem prevention and counseling* (pp. 49-70). Westport CT: Quorum Books.

Buckley, W. (1967). *Sociology and modern systems theory.* Englewood Cliffs, NJ: Prentice-Hall.

Burden, D. S., & Googins, B. (1987). *Balancing job and homelife study: Summary of findings*. Boston: Boston University School of Social Work.

Bureau of National Affairs, Inc. (1986). *Work and family: A changing dynamic*. Washington, DC: Bureau of National Affairs.

Burke, R. J., & Bradshaw, P. (1981). Occupation and life stress in the family. *Small Group Behavior, 12,* 329–375.

Burke, R. J., & Greenglass, E. R. (1987). Work and family. In C. L. Cooper & I. T. Robertson (Eds.), *International Review of Industrial and Organizational Psychology* (pp. 273–320). New York: John Wiley & Sons.

Burke, R. J., & Weir, T. (1975). Giving and receiving help with work and non-work related problems. *Journal of Business Administration, 6,* 59–78.

——— . (1977a). Husband-wife helping-relationships: The "mental health" function in marriage. *Psychological Reports, 40,* 911–925.

——— . (1977b). Marital helping relationships: The moderator between stress and well-being. *Journal of Psychology, 95,* 121–130.

——— . (1982). Husband-wife helping relationships as moderators of experienced stress: The "mental hygiene" function in marriage. In H. I. McCubbin, A. E. Cauble, & J. M. Patterson (Eds.), *Family stress, coping, and social support* (pp. 221–238). Springfield, IL: Charles C. Thomas.

Burr, W. R. (1973). *Theory construction and the sociology of the family*. New York: John Wiley & Sons.

Burr, W. R., Leigh, G. K., Day, R. D., & Constantine, J. (1979). Symbolic interaction and the family. In W. R. Burr, R. Hill, F. I. Nye, & I. L. Reiss (Eds.), *Contemporary theories about the family* (Vol. 2, pp. 42–111). New York: Free Press.

Byers, S. K. (1987). Organizational stress: Implications for health promotion managers. *American Journal of Health Promotion, 2*(1), 21–27.

Byrne, D. (1971) *The attraction paradigm*. New York: Academic Press.

Campbell, A., Converse, P. E., & Rogers, W. L. (1976). *The quality of life: Perceptions, evaluations, and satisfactions*. New York: Russell Sage Foundation.

Caplan, R. D. (1987). Person-environment fit theory and organizations: Commensurate dimensions, time perspectives, and mechanisms. *Journal of Vocational Behavior, 31,* 248–267.

Caplan, R. D., Cobb, S., French, J. R. P., Jr., Harrison, R. V., Pinneau, S. R., Jr. (1975). *Job demands and worker health: Main effects and occupational differences* (Department of Health, Education and Welfare HEW [NIOSH] Publication No. 75–160). Washington, DC: U.S. Government Printing Office.

Carnes, P. (1981). *Understanding us: Enrichment program for families*. Minneapolis: Interpersonal Communication Program.

Caron, W., & Olson, D. H. (1984). *Family satisfaction and perceived-ideal discrepancy on FACES II*. St. Paul: Family Social Science, University of Minnesota.

Catalyst, (1984). *Work and family seminars: Corporations' responses to employees' needs*. New York: Author.

Cate, R. M., Lloyd, S. A., & Henton, J. M. (1985). The effect of equity, equality and reward level on the stability of students' relationships. *Journal of Social Psychology, 125,* 715–721.

Cate, R. M., Lloyd, S. A., Henton, J. M., & Larson, J. H. (1982). Fairness and reward level as predictors of relationship satisfaction. *Social Psychology Quarterly, 45,* 177–181.

Cate, R. M., Lloyd, S. A., & Long, E. (1988). The role of rewards and fairness in developing premarital relationships. *Journal of Marriage and the Family, 50,* 443–452.

Chadwick-Jones, J. K. (1976). *Social exchange theory: Its structure and influence in social psychology.* New York: Academic Press.

Chatman, J. A. (1989). Improving interactional organizational research: A model of person-organizational fit. *Academy of Management Review, 14,* 333–349.

Christensen, H. T. (1964). The intrusion of values. In H. T. Christensen (Ed.), *Handbook of marriage and the family* (pp. 969–1006). Chicago: Rand McNally.

Cohen, J., & Cohen, P. (1975). *Applied multiple regression/correlation analysis for the behavioral sciences.* Hillsdale, NJ: Lawrence Erlbaum Associates.

Constantine, L. L. (1986). *Family paradigms: The practice of theory in family therapy.* New York: Guilford Press.

Cooper, C. L., & Marshall, J. (1978). Sources of managerial and white collar stress. In C. L. Cooper & R. Payne (Eds.), *Stress and work* (pp. 81–105). Chichester, England: John Wiley & Sons.

Coser, L. M. (1974). *Greedy institutions.* New York: Free Press.

Coser, L. A., & Coser, R. L. (1974). The housewife and her "greedy family." In L. A. Coser, *Greedy institutions* (pp. 89–100). New York: Free Press.

Coverman, S., & Sheley, J. F. (1986). Change in men's housework and child-care time, 1965–1975. *Journal of Marriage and the Family, 48,* 413–422.

Cronbach, L. J. (1951). Coefficient alpha and the internal structure of tests. *Psychometrika, 16,* 297–334.

——— . (1958). Proposals leading to analytic treatment of social perception scores. In R. Tagiuri & L. Petrullo (Eds.), *Person perception and interpersonal behavior* (pp. 353–379). Stanford, CA: Stanford University Press.

Cronbach, L. J., & Furby, L. (1970). How should we measure "change"—or should we? *Psychological Bulletin, 74,* 68–80.

Crouter, A. C. (1984). Spillover from family to work: The neglected side of the work-family interface. *Human Relations, 37,* 425–442.

Culbert, S. A., & Renshaw, J. R. (1972). Coping with the stresses of travel as an opportunity for improving the quality of work and life. *Family Process, 11,* 321–337.

Curran, D. (1983). *Traits of a healthy family.* Minneapolis: Winston Press.

Deal, T. E., & Kennedy, A. A. (1982). *Corporate cultures: The rites and rituals of corporate life.* Reading, MA: Addison-Wesley.

Denton, W. (1986). Introduction to marriage and family enrichment: A shift in paradigm. In W. Denton (Ed.), *Marriage and family enrichment* (pp. 3–6). New York: Haworth Press.

Devilbiss, M. C., & Perrucci, C. C. (1982). Effects of role multiplicity on U.S. Army personnel. *Journal of Political and Military Sociology, 10,* 1–13.

Dinkmeyer, D., & Carlson, J. (1986). Time for a better marriage. In W. Denton (Ed.), *Marriage and family enrichment* (pp. 19–28). New York: Haworth Press.

Donatelle, R. J., & Hawkins, M. J. (1989). Employee stress claims: Increasing implications for health promotion programming. *American Journal of Health Promotion, 3*(1), 19–25.

Draughn, P. S. (1989). Middle-aged men: The work/family relationship. *Family Perspective, 23,* 15–29.

Dunst, C., Trivette, C., & Deal, A. (1988). *Enabling and empowering families: Principles and guidelines for practice.* Cambridge, MA: Brookline Books.

Dyer, P. M., & Dyer, G. H. (1986). Leadership training for marriage and family enrichment. In W. Denton (Ed.), *Marriage and family enrichment* (pp. 97–110). New York: Haworth Press.

Edmonds, V. H. (1967). Marital conventionalization: Definition and measurement. *Journal of Marriage and the Family, 29,* 681–688.

Edwards, J. (1969). Familial behavior as social exchange. *Journal of Marriage and the Family, 31,* 518–526.

Ellis, A. (1962). *Reason and emotion in psychotherapy.* New York: Lyle Stuart.

——— . (1970) *The essence of rational psychotherapy: A comprehensive approach to treatment.* New York: Institute for Rational Living.

——— . (1971) *Growth through reason.* Palo Alto, CA: Science and Behavior Books.

——— . (1977). The basic clinical theory of rational-emotive therapy. In A. Ellis & R. Grieger (Eds.), *Handbook of rational-emotive therapy* (pp. 3–34). New York: Springer.

——— . (1978). What people can do for themselves to cope with stress. In C. L. Cooper & R. Payne (Eds.), *Stress at work* (pp. 209–222). Chichester, England: John Wiley & Sons.

Ellis, A., & Harper, R. (1961). *A guide to rational living.* Beverly Hills, CA: Leighton.

——— . (1979). *A new guide to rational living.* Hollywood, CA: Wilshire.

Emerson, R. (1976). Social exchange theory. In A. Inkeles, J. Coleman, & N. Smelser (Eds.), *Annual review of sociology* (pp. 335–362). Palo Alto, CA: Annual Reviews.

England, P., & Farkas, G. (1986). *Households, employment, and gender: A social, economic, and demographic view.* New York: Aldine.

Epstein, N. B., Baldwin, L. M., & Bishop, D. S. (1983). The McMaster family assessment device. *Journal of Marital and Family Therapy, 9,* 171–180.

Epstein, N., Bishop, D., & Baldwin, L. (1982). McMaster model of family functioning: A view of the normal family. In F. Walsh (Ed.), *Normal family processes* (pp. 115–141). New York: Guilford Press.

Erickson, R. J., & Wharton, A. S. (1989, November). *Emotion management: The neglected link between work and family life.* Paper presented at the Pre-Conference Theory Construction and Research Methodology Workshop, National Council on Family Relations, New Orleans, LA.

Evans, P., & Bartolome, F. (1980). The relationship between professional life and private life. In C. B. Derr (Ed.), *Work, Family and Career* (pp. 281–317). New York: Praeger.

——— . (1984). The changing pictures of the relationship between career and family. *Journal of Occupational Behavior, 5,* 9–21.

——— . (1986). The dynamics of the work-family relationships in managerial lives. *International Review of Applied Psychology, 35,* 371–395.

Farkas, G. (1976). Education, wage rates, and the division of labor between husband and wife. *Journal of Marriage and the Family, 38,* 473–483.

Finkelstein, J. A., & Ziegenfuss, J. T., Jr. (1978). Diagnosing employees' personal problems. *Personnel Journal, 57,* 633–636, 643.

Fisher, B. L., Giblin, P. R., & Hoopes, M. H. (1982). Healthy family functioning: What therapists say and what families want. *Journal of Marital and Family Therapy, 8,* 273–284.

Fowlkes, M. R. (1987). Role combinations and role conflict: Introductory perspective. In F. J. Crosby (Ed.), *Spouse, parent, worker* (pp. 3–10). New Haven: Yale University Press.

French, J. R. P., Jr., Caplan, R. D., & Harrison, R. V. (1982). *The mechanisms of job stress and strain*. Chichester, England: John Wiley & Sons.

French, J. R. P., Jr., & Kahn, R. L. (1962). A programmatic approach to studying the industrial environment and mental health. *Journal of Social Issues, 18*(3), 1–47.

French, J. R. P., Jr., Rogers, W., & Cobb, S. (1974). A model of person-environment fit. In G. V. Coelho, D. A. Hamburgh, & J. E. Adams (Eds.), *Coping and adaptation* (pp. 316–333). New York: Basic Books.

French, W. L., & Bell, C. H., Jr. (1984). *Organizational development: Behavioral science interventions for organization improvement* (3rd ed.). Englewood Cliffs, NJ: Prentice-Hall.

Friedman, D. (1987). Notes on "Toward a theory of value in social exchange." In K. S. Cook (Ed.), *Social exchange theory* (pp. 47–58). Newbury Park, CA: Sage.

Friedman, D. E. (1987). *Family-supportive policies: The corporate decision-making process*. New York: Conference Board.

Galinsky, E. (1986). Family life and corporate policies. In M. W. Yogman, & T. B. Brazelton (Eds.), *In support of families* (pp. 109–145). Cambridge, MA: Harvard University Press.

Galinksy, E., & Hughes, D. (1987, August). *The Fortune Magazine child care study*. Paper presented at the 1987 Annual Convention of the American Psychological Association, New York, NY.

Galinsky, E., Hughes, D., & David, J. (1990). Trends in corporate family-supportive policies. *Marriage and Family Review, 15*(3/4) 75–94.

Galinsky, E., & Stein, P. J. (1990). The impact of human resource policies on employees. Balancing work/family life. *Journal of Family Issues, 11,* 368–383.

Galvin, K. M., & Brommel, B. J. (1986). *Family communication: Cohesion and change* (2nd ed.). Glenview, IL: Scott, Foresman and Company.

Garbarino, J. (1983). Social support networks: Rx for the helping professions. In J. K.Whittaker & J. Garbarino (Eds.), *Social support networks: Informal helping in the human services* (pp. 3–28). New York: Aldine De Gruyter.

Giblin, P. (1986). Research and assessment in marriage and family enrichment: A meta-analysis study. In W. Denton (Ed.), *Marriage and family enrichment* (pp. 79–96). New York: Haworth Press.

Giblin, P., Sprenkle, D. H., & Sheehan, R. (1985). Enrichment outcome research: A meta-analysis of premarital, marital, and family interventions. *Journal of Marital and Family Therapy, 11,* 257–271.

Gilford, R., & Bengtson, V. (1979). Measuring marital satisfaction in three generations: Positive and negative dimensions. *Journal of Marriage and the Family, 41,* 381–398.

Glenn, N. D. (1987a). Continuity versus change, sanguineness versus concern. *Journal of Family Issues, 8,* 348–354.

———. (1987b). Social trends in the United States: Evidence from sample surveys. *Public Opinion Quarterly, 51,* S109–S126.

———. (1988, June). *Some limitations of longitudinal and cohort designs in social and behavioral research*. Paper presented at Conference on Health Services Research Methodology: A Focus on AIDS, Tucson, AZ.

———. (1989). A flawed approach to solving the identification problem in the estimation of mobility effect models: A comment on Brody and McRae. *Social Forces, 68,* 789–795.

Glenn, N. D., & Weaver, C. N. (1988). The changing relationship of marital status to reported happiness. *Journal of Marriage and the Family, 50,* 317–324.

Glick, P. C. (1989). The family life cycle and social change. *Family Relations, 38,* 123–129.

Goode, W. J. (1960). A theory of role strain. *American Sociological Review, 25,* 483–496.

Gove, W. R., Hughes, M., & Style, C. B. (1983). Does marriage have positive effects on the psychological well-being of the individual? *Journal of Health and Social Behavior, 24,* 122–131.

Gove, W. R., Style, C. B., & Hughes, M. (1990). The effects of marriage on the well-being of adults. *Journal of Family Issues, 11,* 4–35.

Greenhaus, J. H., & Beutell, N. J. (1985). Sources of conflict between work and family roles. In B. C. Miller & D. H. Olson (Eds.), *Family studies: Review yearbook* (3rd ed., pp. 299–319). Beverly Hills, CA: Sage.

Grush, J. E., & Yehl, J. G. (1979). Marital roles, sex differences, and interpersonal attraction. *Journal of Personality and Social Psychology, 37*(1), 116–124.

Guerney, B. G., Jr. (1977). *Relationship enhancement: Skill training programs for therapy, problem prevention, and enrichment.* San Francisco: Jossey-Bass.

——— . (1985). The medical versus the educational model as a base for family therapy research. In L. L. Andreozzi & R. F. Levant (Eds.), *Integrating research and clinical practice* (pp. 71–79). Rockville, MD: Aspen Systems.

Guerney, B., Jr., & Maxson, P. (1990). Marital and family enrichment research: A decade review and look ahead. *Journal of Marriage and the Family, 52,* 1127–1135.

Gutek, B. A., Repetti, R. L., & Silver, D. L. (1988). Nonwork roles and stress at work. In C. L. Cooper & R. Payne (Eds.), *Causes, coping and consequences of stress at work* (pp. 141–174). Chichester, England: John Wiley & Sons.

Hall, D. T., & Hall, F. S. (1980). Stress and the two-career couple. In C. L. Cooper & R. Payne (Eds.), *Current concerns in occupational stress* (pp. 243–266). Chichester, England: John Wiley & Sons.

Hamilton, G. (1929). *A research in marriage.* New York: Boni.

Handy, C. (1978). The family: Help or hindrance? In C. L. Cooper & R. Payne (Eds.), *Stress at work* (pp. 107–123). Chichester, England: John Wiley & Sons.

Harrison, R. (1972). Understanding your organization's character. *Harvard Business Review, 3,* 119–128.

Harrison, R. V. (1978). Person-environment fit and job stress. In C. L. Cooper & R. Payne (Eds.), *Stress at work* (pp. 175–205). Chichester, England: John Wiley & Sons.

Hartman, A., & Laird, J. (1983). *Family-centered social work practice.* New York: Free Press.

Hatfield, E., & Traupmann, J. (1981). Intimate relationships: A perspective from equity theory. In S. Duck & R. Gilmour (Eds.), *Personal Relationships 1: Studying personal relationships* (pp. 165–178). London: Academic Press.

Hayghe, H. (1986). Rise in mothers' labor force activity includes those with infants. *Monthly Labor Review, 109,* 43–45.

Heath, A. (1976). *Rational choice theory and social exchange.* New York: Cambridge University Press.

Hertz, R. (1986). *More equal than others.* Berkeley: University of California Press.

Hess, R., & Handel, G. (1959). *Family worlds.* Chicago: University of Chicago Press.

Hill, R. (1949). *Families under stress.* New York: Harper & Row.

Hill, R. B. (1971). *The strengths of black families.* New York: Emerson Hall.

Hinde, R. A. (1979). *Toward understanding relationships*. London: Academic Press.

———. (1981). The bases of a science of interpersonal relationships. In S. Duck & R. Gilmour (Eds.), *Personal Relationships 1: Studying personal relationships* (pp. 1–22). London: Academic Press.

Hochschild, A. R. (1983). *The managed heart*. Berkeley: University of California Press.

Hof, L., & Miller, W. R. (1981). *Marriage enrichment: Philosophy, process, and program*. Bowie, MD: Robert J. Brady Co.

Hofferth, S. L., & Moore, K. A. (1979). Women's employment and marriage. In R. E. Smith (Ed.), *The subtle revolution* (pp. 99–124). Washington, DC: Urban Institute.

Holahan, C. K., & Gilbert, L. A. (1979a). Interrole conflict for working women: Careers versus jobs. *Journal of Applied Psychology, 64,* 86–90.

———. (1979b). Conflict between major life roles: Women and men in dual career couples. *Human Relations, 32,* 451–467.

Holman, T. B., & Jacquart, M. (1988). Leisure-activity patterns and marital satisfaction: A further test. *Journal of Marriage and the Family, 50,* 69–77.

Homans, G. C. (1950). *The human group*. New York: Harcourt, Brace.

———. Social behavior as exchange. *American Journal of Sociology, 63,* 597–606.

———. *Social behavior: Its elementary forms*. New York: Harcourt, Brace & World.

Hoopes, M. H., Fisher, B. L., & Barlow, S. H. (1984). *Structured family facilitation programs: Enrichment, education, and treatment*. Rockville, MD: Aspen Systems.

House, J. S. (1981). *Work stress and social support*. Reading, MA: Addison-Wesley.

House, J. S., & Wells, J. A. (1978). Occupational stress, social support, and health. In A. McLean, G. Black, & M. Colligan (Eds.), *Reducing occupational stress: Proceeding of a conference* (pp. 8–29). Washington, DC: DHEW (NIOSH) Publication 78–140.

Houston, B. K. (1987). Stress and coping. In C. R. Snyder & C. E. Ford (Eds.), *Coping with negative life events* (pp. 373–399). New York: Plenum Press.

Huseman, R. C., Hatfield, J. D., & Miles, E. W. (1987). A new perspective on equity theory: The equity sensitivity construct. *Academy of Management Review, 12,* 222–234.

Jackson, S. E., & Maslach, C. (1982). After-effects of job related stress: Families as victims. *Journal of Occupational Behavior, 3,* 63–77.

Kabanoff, B. (1980). Work and non-work: A review of models, methods and findings. *Psychological Bulletin, 88,* 60–77.

Kahn, R. L. (1981). *Work and health*. New York: Wiley Interscience.

Kahn, R., Hein, K., House, J., Kasl, S., & McLean, A. (1982). Report on stress in organizational settings. In G. R. Elliott & C. Eisdorfer (Eds.), *Stress and human health* (pp. 81–117). New York: Springer Publishing.

Kahn, R. L., Wolfe, D. M., Quinn, R., Snoek, J. D., & Rosenthal, R. A. (1964). *Organizational stress*. New York: John Wiley & Sons.

Kamerman, S. B., & Kahn, A. J. (1987). *The responsive workplace: Employers and a changing labor force*. New York: Columbia University Press.

Kamerman, S. B., & Kingston, P. W. (1982). Employer responses to the family responsibilities of employees. In S. B. Kamerman & C. D. Hayes (Eds.), *Families that work* (pp. 144–208). Washington, DC: National Academy Press.

Kanter, R. M. (1977a). *Men and women of the corporation*. New York: Basic Books.

_____ . (1977b). *Work and family in the United States: A critical review and agenda for research and policy.* New York: Russell Sage Foundation.

Kantor, D., & Lehr, W. (1975). *Inside the family: Toward a theory of family process.* San Francisco: Jossey-Bass.

Karpel, M. A. (1986). Questions, obstacles, contributions. In M. A. Karpel (Ed.), *Family resources: The hidden partner in family therapy* (pp. 3–61). New York: Guilford Press.

Katz, D., & Kahn, R. L. (1978). *The social psychology of organizations* (2nd ed.). New York: John Wiley & Sons.

Kelley, H. H. (1979). *Personal relationships: Their structures and processes.* Hillsdale, NJ: Erlbaum.

Kelley, H. H., Berscheid, E., Christensen, A., Harvey, J. H., Huston, T. L. Levinger, G., McClintock, E., Peplau, L. A., & Peterson, D. R. (1983). Analyzing close relationships. In H. H. Kelley, E. Berscheid, A. Christensen, J. H. Harvey, T. L. Huston, G. Levinger, E. McClintock, L. A. Peplau, & D. R. Peterson (Eds.), *Close relationships* (pp. 20–67). New York: W. H. Freeman and Company.

Kelley, H. H., & Thibaut, J. W. (1978). *Interpersonal relations: A theory of interdependence.* New York: John Wiley & Sons.

Kelly, R. F., & Voydanoff, P. (1985). Work/family role strain among employed parents. *Family Relations, 34,* 367–374.

Kerlinger, F. N., & Pedhazur, E. J. (1973). *Multiple regression in behavioral research.* New York: Holt, Rinehart and Winston.

Kessler, R. C., & Essex, M. (1982). Marital status and depression: The importance of coping resources. *Social Forces, 61,* 484–507.

Kingston, P. W. (1990). Illusions and ignorance about the family-responsive workplace. *Journal of Family Issues, 11,* 438–454.

Kingston, P. W., & Nock, S. L. (1987). Time together among dual-earner couples. *American Sociological Review, 52,* 391–400.

Klein, D. M., & Hill, R. (1979). Determinants of family problem-solving effectiveness. In W. R. Burr, R. Hill, F. I. Nye, & I. R. Reiss (Eds.), *Contemporary theories about the family: Vol. 1* (pp. 493–548). New York: Free Press.

Kluckhohn, C. (1951). Values and value orientations in the theory of action: An exploration of definition and classification. In T. Parsons & E. A. Shils (Eds.), *Toward a general theory of action* (pp. 388–433). Cambridge, MA: Harvard University Press.

Kluckhohn, F. R., & Strodtbeck, F. L. (1961). *Variations in value orientations.* Evanston, IL: Row, Peterson.

Kobasa, S. (1979). Stressful life events, personality, and health: An inquiry into hardiness. *Journal of Personality and Social Psychology, 37,* 1–11.

Kobasa, S., Maddi, S. R., & Courington, S. (1981). Personality and constitution as mediators in the stress-illness relationship. *Journal of Health and Social Behavior, 22,* 368–378.

Kohn, M. L. (1963). Social class and parent child relationships: An interpretation. *American Journal of Sociology, 68,* 471–480.

_____ . (1969). *Class and conformity: A Study in values.* Homewood, IL: Dorsey Press.

Koos, E. (1946). *Families in trouble.* New York: King's Crown Press.

Kopelman, R. E., Greenhaus, J. H., & Connolly, T. F. (1983). A model of work, family, and interrole conflict: A construct validation study. *Organizational Behavior and Human Performance, 32,* 198–215.

L'Abate, L. (1990). *Building family competence: Primary and secondary prevention strategies.* Newbury Park, CA: Sage.

Ladewig, B. H., & McGee, G. W. (1986). Occupational commitment, a supportive family environment, and marital adjustment: Development and estimation of a model. *Journal of Marriage and the Family, 48,* 821-829.

La Gaipa, J. L. (1977). Interpersonal attraction and social exchange. In S. Duck (Ed.), *Theory and practice in interpersonal attraction* (pp. 129-164). London: Academic Press.

——— . (1981). A systems approach to personal relationships. In S. Duck & R. Gilmour (Eds.), *Personal relationships 1: Studying personal relationships* (pp. 67-89). London: Academic Press.

Lamb, M. (1987, June). "Will the real new father please stand up?" *Parents*, pp. 77-80.

Lambert, S. J. (1990). Processes linking work and family: A critical review and research agenda. *Human Relations, 43,* 239-257.

Langman, L. (1987). Social stratification. In M. B. Sussman & S. K. Steinmetz (Eds.), *Handbook of marriage and the family* (pp. 211-249). New York: Plenum Press.

LaRossa, R. (1988). Fatherhood and social change. *Family Relations, 37,* 451-457.

Larzelere, R. E., & Klein, D. M. (1987). Methodology. In M. B. Sussman & S. K. Steinmetz (Eds.), *Handbook of marriage and the family* (pp. 125-155). New York: Plenum Press.

Lavee, Y., McCubbin, H. I., & Patterson, J. M. (1985). The double ABCX model of family stress and adaptation: An empirical test by analysis of structural equations with latent variables. *Journal of Marriage and the Family, 47,* 811-825.

Lawler, E. E., III (1973). *Motivation in work organizations.* Monterey, CA: Brooks/Cole.

Lazarus, R. S. (1976). *Patterns of adjustment* (3rd ed.). New York: McGraw-Hill.

Lazarus, R. S., & Folkman, S. (1984). *Stress, appraisal, and coping.* New York: Springer Publishing.

LeCroy, C. W., Carrol, P., Nelson-Becker, H., & Sturlaugson, P. (1989). An experimental evaluation of the caring days technique for marital enrichment. *Family Relations, 38,* 15-18.

Leik, R., & Leik, S. (1972). *Interpersonal commitment as a balancing mechanism in social exchange.* Paper presented at the Pacific Sociological Association Meeting, Scottsdale, AZ.

——— . (1977). Transition to interpersonal commitment. In R. L. Hamblin & J. H. Kunkel (Eds.), *Behavioral theory in sociology* (pp. 299-322). New Brunswick, NJ: Transaction.

Levi, L. (1975). *Emotions: Their parameters and measurement.* New York: Raven Press.

Levinger, G. (1965). Marital cohesiveness and dissolution: An integrative review. *Journal of Marriage and the Family, 27,* 19-28.

——— . (1979a). A social psychological perspective on marital dissolution. In G. Levinger & O. C. Moles (Eds.), *Divorce and separation: Context, causes, and consequences* (pp. 37-60). New York: Basic Books.

——— . (1979b). A social exchange view of the dissolution of pair relationships. In R. L. Burgess & T. L. Huston (Eds.), *Social exchange in developing relationships* (pp. 169-193). New York: Academic Press.

——— . (1983). Development and change. In H. H. Kelley, E Berscheid, A. Christensen, J. H. Harvey, T. L. Huston, G. Levinger, E. McClintock, L. A. Peplau, & D. R. Peterson (Eds.), *Close relationships* (pp. 315-359). New York: W. H. Freeman and Company.

——— . (1986). Compatibility in relationships. *Social Science, 71*(2/3), 173-177.

Levinger, G., & Snoek, J. D. (1972). *Attraction in relationship: A new look at interpersonal attraction.* Morristown, NJ: General Learning Press.

Lewin, K. (1935). *A dynamic theory of personality.* New York: McGraw-Hill.

——— . (1951). *Field theory in social science.* New York: Harper & Row.

Lewis, J. M., Beavers, W. R., Gossett, J. T., & Phillips, V. (1976). *No single thread.* New York: Brunner/Mazel.

Lewis, R., & Spanier, G. (1979). Theorizing about the quality and stability of marriage. In W. R. Burr, R. Hill, F. I. Nye, & I. L. Reiss (Eds.), *Contemporary theories about the family* (Vol. 1, 268-294). New York: Free Press.

Lewis-Beck, M. S. (1980). *Applied regression: An introduction.* Beverly Hills, CA: Sage.

Lippitt, G. L. (1982). *Organizational renewal: A holistic approach to organization development* (2nd ed.). Englewood Cliff, NJ: Prentice-Hall.

Litwak, E., Messeri, P., Wolfe, S., Gorman, S., Silverstein, M., & Guilarte, M. (1989). Organizational theory, social supports, and mortality rates: A theoretical convergence. *American Sociological Review, 54,* 49-66.

Litwak, E., & Meyer, H. F. (1966). A balance theory of coordination between bureaucratic organizations and community primary groups. *Administrative Science Quarterly, 11,* 33-58.

Lloyd, S. A., Cate, R. M., & Henton, J. M. (1982). Equity and rewards as predictors of satisfaction in casual and intimate relationships. *Journal of Psychology, 110,* 43-48.

Locke, E. A. (1969). What is job satisfaction? *Organizational behavior and human performance, 4,* 309-336.

——— . (1976). The nature and consequences of job satisfaction. In M. D. Dunnette (Ed.), *Handbook of industrial and organizational psychology* (pp. 1297-1349). Chicago: Rand McNally.

Lofquist, L. H., & Davis, R. V. (1984). Research on work adjustment and satisfaction: Implications for career counseling. In S. D. Brown & R. W. Lent (Eds.), *Handbook of counseling psychology* (pp. 216-237). New York: John Wiley & Sons.

Louis Harris and Associates, Inc. (1981). *Families at work.* Minneapolis, MN: General Mills.

Luft, J. (1969). *Of human interaction.* Palo Alto, CA: National Press Books.

Mace, D. R. (Ed.). (1983). *Prevention in family services.* Beverly Hills, CA: Sage.

——— . (1983). What this book is about. In D. R. Mace (Ed.), *Prevention in family services* (pp. 15-25). Beverly Hills, CA: Sage.

Mace, D. R., & Mace, V. (1978). Measure your marriage potential: A simple test that tells couples where they are. *The Family Coordinator, 27,* 63-67.

——— . (1980). Enriching marriages: The foundation stone of family strength. In N. Stinnett, B. Chesser, J. DeFrain, & P. Knaub (Eds.), *Family strengths: Positive models for family life* (pp. 89-110). Lincoln: University of Nebraska Press.

——— . (1986). The history and present status of the marriage and family enrichment movement. In W. Denton (Ed.), *Marriage and family enrichment* (7-18). New York: Haworth Press.

Mahoney, M. J., & Arnoff, D. B. (1978). Cognitive and self-control therapies. In S. Garfield & A. Bergin (Eds.), *Handbook of psychotherapy and behavior change: An empirical analysis* (pp. 689-722). New York: John Wiley & Sons.

Mandler, G (1975). *Mind and emotion.* New York: John Wiley & Sons.

Mangam, I. L. (1981). Relationships at work: A matter of tension and tolerance. In S. Duck & R. Gilmore (Eds.), *Personal relationships. 1: Studying personal relationships* (pp. 197–214). London: Academic Press.

Marks, G. (1977). Multiple roles and role strain: Some notes on human energy, time and commitment. *American Sociological Review, 42,* 921–936.

Marshall, C. (1988). Family influences on family members' job performance. *Family Perspective, 22,* 273–291.

McBroom, W. H. (1984). Changes in sex-role orientations: A five year longitudinal comparison. *Sex Roles, 11,* 583–592.

McClintock, E. (1983). Interaction. In H. H. Kelley, E. Berscheid, A. Christensen, J. H. Harvey, T. L. Huston, G. Levinger, E. McClintock, L. A. Peplau, & D. R. Peterson (Eds.), *Close Relationships* (pp. 68–109). New York: W. H. Freeman and Company.

McCubbin, H. I., & Patterson, J. (1983). *One thousand army families: Strengths, coping, and supports.* St. Paul: University of Minnesota.

McCubbin, H. I., & Thompson, A. I. (1987). Family typologies and family assessment. In H. I. McCubbin & A. I. Thompson (Eds.), *Family assessment inventories for research and practice* (pp. 35–49). Madison: University of Wisconsin.

McCubbin, M. A., & McCubbin, H. I. (1987). Family stress theory and assessment: The T-Double ABCX Model of family adjustment and adaptation. In H. I. McCubbin and A. I. Thompson (Eds.), *Family assessment inventories for research and practice* (pp. 1–32). Madison: University of Wisconsin.

McDonald, G. W. (1981). Structural exchange and marital interaction. *Journal of Marriage and the Family, 43,* 825–839.

McDonald, G. W., & Cornille, T. A. (1988). Internal family policy making and family problem solving: Toward a structural exchange model of family goal achievement. In D. M. Klein & J. Aldous (Eds.), *Social stress and family development* (pp. 246–263). New York: Guilford Press.

McGoldrick, M., Pearce, J. K., & Giordano, J. (Eds.). (1982). *Ethnicity and family therapy.* New York: Guilford Press.

McGregor, D. (1960). *The human side of enterprise.* New York: McGraw-Hill.

McNeely, R. L., & Fogarty, B. A. (1988). Balancing parenthood and employment: Factors affecting company receptiveness to family-related innovations in the workplace. *Family Relations, 37,* 189–195.

Mellman, M., Lazarus, E., & Rivlin, A. (1990). Family time, family values. In D. Blankenhorn, S. Bayme, & J. B. Elshtain (Eds.), *Rebuilding the nest: A new commitment to the American family* (pp. 73–92). Milwaukee, WI: Family Services America.

Menaghan, E. G. (1983). Individual coping efforts and family studies: Conceptual and methodological issues. In H. I. McCubbin, M. B. Sussman, & J. M. Patterson (Eds.), *Social stress and the family* (pp. 113–135). New York: Haworth Press.

Merrick, T. W., & Tordella, S. J. (1988). Demographics: People and markets. *Population Bulletin, 43,* 1–48.

Merton, R. K. (1957). *Social theory and social structure* (rev. ed.). New York: Free Press.

Miller, D., & Swanson, G. (1958). *The changing American parent.* New York: John Wiley & Sons.

Miller, J. G. (1978). *Living systems.* New York: McGraw-Hill.

Miller, S., Nunnally, E. W., & Wackman, D. B. (1979). *Talking together*. Minneapolis, MN: Interpersonal Communication Programs.

Mindel, C. H., & Habenstein, R. W. (Eds.). (1976). *Ethnic families in America: Patterns and variations*. New York: Elsevier.

Mobley, W. H., Griffeth, R. W., Hand, H. H., & Meglino, B. M. (1979). Review and conceptual analysis of the employee turnover process. *Psychological Bulletin, 86*, 493-522.

Montgomery, J. (1982). *Family crisis as process*. Washington, DC: University Press of America.

Moos, R. H. (1986a). Work as a human context. In M. S. Pallak & R. Perloff (Eds.), *Psychology and work: Productivity, change, and employment* (pp. 9-52). Washington, DC: American Psychological Association.

——— . (1986b). *Work environment scale manual* (2nd ed.). Palo Alto, CA: Consulting Psychologists Press.

——— . (1990). Conceptual and empirical approaches to developing family-based assessment procedures: Resolving the case of the Family Environment Scale. *Family Process, 29*, 199-208.

Moos, R. H., & Billings, A. (1982). Conceptualizing and measuring coping resources and processes. In L. Goldberger & S. Breznitz (Eds.), *Handbook of stress: Theoretical and clinical aspects*. New York: Macmillan.

Moos, R. H., & Moos, B. S. (1984). Clinical applications of the family environment scale. In E. E. Filsinger (Ed.), *Marriage and family assessment: A sourcebook for family therapy* (pp. 253-273). Beverly Hills, CA: Sage.

——— . (1986). *Family environment scale manual* (2nd ed.). Palo Alto: Consulting Psychologists Press.

Mortimer, J. T., & London, J. (1984). The varying linkages of work and family. In P. Voydanoff (Ed.), *Work and the family: Changing roles of men and women* (pp. 20-42). Palo Alto, CA: Mayfield Publishing.

Murray, H. A. (1938). *Explorations in personality*. New York: Oxford University Press.

Murstein, B. I., Cerreto, M., MacDonald, M. G. (1977). A theory and investigation of the effect of exchange-orientation on marriage and friendship. *Journal of Marriage and the Family, 39*, 543-548.

Near, J. P., Rice, R. W., & Hunt, R. G. (1980). The relationship between work and nonwork domains: A review of empirical research. *Academy of Management Review, 5*, 415-429.

Neenan, P. A. (1989). Marital quality and job satisfaction of male air force personnel: A test of the spillover hypothesis. In G. L. Bowen & D. K. Orthner (Eds.), *The organization family: Work and family linkages in the U.S. military*. New York: Praeger.

Nieva, V. F. (1985). Work and family linkages. In L. Larwood, A. H. Stromberg, & B. A Gutek (Eds.), *Women and work: An annual review* (Vol. 1, pp. 169-190). Beverly Hills, CA: Sage.

Norusis, M. J. (1986). *The SPSS guide to data analysis*. Chicago: SPSS Inc.

Nunnally, J. C. (1967). *Psychometric theory*. New York: McGraw-Hill.

Nye, F. I. (1967). Values, family, and a changing society. *Journal of Marriage and the Family, 27*, 241-247.

——— . (1978). Is choice and exchange theory the key? *Journal of Marriage and the Family, 40*, 219-233.

————. (1979). Choice, exchange and the family. In W. R. Burr, R. Hill, F. I. Nye, & I. L. Reiss (Eds.), *Contemporary theories about the family* (Vol. 2, pp. 1-41). New York: Free Press.

Olson, D. H. (1986). Circumplex model VII: Validation studies and FACES III. *Family Process, 25,* 337-351.

Olson, D., & McCubbin, H. I. (1983). *Families: What makes them work.* Beverly Hills, CA: Sage.

Olson, D. H., McCubbin, H. I., Barnes, H., Larsen, A., Muxen, M., & Wilson, M. (1985). *Family inventories.* (rev. ed.). St. Paul: University of Minnesota.

Olson, D. H., & Portner, J. (1984). Family adaptability and cohesion evaluation scales. In E. E. Filsinger (Ed.), *Marriage and family assessment: A sourcebook for family therapy* (pp. 299-315). Beverly Hills, CA: Sage.

Olson, D. H., Russell, C. S., & Sprenkle, D. H. (1983). Circumplex model of marital and family assessment: VI. Theoretical update. *Family Process, 22,* 69-83.

Oppenheimer, V. K. (1974). The life-cycle squeeze: The interaction of men's occupational and family life cycles. *Demography, 11,* 227-245.

————. (1982). *Work and the family: A study in social demography.* New York: Academic Press.

O'Reilly, C. A., III, Chatman, J., & Caldwell, D. (1990). *People and organizational cultures: A Q-sort approach to assessing person-organization fit.* Working paper, University of California at Berkeley.

Orthner, D. K. (1989, November). *Changing family values and norms: An institution in transition.* Paper presented at the conference organized by the Institute for American Values, Stanford University, CA.

————. (1990). The family in transition. In D. Blankenhorn, S. Bayme, & J. B. Elshtain (Eds.), *Rebuilding the nest: A new commitment to the American family* (pp. 93-118). Milwaukee, WI: Family Service America.

Orthner, D. K., & Bowen, G. L. (1982a). *Families-in-blue: Insights from air force families in the Pacific.* Greensboro, NC: Family Development Press.

————. (1982b). Attitudes toward family enrichment and support programs among air force families. *Family Relations, 31,* 415-424.

Orthner, D. K., Bowen, G. L., & Beare, V. G. (1990). The organization family: A question of work and family boundaries. *Marriage and Family Review,* 15(3/4), 15-36.

Orthner, D. K., & Pittman, J. F. (1986). Family contributions to work commitments. *Journal of Marriage and the Family, 48,* 573-581.

O'Toole, J. J. (1979). Corporate and managerial cultures. In C. L. Cooper (Ed.), *Behavior problems in organizations* (pp. 7-28). New York: Prentice-Hall.

Otto, H. (1962). What is a strong family? *Marriage and Family Living, 25,* 77-81.

————. (1963). Criteria for assessing family strength. *Family Process, 2,* 329-337.

————. (1964). The personal and family strengths research projects. *Mental Hygiene, 48,* 439-450.

————. (1975). *The use of family strength concepts and methods in family life education.* Beverly Hills, CA: Holistic Press.

————. (1979). Developing human and family potential. In N. Stinnett, B. Chesser, & J. Defrain (Eds.), *Building family strengths: Blueprints for action* (pp. 39-50). Lincoln: University of Nebraska Press.

Ouchi, W. G. (1981). *Theory Z.* New York: Avon Books.

Pankhurst, J. G., & Houseknecht, S. K. (1983). The family, politics, and religion in the 1980s: In fear of the new individualism. *Journal of Family Issues, 4,* 5–34.

Pearlin, L., & Johnson, J. (1977). Marital status, life strains and depression. *American Sociological Review, 42,* 704–715.

Pearlin, L. I., & Schooler, C. (1978). The structure of coping. *Journal of Health and Social Behavior, 19,* 2–21.

Pervin, L. A. (1987). Person-environment congruence in the light of the person-situation controversy. *Journal of Vocational Behavior, 31,* 222–230.

Peters, T. J., & Waterman, R. H. (1982). *In search of excellence.* New York: Harper & Row.

Piotrkowski, C. S. (1979). *Work and the family system: A naturalistic study of working class and lower middle class families.* New York: Free Press.

Piotrkowski, C. S., & Crits-Christoph, P. (1981). Women's jobs and family adjustment. *Journal of Family Issues, 2,* 126–147.

Piotrkowski, C. S., Rapoport, R. N., & Rapoport, R. (1987). Families and work. In M. B. Sussman & S. K. Steinmetz (Eds.), *Handbook of Marriage and the Family* (pp. 251–283). New York: Plenum Press.

Pittman, J. F., & Orthner, D. K. (1988). Gender differences in the prediction of job commitment. In E. B. Goldsmith (Ed.), *Work and family: Theory, research, and applications* (pp. 227–248). Newbury Park, CA: Sage.

Pleck, J. H. (1977). The work-family role system. *Social Problems, 24,* 417–424.

——— . (1985). *Working wives/working husbands.* Beverly Hills, CA: Sage.

Pleck, J., & Staines, G. (1985). Work schedules and family life in two-career couples. *Journal of Family Issues, 6,* 61–82.

Pollak, O. (1967). The outlook for the American family. *Journal of Marriage and the Family, 29,* 193–205.

Popenoe, D. (1989). The family transformed. *Family Affairs, 2*(2–3), 1–5.

Powell, G. N. (1988). *Women and men in management.* Newbury Park, CA: Sage.

Presser, H. (1988). Shift work and child care among young dual-earner American parents. *Journal of Marriage and the Family, 50,* 133–148.

Raabe, P. H., & Gessner, J. (1988). Employer family-supportive policies: Diverse variations on the theme. *Family Relations, 37,* 196–202.

Rallings, E. M., & Nye, F. I. (1979). Wife-mother employment, family and society. In W. R. Burr, R. Hill, F. I. Nye, & I. L. Reiss (Eds.), *Contemporary theories about the family* (Vol. 1, pp. 203–226). New York: Macmillan.

Rapoport, R., & Rapoport, R. (1965). Work and family in contemporary society. *American Sociological Review, 30,* 381–394.

Ravlin, E. C., & Meglino, B. M. (1989). The transitivity of work values: Hierarchical preference ordering of socially desirable stimuli. *Organizational Behavior and Human Decision Processes, 44,* 494–508.

Rekers, G. (Ed.). (1985). *Family building: Six qualities of a strong family.* Ventura, CA: Regal Books.

Renne, K. (1971). Health and marital experience in an urban population. *Journal of Marriage and the Family, 33,* 338–348.

Renshaw, J. R. (1976). An exploration of the dynamics of the overlapping worlds of work and family. *Family Process, 15,* 143–166.

Repetti, R. L. (1987). Linkages between work and family roles. In S. Oskamp (Ed.), *Applied social psychology annual: Vol. 7* (pp. 98–127). Beverly Hills, CA: Sage.

Reubens, B. G., & Reubens, E. P. (1979). Women workers, nontraditional occupations and full employment. In A. F. Cahn (Ed.), *Women in the U.S. labor force* (pp. 103–126). New York: Praeger.

Revicki, D. A., & May, H. J. (1985). Occupational stress, social support, and depression. *Health Psychology, 4*(1), 61–77.

Rice, R. W., McFarlin, D. B., Hunt, R. G., & Near, J. P. (1985). Organizational work and the perceived quality of life: Toward a conceptual model. *Academy of Management Review, 10*, 296–310.

Ridenour, R. I. (1984). The military, service families, and the therapist. In F. W. Kaslow and R. I. Ridenour (Eds.), *The military family* (pp.1–17). New York: Guilford Press.

Rodman, H. (1963). The lower-class value stretch. *Social Forces, 42*, 205–215.

——— . (1971). *Lower-class families*. New York: Oxford University Press.

Rokeach, M. (1968). *Beliefs, attitudes, and values*. San Francisco: Jossey-Bass.

——— . (1973). *The nature of human values*. New York: Free Press.

Roosa, M. W., & Beals, J. (1990). Measurement issues in family assessment: The case of the Family Environment Scale. *Family Process, 29*, 191–198.

Rosenblatt, A., & Greenberg, J. (1988). Depression and interpersonal attraction: The role of perceived similarity. *Journal of Personality and Social Psychology, 55*, 112–119.

Rotter, J. B. (1966). Generalized expectations for internal versus external control of reinforcement. *Psychological Monographs: General and Applied, 80*, 1–28.

Rubin, Z. (1973). *Liking and loving: An invitation to social psychology*. New York: Holt.

Rudd, N. M., & McKenry, P. C. (1986). Family influences on the job satisfaction of employed mothers. *Psychology of Women Quarterly, 10*, 363–372.

Sabatelli, R. M. (1984). A marital comparison level index: A measure for assessing outcomes relative to expectations. *Journal of Marriage and the Family, 46*, 651–662.

——— . (1988a). Exploring relationship satisfaction: A social exchange perspective on the interdependence between theory, research, and practice. *Family Relations, 37*, 217–222.

——— . (1988b). Measurement issues in marital research: A review and critique of contemporary survey instruments. *Journal of Marriage and the Family, 50*, 891–915.

Sampson, E. E. (1978). Scientific paradigms and social values. Wanted: A scientific revolution. *Journal of Personality and Social Psychology, 36*, 1332–1343.

Satir, V. (1972). *Peoplemaking*. Palo Alto, CA: Science and Behavior Books.

Savery, L. K. (1988). The influence of social support on the reaction of an employee. *Journal of Managerial Psychology, 3*(1), 27–31.

Scanzoni, J. H. (1970). *Opportunity and the family*. New York: Free Press.

——— . (1972). *Sexual bargaining: Power politics in the American marriage*. Englewood Cliffs, NJ: Prentice-Hall.

——— . (1975). Sex roles, economic factors and marital solidarity in black and white marriages. *Journal of Marriage and the Family, 37*, 130–144.

——— . (1978). *Sex roles, women's work, and marital conflict: A study of family change*. Lexington, MA: Lexington Books.

——— . (1979a). Social exchange and behavioral interdependence. In T. L. Huston, & R. L. Burgess (Eds.), *Social exchange and developing relationships* (pp. 61–98). New York: Academic Press.

——— . (1979b). A historical perspective on husband-wife bargaining power and marital dissolution. In G. Levinger & O. C. Moles (Eds.), *Divorce and separation* (pp. 20–36). New York: Basic Books.

Scanzoni, J., & Fox, G. L. (1980). Sex roles, family and society: The seventies and beyond. *Journal of Marriage and the Family, 42,* 743–756.

Scanzoni, J., Polonko, K., Teachman, J., & Thompson, L. (1989). *The sexual bond: Rethinking families and close relationships.* Newbury Park, CA: Sage.

Scanzoni, J., & Szinovacz, M. (1980). *Family decision making: A developmental sex role model.* Beverly Hills, CA: Sage.

Scheibe, K. E. (1970). *Beliefs and values.* New York: Holt, Rinehart and Winston.

Schein, E. H. (1984). Coming to a new awareness of organizational culture. *Sloan Management Review, 25,* 3–16.

———. (1985). *Organizational culture and leadership.* San Francisco: Jossey-Bass.

Schumm, W. R., McCollum, E. E., Bugaighis, M. A., Jurich, A. P., & Bollman, S. R. (1986). Characteristics of the Kansas Family Life Satisfaction Scale in a regional sample. *Psychological Reports, 58,* 975–980.

Schumm, W. R., Nichols, C. W., Schectman, K. L., & Grigsby, C. C. (1983). Characteristics of responses to the Kansas Marital Satisfaction Scale by a sample of 84 married mothers. *Psychological Reports, 53,* 567–572.

Schumm, W. R., Paff-Bergin, L. A., Hatch, R. C., Obiorah, F. C., Copeland, J. M., Meens, L. D., & Bugaighis, M. A. (1986). Concurrent and discriminate validity of the Kansas Marital Satisfaction Scale. *Journal of Marriage and the Family, 48,* 381–387.

Schwartz, P. (1987). The family as a changed institution. *Journal of Family Issues, 8,* 455–459.

Schwartzman, J. (1985). Macrosystemic approaches to family therapy: An overview. In J. Schwartzman (Ed.), *Families and other systems: The macrosystemic context of family therapy.* New York: Guilford Press.

Seashore, S. E., & Taber, T. D. (1976). Job satisfaction indicators and their correlates. In A. D. Biderman & T. F. Drury (Eds.), *Measuring work quality for social reporting* (pp. 89–124). New York: John Wiley and Sons.

Segal, M. W. (1989). The nature of work and family linkages: A theoretical perspective. In G. L. Bowen & D. K. Orthner (Eds.), *The organization family: Work and family linkages in the U.S. military* (pp. 3–36). New York: Praeger.

Sekaran, U. (1983). How husbands and wives in dual-career families perceive their family and work worlds. *Journal of Vocational Behavior, 22,* 288–302.

———. (1986). *Dual-career families.* San Francisco: Jossey-Bass.

Shinn, M., Wong, N. W., Simko, P. A., & Ortiz-Torres, B. (1989). Promoting the well-being of working parents: Coping, social support, and flexible job schedules. *American Journal of Community Psychology, 17,* 31–55.

Shirom, A. (1989). Burnout in work organizations. In C. L. Cooper & I. Robertson (Eds.), *International review of industrial and organizational psychology* (pp. 25–48). New York: John Wiley & Sons.

Shouksmith, G. (1987). Emerging personnel values in changing societies. In B. M. Bass & P. J. D. Drenth (Eds.), *Advances in organizational psychology: An international review* (pp. 19–33). Newbury Park, CA: Sage.

Sieber, S. (1974). Toward a theory of role accumulation. *American Sociological Review, 39,* 567–578.

Silverzweig, S., & Allen, R. F. (1976). Changing the corporate culture. *Sloan Management Review, 17,* 33–49.

Simpson, I. H., & England, P. (1981). Conjugal work roles and marital solidarity. *Journal of Family Issues, 2,* 180-204.

Small, S. A. & Riley, D. (1990). Toward a multidimensional assessment of work spillover into family life. *Journal of Marriage and the Family, 52,* 51-61.

Smith, D. S. (1985). Wife employment and marital adjustment: A cumulation of results. *Family Relations, 34,* 483-490.

Snyder, D. K. (1979). Multidimensional assessment of marital satisfaction. *Journal of Marriage and the Family, 41,* 813-823.

Spanier, G. B. (1972). Romanticism and marital adjustment. *Journal of Marriage and the Family, 34,* 481-487.

────── . (1976). Measuring dyadic adjustment: New scales for assessing the quality of marriage and similar dyads. *Journal of Marriage and the Family, 38,* 15-28.

Spanier, G. B., & Cole, C. L. (1976). Toward clarification and investigation of marital adjustment. *International Journal of Sociology of the Family, 6,* 121-146.

Spanier, G. B., & Filsinger, E. E. (1984). The dyadic adjustment scale. In E. E. Filsinger (Ed.), *Marriage and family assessment: A sourcebook for family therapy* (pp. 155-168). Beverly Hills, CA: Sage.

Spiegel, J. (1971). *Transactions: The interplay between individual, family, and society.* New York: Science House.

────── . (1982). An ecological model of ethnic families. In M. McGoldrick, J. K. Pearce, & J. Giordana (Eds.), *Ethnicity and family therapy: An overview* (pp. 31-51). New York: Guilford Press.

Spokane, A. R. (1987). Conceptual and methodological issues in person-environment fit research. *Journal of Vocational Behavior, 31,* 217-221.

SPSS, Inc. (1986). *SPSS^X user's guide* (2nd ed.). Chicago: Author.

Statuto, C. M., Ooms, T., Brand, S., & Pittman, K. (1984). *Families in the eighties: Implications for employers and human services.* Washington, DC: Catholic University of America.

Stein, H. F. (1985). Values and family therapy. In J. Schwartzman (Ed.), *Families and other systems: The macrosystemic context of family therapy* (pp. 201-243). New York: Guilford Press.

Stillman, F., & Bowen, G. L. (1985). Corporate support mechanisms for families: An exploratory study and agenda research and evaluation. *Evaluation and Program Planning, 8,* 309-314.

Stinnett, N. (1979). Strengthening families. *Family Perspective, 13,* 3-9.

Stinnett, N., & DeFrain, J. (1985). *Secrets of strong families.* Boston: Little, Brown.

Stinnett, N., & Sauer, K. (1977). Relationship characteristics of strong families. *Family Perspective, 11* (4), 3-11.

Stuart, R. (1980). *Helping couples change: A social learning approach to marital therapy.* New York: Guilford Press.

Sussman, M. B. (1977). Family, bureaucracy, and the elderly individual: An organizational/linkage perspective. In E. Shanas & M. B. Sussman (Eds.), *Family, Bureaucracy, and the Elderly* (pp. 2-20). Durham, NC: Duke University Press.

Taylor, F. W. (1947). *Scientific management.* New York: Harper & Row.

Teachman, J. D., Polonko, K. A., & Scanzoni, J. (1987). Demography of the family. In M. B. Sussman & S. K. Steinmetz (Eds.), *Handbook of marriage and the family* (pp. 3-36). New York: Plenum Press.

Terman, L. M., Buttenweiser, P., Ferguson, L. W., Johnson, W. B., & Wilson, D. P. (1938). *Psychological factors in marital happiness.* New York: McGraw-Hill.

Tharp, R. G. (1963). Psychological patterning in marriage. *Psychological Bulletin, 60,* 97–117.

Thibaut, J. W., & Kelley, H. H. (1959). *The social psychology of groups.* New York: John Wiley & Sons.

Thoits, P.A. (1987). Negotiating roles. In F. J. Crosby (Ed.), *Spouse, parent, worker: On gender and multiple roles* (pp. 11–22). New Haven, CT: Yale University Press.

Thornton, A. (1989). Changing attitudes toward family issues in the United States. *Journal of Marriage and the Family, 51,* 873–893.

Tiggle, R. B., Peters, M. D., Kelley, H. H., & Vincent, J. (1982). Correlational and discrepancy indices of understanding and their relation to marital satisfaction. *Journal of Marriage and the Family, 44,* 209–215.

Tolman, E. C. (1932). *Purposive behavior in animals and men.* New York: Century.

Turner, J. H. (1978). *The structure of sociological theory.* Homewood, IL: Dorsey.

Turner, J. H., & Musick, D. (1985). *American dilemmas: A sociological interpretation of enduring social issues.* New York: Columbia University Press.

Van Der Veen, F., Huebner, B., Jorgens, B., & Neja P. (1964). Relationship between the parents' concept of the family and family adjustment. *American Journal of Orthopsychiatry, 34,* 45–55.

Vincent, C. E. (1966). Familia spongia: The adaptive function. *Journal of Marriage and the Family, 28,* 29–36.

Vocational Education Work and Family Institute (1983). *Study of work-family issues in Minnesota.* St. Paul, MN: Author.

Voydanoff, P. (1980a). Work roles as stressors in corporate families. *Family Relations, 29,* 489–494.

———. (1980b) *The implications of work-family relationships for productivity* (Work in America Institute Studies in Productivity, No. 13). Scarsdale, NY: Work in America Institute.

———. (1980c, October). *Work-family life cycles.* Paper presented at the workshop on theory construction and research methodology, National Council on Family Relations, Boston, MA.

———. (1987). *Work and family life.* Newbury Park, CA: Sage.

Voydanoff, P., & Donnelly, B. W. (1989). Work and family roles and psychological distress. *Journal of Marriage and the Family, 51,* 923–932.

Voydanoff, P., & Kelly, R. F. (1984). Determinants of work-related family problems among employed parents. *Journal of Marriage and the Family, 46,* 881–892.

Vroom, V. H. (1964). *Work and motivation.* New York: John Wiley & Sons.

Walsh, F. (1982). Conceptualizations of normal family functioning. In F. Walsh (Ed.), *Normal family processes* (pp. 3–42). New York: Guilford Press.

Walster, E., Walster, G. W., & Berscheid, E. (1978). *Equity: Theory and research.* Boston: Allyn & Bacon.

White, L., & Keith, B. (1990). The effects of shift work on the quality and stability of marital relations. *Journal of Marriage and the Family, 52,* 453–462.

Whyte, W. H., Jr. (1956). *The organization man.* New York: Simon & Schuster.

Wilensky, H. L. (1960). Work, careers and social integration. *International Social Science Journal, 12,* 543–560.

Wilkinson, D. (1987). Ethnicity. In M. B. Sussman & S. K. Steinmetz (Eds.), *Hand-book of marriage and the family* (pp. 183–210). New York: Plenum Press.

Yalom, I. D. (1970). *The theory and practice of group psychotherapy*. New York: Basic Books.

Yankelovich, D. (1979). Work, values and the new breed. In C. Kerr & J. Rosow (Eds.), *Work in America: The decade ahead* (pp. 3–26). New York: Van Nostrand Reinhold.

——— . (1981). *New rules*. New York: Bantam.

Index

adolescents, 138
Aldous, J., 3
Anderson, S. A., 77, 86, 111, 118
Antonovsky, A., 50
Army couples, model test on: causal conditions and, 68, 87, 98; conductors of, 67; data analysis and, 88–91, 93; data source for, 68; demographic variables and, 88, 98; marital satisfaction analysis and, 84–86; procedures for, 69; purpose of, 67; results of, 93, 95, 97–98; social desirability and, 86, 98; sponsor of, 67; subjects for, 69

Bartolome, F., 146, 147
Beck, A. T., 49
beliefs defined, 48, 50
Bem, D. J., 48
Berscheid, Ellen, 31–32, 39–42
Beutell, N. J., 139
Borden, V. M., 53, 55
Bowen, Gary, 29, 58
Bradbury, T. N., 31–32
Bureau of Labor Statistics, 133
Burke, Ronald, 4, 141, 142, 143–44
Burr, W. R., 35
Byrne, Don, 38

Caliber Associates, 67
Caplan, R. D., 72, 99, 101, 102–3
Caron, W., 44
Cate, R. M., 36
causal conditions, 47, 48, 68, 87, 98. *See also* influences on value-behavior congruency
Chatman, Jennifer, 24
Cobb, S., 60
Cole, C. L., 32, 85, 118
Constantine, L. L., 8, 33
Consulting Psychologists Press, 15
corporate couples, model test on: data analysis of, 119–21; data source for, 104; demographic variables and, 119; marital satisfaction analysis, 118, 120–21; procedures for, 104–5; regression analysis and, 123, 128; results of, 121–23, 128; social desirability and, 119; subjects for, 104; VBC model evaluation and, 128–29
corporations, modern: behavioral and social science use by, 1; benefits to employees by, 4–5; family segregation from, 2–3; lack of marital enrichment programs by, 4–5, 150; management focus of, 1, 3–4; MAP

ABOUT THE AUTHOR

GARY L. BOWEN is Associate Professor and Chairperson, Services to Families and Children Specialization, School of Social Work, the University of North Carolina at Chapel Hill. He has worked extensively over the last decade as a researcher, consultant, and trainer with all four service branches in the Department of Defense. Dr. Bowen has published extensively on the nature of work and family linkages and is co-editor, with Dr. Dennis Orthner, of *The Organization Family: Work and Family Linkages in the U.S. Military* (Praeger, 1989).